The God of the OT was a
wrathful, vengeful god...
The God of the NT in Christ
was a pick up your cross
and follow me god.

The God of the 20th century
is a Santa Claus god...

Religious Television

COMMUNICATION

AND HUMAN VALUES

A series developed by the Centre for the Study of Communication
and Culture, London, England, in cooperation with the
World Association for Christian Communication, London.

Religious Television

The American Experience

Peter G. Horsfield

Longman
New York & London

RELIGIOUS TELEVISION
The American Experience

Longman Inc., 1560 Broadway, New York, N.Y. 10036
Associated companies, branches, and representatives
throughout the world.

Developmental Editor: Gordon T. R. Anderson
Editorial and Design Supervisor: Ferne Y. Kawahara
Manufacturing Supervisor: Marion Hess

Library of Congress Cataloging in Publication Data
Horsfield, Peter G.
  Religious television.
  (Communication and human values)
  Bibliography: p.
  Includes index.
  1. Television in religion—United States. I. Title.
II. Series.
BV656.3.H67   1984   269'.2   83-11313
LSBN 0-582-28432-5

Manufactured in the United States of America
Printing: 9 8 7 6 5 4 3 2   Year: 92 91 90 89 88 87 86 85 84

To Marilyn

Contents

Foreword

The story of life—why it began, what it means, how it should be conducted—used to be the story of religion. Its telling related otherwise disparate members of far-flung communities to one another. Today, however, that story is told by television.

Television presents most of what we know (or think we know) in common. It tells us about the events, arts, sciences, mores, and governance of societies. It tells most of the stories to most of the people most of the time. Our children are no longer nurtured solely within the family, the church, and the school. Nor do they encounter the outside culture on terms established mainly by those social institutions. They are born into homes where television brings in the dominant outside culture an average of six and a half hours a day. The task of introducing children to the norms and roles of the community has changed hands. With a television pulpit in every home and tireless preachers delivering messages from and audiences to the corporate sponsor, religion faces its most formidable challenge in history.

What is, and what should be, the response? The answer depends on historical, theological, and sociopolitical conditions and positions. But the question must be posed anew and the answers worked out in light of the essential background which Peter Horsfield provides in this book. Dr. Horsfield offers more than short-term answers, however. He provides a map, a perspective, and a realistic assessment of the obstacles to any course of action.

Most recent research on television and religion, summarized in this book, has been stimulated by the advent of the "electronic church." But as Dr. Horsfield makes clear, the "electronic church" is, in fact, not really new. What is new is its prominence, born of its emergence at a particular point in political history, and born of technological and policy changes that have favored it over other religious institutions in their use of television.

The fact that these developments have seemed to favor the emergence of politically conservative and theologically fundamentalist programs (as has been the charge) can be partially explained by policy decisions made by networks and "conventional" churches years ago. The major, prominent churches in existence at the onset of uniform federal regulation committed themselves to a style of broadcast presence ("free" or "sustaining" time) and a model of broadcasting which held firm until mid-1971. At that time the conservative, independent, and fundamentalist churches that had been left out of this system seemingly burst onto the national scene with their own network and markets created via cable, satellite, and "religious only" UHF-TV.

Public discussion and press treatment of religious broadcasting have tended to concentrate on this "electronic church"—the eight or ten largest, most prominent, and best financed of these organizations. But there are, in fact, over eighty syndicated religious series and hundreds of local or regional productions, series, and broadcast church services on television, and many more on radio. It is a vast and varied field.

The popularity and staying power of religious broadcasting can be illuminated by the results of our own research on television. The power-oriented, violence-saturated world portrayed on television tends to cultivate in its regular viewers a sense of mistrust and insecurity and perceptions of a "mean world." Simple, strong, tough measures and hard-line postures—political or religious, or both—appeal to anxious and apprehensive viewers. Reliable ritual speaks to them—confirming the fears, feeding the hopes, and cultivating the assumptions television shaped in the first place and through which it dominates the cultural climate in which political parties, traditional religions, and all other institutions must now find their way.

The map and guidelines Dr. Horsfield provides will help the reader to do just that. He looks at religious television calmly, systematically investigating its history and assumptions and sorting out the potential relationships between religion and television. Dr. Horsfield performs a service, in both the scope and the perspective he has assumed, by illuminating some of the following choices and possible consequences for religious television.

Is the still emergent "electronic church" riding the crest of the wave of television-induced anxieties or is it making waves of its own? Is it religion at all or is it television—just another program built around financial appeals and a mail-order scheme? Can a message of integrity and perspective, different from that of the television ritual but addressed to the same audience, penetrate conventional viewer perceptions and expectations? Can television convey a successful challenge to its own vision of the world? Can mainline religion (or any institution other than business) "use" television for its purposes or must it become co-opted into the television world-view? These are a few of the questions to ponder.

If television has shaped religion, as this book suggests, can religion also shape television? Through his careful review of history, research, and policy, Dr. Horsfield found some indication that the whole enterprise of religious broadcasting may have been overly influenced by the present institutional structure of television. So this book also shows a way to explore religion's possible influence on television. It may well be that only by working to restructure the cultural order—and its mainstream, television—can religion reclaim its historic moral position.

George Gerbner
Stewart Hoover

Annenberg School of Communications
University of Pennsylvania, Philadelphia

Preface

The modern evangelical movement in America burst onto the public stage in the national election year of 1976. Though evangelicalism had always been an element in American religious life and had been growing in strength for several previous decades, it was the candidacy and election of a self-proclaimed "born-again" Southern evangelical as American president which brought the phenomenon to widespread public attention.

This awakening interest in the evangelical movement led to an immediate interest in its most visible manifestation: evangelical television. The public was generally surprised at the advanced technological competence of the evangelical broadcasters, the extent of their large organizations, and the size of their budgets. *Newsweek* in 1976 reflected a common feeling when it called the evangelical movement "the most significant and overlooked religious phenomenon of the 1970s."

The fact that the growth of evangelical broadcasting had occurred largely unnoticed led many to believe that the broadcasters had in fact been operating in secret and were intent on some kind of social or political duplicity. For many, this suspicion appeared to be confirmed in the following election year, when some of the broadcasters formed active coalitions with the "new right" politicians and political groups with a view to countering some of the liberals' moral and political advances of the 1960s. For some fearful observers, the growth of evangelical broadcasting represented a massive takeover by the political and moral right and a plot to establish a religious republic with the evangelical and fundamentalist broadcasters as the major spokespersons. More moderately, some journalists observed that the television preachers, by unifying and motivating otherwise inactive voters, could hold the key to the election.

The election itself removed much of the ambiguity in which this kind of speculation flourished. Since that time the widespread interest in religious broadcasting has largely faded. The media's handling of the phenomenon of religious television can now be seen to have been both polarized and exaggerated, lacking historical and empirical perspective and shaped to a large extent by the media's preference for sensation and confrontation in the

preelection atmosphere. Several of the major commercial religious broadcasters can be seen also to have craftily used this media bias to advance their
own particular causes.

The preoccupation with the political aspects of religious television,
though, has tended to ignore and obscure other important dimensions of
the phenomenon. The recent trends in religious television raise questions
and issues which are of importance not only for political observers, but also
for religious communicators, sociologists, and those concerned with
understanding how television functions in American society. One of the
principal issues is the social power of television itself, for a study of religious
television in American society provides a case study of what happens when
a strongly ideological social group such as a religious organization confronts
the established and also strongly ideological American television industry.

What can be seen from a study of religious uses of television in America
is that over the past several years there has developed a marked imbalance
in the presentation of American religious faith and culture. While there are
several factors contributing to this imbalance, the dominant factor is the
economic and functional interests of the commercial television industry.
These interests have found it advantageous to their own cause to promote
a minority religious expression on television because this particular expression reinforces television's own economic and mythological intentions.
Further, television has permitted this viewpoint to replace other religious
viewpoints, even though these others are more representative of more
popular American religious traditions. Television's managers have exercised
a powerful censoring effect on the expression of religious faith in America,
giving them consequentially an exaggerated influence over the development
of American religious culture and institutions and possibly over the nature
of American and even global religious life.

The evangelical and fundamentalist traditions of Christianity, which
have benefitted most from this situation, justify their inequable communi-
cative power in terms which, in the light of this analysis, can be seen to be
false and self-deluding. When considered against impartial research data
their strategy in relation to television appears largely to have failed. This
failure, in combination with other religious approaches to television,
suggests that none of the major strategies employed by the major American
religious traditions have been effective in overcoming the awesome power
of the television industry itself. The message of these religious traditions has
been reduced to blend with television's own intention to function as the
adequate religion of contemporary society.

These theses are examined and supported through this study. Part I
provides a historical overview of the development of religious television in
America and an analysis of the factors which have contributed to its
particular structure and the issues raised by it. Part II provides a survey of
empirical research relevant to the various issues in religious television and

through this survey clarifies many of the questions which have been raised in relation to the religious use of television. Part III provides a projection of the future of current trends in religious television in America and elements of a strategy for a realistic use of television in the total mission of the church.

This book represents the culmination of six years of doctoral work and research in theology and mass communication at Boston University Graduate School. I want to acknowledge the help in that program given by many, but particularly by J. Robert Nelson, Professor of Systematic Theology, and F. Earle Barcus, Professor of Communication Research. The Boston University School of Theology Library was most helpful in obtaining many idiosyncratic titles and microfilms on which this research strongly depends. There were some broadcasters and program agencies of different churches who gave me access to their files and made otherwise private research available to me for use in the study. Mention should be made particularly of Bill Fore of the National Council of Churches Communication Commission and the Christian Broadcasting Network in Virginia. The secrecy and suspicion of so many other broadcasters is regrettable and can only be detrimental to the overall cause of Christ and his kingdom. I wish to acknowledge also the personal help and support given by the two churches of which I was pastor during the period of study and writing: The Arlington Heights United Methodist Church in Massachusetts and The Gap Uniting Church in Brisbane, Australia. The experience within these churches has provided a necessary perspective from which to view the phenomenon of religious television. My editor, Robert White of the Centre for the Study of Communication and Culture in London, has provided many pages of comments, criticisms, and suggestions which could well be published themselves as a commentary on the whole subject of religious broadcasting and its impact on culture. The book is dedicated to my wife, Marilyn, whose theological and psychological insights and comments have added significantly to the level of analysis in the book.

Finally, I would be pleased to bequeath to the first comer the constant flow of direct mail I have received from broadcasters as a consequence of my having established contact with them. I fear that I shall be loved, inspired, prayed for, thought specially of, possibility-powered, and something-specialled to an early death.

Peter G. Horsfield

PART **I**

The Development of
Religious Television

1
The Emergence of Religious Television

The First Twenty Years

Religious programs on television are not a new phenomenon: they have been a part of the schedule since television's first year of operation, just as religious programs were some of the earlier types of broadcasts on radio.

The early years of television were dominated by the three major faith groups: the Roman Catholics, Protestants, and Jews. By the time the networks had developed television, they had had several decades of experience with religious groups on radio. They had worked out many strategies for dealing with the large number of religious groups who wanted to broadcast their messages, and with the religious mavericks whose fire-and-brimstone preaching could be dangerously libellous.

The practice of the networks was to deal primarily with only the reputable and mainline religious groups. Catholics were represented by the National Council of Catholic Men, Jews by the Jewish Seminary of America, and Protestants by the Federal Council of Churches of Christ. Each of these three groups had enjoyed a working relationship with the radio networks and when television networks emerged these relationships were extended into the new medium.

The practice of the networks was to produce religious programs, either by making production facilities, technical services and some budget resources available to the religious groups for the production of their own programs, or by using these religious agencies as consultants on their own religious programs. These programs were then fed to affiliate stations for airing on "sustaining-time," or public-service time. Local stations often acted similarly, producing religious programs in association with local church bodies or representative councils.

The arrangement was mutually beneficial. For the networks and their affiliates it supplied one of the means by which they met the requirements of the Federal Communications Commission (FCC). Most stations broadcast a certain amount of religious programming as part of their license obligation to operate in the public interest. By working with these established religious groups, the networks were able to maintain substantial control over the content of the religious programs and thus avoid controversial material which could have caused legal or broadcasting repercussions. The CBS network, for example, adopted this policy in 1933 after it was involved in legal problems caused by the radio broadcasts over its stations of the controversial priest, Father Charles Coughlin.

By dealing with representative groups, the networks also avoided the problems of trying to manage the numerous individual denominations and independent religious groups, all of whom wanted to gain free access to television's airwaves.

The arrangement was also most beneficial for the established religious groups. It gave them access to free air-time, the valuable technical and in some cases budgetary resources of the networks, and a large measure of control over the content of religious faith communicated by television.

In working to maintain this favorable relationship with the networks, however, the mainline groups were under continual pressure. The networks maintained substantial control over the content of religious programming produced under their auspices, and they worked continually to fit the religious perspective into their own particular perspectives. The religious organizations working with the networks were forced to make compromises in the face of this substantial censoring or levelling effect on the presentation of religious faith.

The compromise was not always one-way, however. Though the networks sought to make all religious programming emphasize broad religious truths rather than individual tenets of denominations and to avoid dealing with controversial economic and social issues which were of religious significance, many programs produced by the churches in relation with the networks were critical or prophetic in nature. For example "Duty Bound," an NBC one-hour religious special on March 11, 1972, drew more than 10,000 letters in response.

Programming on all three networks has also consistently dealt with views, actions, and testimony from the different denominational viewpoints, reflecting the churches' conviction that Christian witness and action cannot be divorced from particular persons and denominational perspectives.

The presentation of relevant and prophetic material did not come without a fight and some mainline broadcasters considered that for the exposure and benefit gained, network programming was not worth it. Everett Parker of the United Church of Christ's Office of Communication eventually withdrew his denomination's participation from network religious programming because he felt that there were more important areas of ministry within television, particularly in the area of media reform.

Other broadcasters expressed similar concerns. Mike Gallagher, who was the Roman Catholic producer for NBC-Catholic programs, criticized the lack of seriousness which characterized the network attitude to religious programs: "I have a rather cynical attitude towards the networks. They're just using religious shows to fulfill their FCC obligations."[1] Dr. Franklin Mack, also of the United Church of Christ, suggested that networks were "more a waste of time in terms of resources for the minimal time and audiences that you can get."[2]

Such an imposed control also drew criticism on theological grounds. Theologian Martin Marty, as early as 1961, suggested that the communication of the Christian faith under such conditions is difficult because the essence of Christianity lies in its *particular* beliefs and affirmations, not just in its general ones. To ask a Christian communicator to reduce his message to "broad truths" is to remove the essence of the Christian faith.[3] Evangelical broadcaster Ben Armstrong has similarly attacked the programs produced under such conditions as "bland discussions about good deeds, rather than the mandates of the gospel."[4]

In general, though, the communication agencies of the established faiths and denominations were prepared to accept the prerequisites of the networks and their affiliates. Not only was the free use of network facilities and air-time too good to pass over, but the communication agencies had been conditioned to the acceptance of broad religious truths over idiosyncratic truths by the ecumenical movement. Their social emphasis on justice and equity also provided justification for network controls which appeared to promote commonality and the socially responsible use of a public medium.

The 1950s therefore became the heyday of network mainline religious programming.[5] Long-running and award-winning programs such as "Lamp Unto My Feet" (CBS), "Directions" (ABC), "Frontiers of Faith" (NBC), and "Look Up and Live" (CBS) all began production in this period.

The proportional use of time which the networks maintained with the various major religious groups was not totally satisfactory for some of the larger individual denominations and the individual fundamentalist and evangelical organizations and they turned to alternative methods of broadcasting as well. Some of the larger Protestant denominations, such as the Southern Baptists, Seventh-Day Adventists, and Lutheran Church–Missouri Synod were of sufficient stature to be able to gain free sustaining-time directly from local stations and they used this to supplement the smaller amount of time they received from the networks. Funds for the production of this denominational programming came exclusively from members of the denominations. These independently syndicated, sustaining-time programs did well. Many of them won numerous awards for quality and have achieved international syndication, such as "The Answer" (Southern Baptist) "Faith for Today" (Seventh Day Adventist), "This Is the Life" (Lutheran Church–Missouri Synod). It has been estimated, for example, that by 1974 the Southern Baptist Radio and Television Commission had nearly 2,500 broadcasts a week on sustaining-time valued at $10 million annually donated by individual local television stations.[6]

Part of the reason for the early successful syndication and acceptance of these independent programs was their quality and dependability. Though produced by evangelical denominations, the programs reflected characteristics similar to other sustaining-time programming: they were low-key in their approach, they were moderate in their doctrine, and they often employed a dramatic format.

There were many other independent Christian groups which had neither the resources nor the stature to attract free time from either networks or local stations for the broadcast of their programs. These were generally evangelical or fundamentalist Protestant groups from the Southern states, most of whom had been active in radio. When television arrived, the more aggressive also moved into programming on the new medium. Because they lacked the advantage of free air-time and the resources of large denominations behind them, those which eventually survived on television were highly competitive in nature and had developed the structure and charisma for attracting substantial financial support from the viewing audience to enable them to purchase commercial air-time from the stations. It was these independent, audience-supported evangelists who came to take over the religious airwaves in the 1960s and 1970s and earned the nickname of the electronic church.

Coming into the 1960s, therefore, there existed primarily a four-part structure in religious television.

1. *Network sustaining-time programs*, produced by networks in association with the Jewish Theological Seminary, the Roman Catholic Church, the National Council of Churches, and several other recognized faiths and denominations.
2. *Syndicated sustaining-time programs*, comprised primarily of programs produced by individual denominations and syndicated nationally.
3. *Local programs*, mostly sustaining-time programs, produced by local television stations either independently or in association with local religious groups or churches.
4. *Paid-time, audience supported syndicated programs*, produced primarily by independent Protestant groups, supported by audience contributions, and aired on time purchased from individual local stations.

In spite of the obvious financial disadvantages of having to purchase all their air-time, raise their own money, and produce their own programs, paid-time programming fared very well. By 1959, 53 percent of all religious time on television was occupied by programs that purchased their air-time, compared to 47 percent by all other types of religious programs.[7] Though much of this air-time was initially in the smaller markets, it illuminates the doggedness which has characterized these smaller religious broadcasters.

"Angel of the Airwaves"

One religious broadcaster who does not fit into any other category was the Roman Catholic bishop, Fulton J. Sheen. Sheen's charisma and career were unusual in the life of the American Roman Catholic Church. Though he was trained as an academic with a strong background in philosophy, Sheen was able to sustain the interest of and communicate to a wide range of people of all faiths.

He began broadcasting in 1928 with a series of radio sermons over the popular radio station WLWL in New York, and continued as the regular speaker on the national "Catholic Hour" program which appeared opposite "Amos 'n' Andy" and was followed immediately by comedian Fred Allen. Of such competition are great religious communicators made!

Sheen's national fame, however, came through national television. He was approached by a commercial television network to present a regular television program with commercial sponsorship (i.e., to compete commercially with other programs). The church had nothing to do with the invitation, nor with sponsorship of the program.

Sheen's program was a marked change from similar programs of the time. He avoided the lavish flourishes of other commercial broadcasts. His program consisted solely of a speech or classroom lecture on a religious or moral subject, presented in a study-type set, with the aid of a blackboard on which he occasionally illustrated a point being made. The only assistance he received throughout the program was from a stagehand who cleaned the board while it was off-camera. Sheen frequently referred to the cleanliness of the board when coming to use it again, attributing its cleanliness to an "angel," who became nationally famous. For many of Sheen's viewers, however, it was Sheen himself who was the real "angel of the airwaves."

The clean blackboard was Sheen's only "trick." The rest of his program was meticulously planned, with Sheen spending about 30 hours each week preparing for the telecast. A day or two before the actual broadcast he would present the talk to friends in Italian and French in order to clarify his comprehension of the subject. The actual program, however, was unrehearsed, partly because Sheen never used notes or a teleprompter and thus could not accurately be predicted. *Time* magazine, which could not believe that he could consistently present a program under such conditions, actually sent a writer to the studio to detect what special tricks Sheen was using.

Sheen's program was ecumenical in its content, ranging over a broad spread of subjects from communism to art, science, war, family life, and personal problems, though the fact that he was a bishop of the Roman Catholic Church was continually apparent to viewers because of his priestly garb and cape. Interest in the program was sustained solely by Sheen's meticulous planning, vocal variety, facial expressions, gestures, the relevance of his content, and the dynamic of his authoritative personality.

His program brought a great response. Between the years 1952 and 1957 he continued to draw a competitive share of the evening television audience. Many bars tuned their television sets to his program; taxi drivers would stop work for a half-hour in order to watch. A blind couple in Minneapolis bought an Admiral television set to express gratitude to the sponsor of his program.[8]

Sheen was paid $26,000 for each program, the money being given to the office which he directed, the Society for the Propagation of the Faith. When he occasionally made a direct appeal for a dime from viewers or listeners for the poor of the world, he would be deluged with coins taped to letters. In one telecast he even mentioned offhandedly that he liked chocolate cookies. His office was subsequently overwhelmed with mailed gifts of cookies.

No other religious program has ever gained such sustained commercial sponsorship and no other religious program has ever drawn the consistently high audience which Sheen attracted during his five-year series. Yet his success in many ways provided a model which was to be adopted by later conservative broadcasters. His success in taming a common medium overcame any theological differences which are normally of major concern to evangelical and fundamentalist Protestants. For this reason, when Sheen appeared as a guest before the 1977 convention of National Religious Broadcasters he was given a standing ovation by these conservative Protestant broadcasters: he was a symbol of a dream of success shared by most of those present.

The Explosion of the 1960s and 1970s

Changes in the relative structures of religious television began to occur during the 1960s. There was a marked decrease in programming which was broadcast on sustaining-time, and a corresponding growth in both the number and size of the independently syndicated evangelical programs which were broadcast on purchased time. These changes accelerated even further in the 1970s.

Some of the growth patterns for these evangelical programs are dramatic. Rex Humbard, for example, began his television ministry in 1953, broadcasting his local church service in Akron, Ohio. From 1953 to 1969 Humbard was able to develop his program and financial support so that he was able to purchase air-time regularly on 68 stations. In the following year, the number of stations carrying his program rose to 110, and an additional 100 stations were added in each of the following two years. In just three years his purchasing capability and syndication quadrupled!

Oral Roberts experienced similar growth with his program. His television ministry began in 1954 with a revivalist program which was syndicated over 16 stations. In 1967 Roberts perceived that television was a medium which required a different approach from the one that he had been using and that had brought him controversial fame on radio. In that year he closed down his television program and began to redesign it. His new program appeared two years later. It comprised a variety show featuring well-known guests and performers, with a message delivered by Roberts in a much smoother, "cooler" style. His formula apparently worked. His Thanksgiving Special in the following year, using his new approach, reached over 27 million people.[9]

Since the late 1960s there has been a rapid growth of independently syndicated evangelical or fundamentalist programs which purchase their air-time from local stations and raise support from their audience. The number of these programs increased from 38 in 1970 to 72 in 1978.[10]

Starting in 1960, independent evangelical organizations also began to purchase and establish their own television stations and to develop their own programming networks. While these groups had owned radio stations in different parts of the country for several decades, the scarcity of television frequencies delayed their entry into the television market. The expansion of UHF-frequency licenses provided them with the opportunity they needed, and by 1978 there were approximately 30 religious television stations with another 30 applications for a television license by religious groups before the FCC.[11]

The impact of this recent growth on the nature of religious television in America has been profound. Programs that purchase their air-time (primarily evangelical and fundamentalist programs) have come to dominate television's regular religious programming. The extent to which they have grown is indicated by their dominance of air-time. While in 1959 programs that purchased their air-time accounted for 53 percent of religious air-time, by 1977 they occupied 92 percent of air-time used for religious programs. As has been noted, much of this air-time was still held in smaller markets and at more marginal times than most of the mainline programming which has continued. However, paid-time programs have virtually eliminated local religious programming, and the pressure they have exerted on the networks through network affiliate stations has caused the networks to reexamine and in some cases reprogram their religious offerings. In 1979, for example, CBS discontinued the long-running "Lamp Unto My Feet" and "Look Up and Live" and substituted another half-hour series "For Our Times" at a different time.

The near elimination of local programming has come about because local stations have found it more profitable to sell time to evangelical and fundamentalist syndicators than to provide time free for public-service programming.

These changes have caused a marked lack of representativeness in the presentation of religious faith on American television. In 1979 more than half of all national airings of religious programs were accounted for by only 10 major evangelical programs. Other religious expressions and traditions were almost forced off the air totally by these (now) wealthy conservative Protestant organizations.

The irony of this situation is that most of these independent broadcasters are associated with National Religious Broadcasters (NRB), a business association of evangelical broadcasters. NRB was formed in 1944 with the primary intent of gaining more and better air-time for their associates. These broadcasters, who once could not get enough time, have been so effective in their struggle that they now hold a virtual monopoly over air-time used for religious programming, having forced most other religious programs off the air by their cut-throat purchase of time. Yet they show none of the consideration for other types of programming which they originally sought for themselves.

The dominance of religious television by this one minority expression of American religious culture assumes more serious implications when it is considered with the factors that have influenced it, which is the substance of our next chapter.

Notes

1. Quoted in Roger Kahle, "Religion and Network Television," M. S. thesis, Columbia University, 1970, pp. II:3–4.
2. Ibid., p. II:12.
3. Martin Marty, *The Improper Opinion*, Philadelphia: Westminster Press, 1961, p. 66.
4. Ben Armstrong, *The Electric Church*, Nashville: Nelson, 1979, p. 133.
5. There is substantial disagreement in the terms used to distinguish the different Christian traditions. Some of the differences become theologically technical, with distinctions drawn not only between mainline and conservative churches, but also between different varieties of evangelicalism, fundamentalism, and pentecostalism. For clarity in this study, the term "mainline" will be used in relation to the Roman Catholic Church and those churches identified with the National Council of Churches. The terms "Evangelical," "Fundamentalist,"

and/or "Conservative" will be used to identify those churches or broadcast groups affiliated with the National Religious Broadcasters or its parent body, National Association of Evangelicals. No attempt will be made to locate a group precisely within the evangelical or fundamentalist distinctions except to serve a particular purpose.

6. J. Harold Ellens, *Models of Religious Broadcasting*, Grand Rapids: W. B. Erdmans, 1974, pp. 107–9.

7. Federal Communications Commission, Submission by the Communications Committee of the United States Catholic Conference and Others in the Matter of Amendment of the Commission's Rules Concerning Program Definitions for Commercial Broadcast Stations, BC Docket No. 78-355, RM-2709, 1979, Table II.

8. Much of this material on Sheen's career and method is drawn from his autobiography *Treasure in Clay*, Garden City: Doubleday & Co., 1980, particularly Chapter 6.

9. Ellens, *Models*, p. 76.

10. Arbitron figures, quoted in Jeffrey Hadden and Charles Swann, *Prime-time Preachers: The Rising Power of Televangelism*, Reading, Mass.: Addison-Wesley, 1981, p. 55.

11. Personal correspondence from Ben Armstrong, Executive Secretary of NRB, on March 31, 1980. Definitions of what constitutes a "religious station" vary significantly, from one owned by an identifiable religious group to one with a specified amount of religious programming.

2

The Making of the Monopoly

There have been many attempts to explain how the paid-time broadcasters have come to dominate the religious programming on television. There have been suggestions that their success has lain simply in their having outhustled the mainline broadcasters, while others have suggested that their success lies in having grasped the essential nature of the medium—more clearly than the mainline broadcasters—and communicating within those terms. Some conservative broadcasters themselves see their growth solely within theological terms, as God's blessing on their sincerity and faithfulness to the Gospel.

A close examination of the changes that have taken place over the past several decades in religious television suggests that the answer is not simple. The nature of religious television in America can be seen to be a function of the interaction of four main players; changes over the past decades have come about because of changes in the relative power and relationships of the four following players: (1) the regulatory agencies of the federal government, which, through the legislative process, provide the structure within which interaction inside the television industry takes place; (2) the television industry, primarily network and local station managements, which control the airwaves within the legislated structure; (3) the viewing public, which selects what it is that will be watched; and (4) the religious broadcasters who provide the material for broadcasts. If one is to understand the present situation in religious television in America, one must consider the part that has been played by each.

The Role of Federal Regulation: The FCC

The Communications Act of 1934 gave the FCC the power of licensing individual stations to broadcast in a particular area over a particular frequency. Included in the license authority given to each station is the requirement that the station is to operate in the interest of the viewing public within its broadcast area. This requirement is an extension of the principle that the airwaves belong to the people and that stations are acting as the agents of the people.

Though the power of determination of the specific content on television remains with the local station management, the FCC has on different occasions offered suggestions on the types of programming that should be present in a station's schedule in order for the station to fulfill the conditions of its license. On each of the occasions that the FCC has elaborated these types of programming, "religion" has been one of the suggested programming categories. Though the FCC does not have the authority to force stations to present religious programming, most broadcasters feel that to ignore the FCC's recommendations would be a decided risk at license renewal time.

In the earlier years of broadcasting, broadcasters promised Congress to provide churches and other public groups with free air-time for the broadcast of their programs in exchange for favorable legislation which did not bind them to such a compulsory arrangement. On the basis of these promises they were also given freedom in other areas.

For a long time this arrangement persisted. Networks and stations provided free air-time for the broadcast of religious programs on a representative basis. Such programs were generally not commercially sponsored because sponsorship for such low-rating programs was difficult to secure. Some broadcast licensees also considered that religious programs were of such a nature that commercial sponsorship was not appropriate.

Changes in this situation began to occur around 1960. In that year, the FCC released a programming statement in which they concluded, under a good deal of pressure from particular groups, that no public-interest basis was to be served by distinguishing between sustaining-time programs (those broadcast on free air-time) and commercially sponsored programs in evaluating a station's performance in the public interest. As long as the required categories of public-interest programs were present, whether they were public service or commercial in nature was no longer to be a subject of consideration in license-renewal evaluations. This statement opened the way for stations to meet FCC regulations equally with programs that paid for their air-time as with programs for which air-time was provided without charge.

This change in FCC policy did not have an immediately dramatic effect on the nature of religious programming; however, it effectively changed the structure within which religious programming was to be considered by releasing stations from any regulatory obligation to provide free air-time for the broadcast of religious programs. As the social climate changed, and as the number of religious programs that were willing and able to pay for airtime increased, television stations found it more profitable to present religious programs that paid them money rather than programs that cost them money. As will be seen, the growth of independent UHF stations markedly increased the pressure on other stations to maximize their profitability, even on religious programming.

Two other policies of the FCC have strongly influenced the nature of religious television. Communication lawyer Linda-Jo Lacey suggests that the FCC has unfairly favored paid-time religious programs over other types by its uneven enforcement of rules regulating religious commercial time and on-air fund raising. Though there are strict regulations governing the raising of money by stations that hold a noncommercial license (e.g. educational stations), the FCC has avoided enforcement of these regulations when it has been a religious group or organization holding such a license, thus making it easier and more profitable for religious organizations to hold noncommercial licenses by lowering the normal restrictions on the raising of money through on-air solicitations, the sale of religious items, and so on. The FCC, for example, has specifically stated that rules governing the amount of commercial time permitted for each hour of programming do not apply to paid-time religious programs. Though they spend a part of each program soliciting funds for their organizations, the FCC has ruled that paid-time religious programs are not commercial-length programs. This means that television stations may sell unlimited time to religious broadcasters without worrying about usual restrictions on commercial time. This uneven enforcement of FCC policy has made it more than normally profitable for stations to sell time to religious broadcasters who are prepared to buy it. Whereas before the low-audience period of Sunday morning was a difficult one in which to sell commercial time, stations have been able to compensate by selling whole blocks of time to the religious broadcasters.

Each of these decisions has favored the paid-time religious broadcasters and severely handicapped the religious broadcasters who have been dependent on public-service time previously granted by the station.[1]

The FCC has also avoided ruling on the representativeness of religious programs in relation to particular issues or religious-affiliation patterns in a viewing area. Normally the "Fairness Doctrine" ensures that various community opinions on a controversial issue are represented on television. The FCC has ruled, however, that the fairness doctrine does not apply to the broadcast of religious material because religion has not reached the level of social controversy. Neither has the FCC attempted to rule on the differentiation of one expression of religious faith over another. In the opinion of the FCC, the representativeness of religious faith presented on television is a matter to be decided solely by a television station if it wishes to venture to do so.

Through these rulings, the FCC has effectively removed itself from the field of religious television. Though much of the function of the FCC is ostensibly to protect community interests against the economic drive of the television industry, because of the hazards of church–state definitions and perhaps its own timidity, it has largely avoided this responsibility in relation to the regulation of religious television. By its avoidance of the issue, however, it has in fact preferred particular religious expressions over others. By relegating the determination of religious programming on television to individual stations, it has placed religious faith into the hands of the economic marketplace, thus giving a distinct advantage to those expressions of religious faith which are economically competitive.

Changes in the Relative Power of Religious Broadcasters

Part of the reason for the takeover of religious television by conservative, paid-time religious broadcasters has been the changes that have occurred in American religious culture, changes that have reduced the power of those broadcasters who represent the mainline denominations while increasing the power of those representing the conservative denominations and groups.

When television first began, the mainline churches were experiencing the peak of their membership and influence in society. Consequently, when the networks and stations sought a representative religious voice they turned to the mainline churches. The mainline cooperative and moderate approach to religious programming also suited the legislative and public-relations needs of the newly emerging medium of television. The evangelicals and fundamentalists, who were not seen as a major force within the mainstream of American cultural and religious life, existed mainly on the fringes of influence within the television industry.

Major changes in this structure began to occur during the 1960s. Membership of mainline denominations in general began to decline, while membership of evangelical denominations and individual religious groups began to increase.[2] In evaluating the changes in religious television, it is necessary to consider some of the reasons for these more general changes.

Many attempts have been made to explain the phenomenon of declining membership in mainline churches, and increasing membership in evangelical denominations, with varying degrees of emphasis placed on different factors. The most recent, and perhaps the most systematic attempt to base conclusions on empirical rather than speculative foundations, has been the symposium edited by Dean Hoge and David Roozen, published under the title *Understanding Church Growth and Decline, 1950–78*.

In their analysis, Hoge and Roozen affirm that the more important phenomenon to explain is not the growth of conservative churches during this period, because prior to the 1960s all churches had been growing; rather, the phenomenon to note is the decline of the mainline churches— why didn't they continue to grow as the conservative churches did? Hoge and Roozen conclude that the main explanation for denominational trends lies in contextual factors: there was a broad cultural shift in the direction of diversity within society which produced a distance from many of the traditional social institutions. This shift in values hit hardest those denominations and churches whose practice and theology were most closely tied to the culture, namely the affluent, educated, individualistic, and culture-affirming mainline denominations.[3] The trend was most observable among college youth who have traditionally been the source of new church members for these denominations. This shift, which first affected college youth, has spread to other youth and also to large sectors of adults, to the extent that some denominations of moderate and conservative theology have also been experiencing membership decline in the past few years.[4]

The period was one of major social trauma, unrest, and confusion. Beginning with the assassination of John Kennedy, in just 10 years Americans witnessed and experienced the Civil Rights movement with its massive challenges to established American values, the Vietnam war and its social and political consequences, student unrest and riots, the assassinations of Robert Kennedy and Martin Luther King, radical changes in the perception and practice of morality and authority, and the crisis of Watergate and the consequent threat to national leadership and traditional national symbols. The mainline churches during this period appeared to be in disarray as they struggled to come to grips not only with the impact and meaning of the social changes taking place around them, but also with their declining strength and the resultant conflict within.

The social situation of the period, on the other hand, created within many the need for clear leadership and unambiguous answers to social and religious questions. Many people, including some disillusioned former members of mainline churches, found these answers within the evangelical churches. Unlike the mainline churches, the conservative churches as a whole had experienced few setbacks as a result of the changing conditions. They therefore presented an image of certainty, strength, and competent leadership and management. In addition to their unambiguous theology, their personal discipline, the distinctiveness of their life-style and morality, and their authoritative structure provided a secure and unambiguous social alternative for those who were confused and battered by the social changes going on around them.

Other studies confirm Hoge and Roozen's thesis. A study by Bibby and Brinkerhoff reinforces the idea that there has not been the same falloff of youth from the conservative churches, and that they have acquired some members from the other churches. In a study of membership additions to

20 evangelical congregations during the period 1966 to 1970, they found that over 70 percent of the new members in these evangelical churches came from other evangelical churches, largely because of geographical or social mobility, while 20 percent of the new members were children of existing members; two groups which the mainline churches found difficult to hold. Of the remaining 10 percent, they found that the majority were people with a previous church background.[5] The authors concluded that

it seems likely that relatively few new members of evangelical churches come from outside the Christian community. . . . conservative church growth is mainly a matter of retaining those who are already familiar with evangelical culture.[6]

Evangelical broadcasting began to play a significant role within this broader social movement. In addition to their identification with the growing evangelical movement, evangelical television programs helped unify the broader movement and give it visibility as a growing alternative. It gave evangelicals contact with and visibility of their national leaders and celebrities, a sense of identification with a wider evangelical community, and reinforcement for their individual personal commitment. In return, the evangelical community, whose focus of commitment is less scattered and whose financial contributions are more generous than members of mainline churches,[7] has faithfully supported such perceived evangelistic efforts with its time (viewing) and money.

During this period, therefore, evangelicalism as a whole began to shift away from the fringes of American society into the country's religious mainstream, shifting the relative power in relation to the television industry away from the mainline broadcasters and their viewpoint to the evangelical broadcasters and their approach to television.

The fact that the evangelicals were not a majority group was of less importance to the television industry than the perception that they were part of a broader movement. Television, which prefers to present movements rather than established realities, began to turn its attention to this group.

At the same time, however, there was a second major factor that contributed to the disproportionate growth of evangelical television programs, viz. the developing sophistication of computer technology. If it had not been for the development of computer sophistication during this same period, the changes now seen in religious television may never have occurred.

One of the problems continually faced by religious broadcasters has been that of handling the large volume of correspondence generated by their programs. This problem has been of critical concern to the paid-time religious broadcasters who are dependent on continuing audience response for their essential income.

The development of sophisticated computer technology and application in the 1960s gave the paid-time broadcasters the tool they needed for handling larger volumes of personal mail, and for solicitation of funds from their viewers. The computer made possible not only computation of responses, but the development of an extended quasi-personal relationship between broadcaster and audience members, similar to that between a pastor and his congregation. It opened the way for mass counseling of individual problems and, through the retention of relevant personal histories, it gave the means to broadcasters to target specific financial appeals accurately to potential givers.

There were both practical and theological factors that caused the computer to be more advantageous to the evangelical than to the mainline broadcasters. It particularly suited the paid-time broadcasters' need to manage a large volume of data at a centralized organization. The mainline broadcasters, who depended more on support from decentralized congregations, did not have the same need and therefore did not experience the same advantage.

Evangelical theology and practice tended also to be more clear-cut, almost dualistic in its concepts. This made it extremely adaptable to the binary characteristics of computerization. The mainline churches, with their more abstract theologies and ethics and their more complex concepts of personal counseling could not conceive of the conduct of personal relationships via a computer.

Evangelicals reflect a more utilitarian attitude toward technology. For most evangelicals the morality of a particular technology lies principally in the morality of the user and his purpose. Most of their energy was spent, therefore, not in debating the social and ethical implications of computer technology (as did the mainline churches), but in adapting them most advantageously to their own purposes.

It has been the computer, perhaps more than any other single factor, which has made possible the development of the power base on which the independent evangelical broadcast organizations are built, namely, audience support. Development of this financial resource has given them their inordinate leverage within the television industry.

A third factor that promoted the growth of the paid-time broadcasters over the mainline broadcasters was the paid-time broadcasters' willingness and ability to adapt their message to the demands of television.

Television in American society has been found increasingly to present a particular world-view. Running through its diverse programming is a coherent and consistent mythical system by which events are interpreted and its diverse activities integrated. This system includes contextual characteristics such as the tendency to simplify and sensationalize events and issues and to promise and provide instant gratification, and conceptual characteristics such as particular and recurring images of power, happiness, meaning, and the nature of success. These characteristics, along with the typical social uses of television which at times approach the level of ritual, have led several thinkers and communication researchers to suggest that television now functions for many people as an integrated religious system.[8] Research has found that this repetitive use of television, along with television's recurring images, influence people's perception of reality.[9]

There are significant parts of evangelical and fundamentalist theology which correspond to television's approach. Evangelical theology places stress on the individual as the effective social unit, corresponding to television's preference for the individualizing of issues and the personalizing of events. Evangelical theology is simple in its conceptual formulations of ideas and events, at times almost stereotypical. It places great emphasis on the overt experiential and emotional aspects of religious faith, making it more appealing and engaging to television viewers than other more mystical or conceptual expressions of Christianity. The urgency of evangelicals' evangelizing activity is communicated well by television as vitality and dynamism compared to the other, more low-key expressions of the mainline churches. Evangelicals have always placed emphasis on dramatic change and interventions of God, making their message more adaptable to television's predilections towards sensationalism. Finally, conservative theology and practice have tended to be strong in their affirmation of traditional American culture, including the values of free enterprise and the validity of its financial rewards. Mainline programs, on the other hand, were often critical of aspects of the American system. Instead of reaffirming central American values, mainline programs often presented the fringes of American life and culture, making them seem out of place in the context of general television programming.

Evangelicals were also more willing than the mainline broadcasters to adapt actively to the requirements of television. They were not afraid to sensationalize, to present images of luxury, affluence, success and grandeur, to entertain, to cater to their viewers' self-interest and consumerism which had been cultivated by commercial television. Paid-time broadcasters therefore extended the evangelical movement, being those who popularized it within terms familiar to most Americans, the terms of television-land. While many mainline and some evangelical leaders criticized the validity of this interpretation of the Christian faith, the paid-time broadcasters intuited accurately that television had become the "real world" for millions of people, one to which the Christian faith must be communicated in terms common to that world. Whether in the process they lost the essence of the Christian message has been a subject of debate among the various religious traditions ever since, and one which shall be considered in a later chapter.

The Differences between Audiences of Religious Programs

It is a common misperception that sustaining-time religious programs have never attracted as large an audience as present paid-time programs. Many network sustaining-time programs have consistently rated higher than even the current large paid-time programs. This misperception has led to an unbalanced support for paid-time programs on the basis that they are more effective in their use of television than the earlier religious programs were. Television station managers have on occasion replaced mainline sustaining-time programs with paid-time programs because, in their opinion, the paid-time programs were attracting larger audiences and therefore meeting the needs of the viewing public to a greater extent than were sustaining-time programs.

While the audiences for paid-time programs have grown in the past decade, the programs do not attract a large audience within the relative terms of the television industry. As will be seen in more detail subsequently, Nielsen figures for 1979 show only five syndicated religious programs that were able to gain equal to or greater than a rating of one. The largest-rating syndicated program, Oral Roberts, gained a national rating of only two.[10] Sustaining-time programs still attract comparably large audiences by religious television standards when they are given comparable broadcast time.[11]

While many sustaining-time programs have had as large or larger audiences than paid-time programs, what has made a big difference in the disproportionate growth of paid-time programs has been the differences in the nature of the audiences between the two types of programming. The audiences of paid-time programs have tended to be more demonstrative and vocal in their support of the programs than have the audiences of sustaining-time programs. It has been this vocalization of the audiences which has carried a power with local television stations disproportionate to the actual size of the audiences. The paid-time audiences' willingness to support their programs financially has made local stations think that the size of the audience for paid-time programs is larger than it actually is.

The audiences of paid-time programs tend also to be more demonstrative in support of their programs than other audiences. This was clearly demonstrated in Texas by evangelist and television programmer James Robison. Robison had created controversy and legal problems for the local station WFAA by his attacks on homosexuality on his television program. Homosexual groups had complained to the station and had demanded equal time for rebuttal of Robison's attacks. The station eventually found it most expeditious to cancel Robison's program. It is indicative of the loyalty of the audience of some evangelical programs that Robison was able to draw 10,000 people to a rally in Dallas to protest the station's cancellation of his program. This demonstration of support, along with threatened legal action, was sufficient to get the station to reinstate his program.

It is unlikely that a sustaining-time program could muster such support. Viewers of sustaining-time religious programs have never been as loyal or demonstrative, nor has this aspect of viewing been cultivated. The effect, however, was that when paid-time programs began to displace sustaining-time programs there was hardly a word of complaint by the audience to station managers. The takeover by paid-time programs in the decade from 1965 to 1975 went virtually unnoticed and unchallenged. It was only in 1976, when the monopoly was virtually complete, that criticisms began to be heard. At this stage, however, the paid-time broadcasters and the station managers were firmly established in their mutually profitable enterprise.

The Economic Interests of the Television Industry

The major factor influencing the growth of the monopoly in religious television in America has been the commercial television industry. The primary reason why the lack of representativeness in the presentation of religious faith on American television has occurred is this situation is most favorable to the economic interests of the television stations themselves.

Television in America is primarily a commercial activity. Eric Barnouw, the broadcast historian, notes that the dominant pressure in influencing the shape of television has been the demands of the advertisers. Television has developed around advertising, the primary purpose being to gather as large an audience as possible to "sell" to the advertisers. When conflicts have emerged between the producers of programs and the requirements of these industrial goals, it has most frequently been the advertisers who have won.[12]

Part of the function of the Communication Act of 1934 was not to change this, but to create a framework of regulation within which this economic motivation could be contained in order to achieve desired social goals as well. While this regulation has encouraged stations to present some religious programming, as has been noted the FCC through its rulings has largely left the determination of the content of this religious programming to the individual station managers.

In the early years of television, most stations made an effort to be representative in their presentation of religious faith. Most retained the outlook that religion was to be viewed as a public service to their viewing areas, and they attempted to maintain a balance in the content of this programming. Representativeness of different points of view was maintained through the broadcast of various network programs, locally produced programs, denominationally syndicated programs, and independent paid-time programs.

It has been seen that this attitude began to change during the 1960s, largely because of the growing intensification of the commercial competitiveness of the television industry in general. Station managers have always been strongly influenced in their programming by the behavior of other station managers and movements within the television industry as a whole. This influence has also applied to religious programming. A survey by the Broadcast Institute of North America in 1971 found that in choosing and scheduling religious programs, station managers were most strongly influenced by the behavior of other station managers rather than by individual local factors such as community interest and response.[13]

The model for change in relation to religious programming came largely from the growing number of independent UHF stations. These new UHF stations generally did not have a network affiliation and therefore were not provided with network programs for public-service airing. These stations also did not have the resources to provide as much public-service air-time as did the larger VHF stations, and were forced to maximize their profitability wherever possible. The use of paid-time religious programs offered the opportunity to make a profit on the sale of air-time, particularly on Sunday mornings, which were normally a slow audience period. These independent stations therefore tended to broadcast more paid-time religious programs than other stations. The Broadcast Institute study found that on the average 58.4 percent of an independent station's religious programming was paid-time programming, compared to 32.3 percent to 42.1 percent for those stations with a network affiliation.[14] With the precedent set by these UHF stations and in the absence of specific direction from the FCC, other stations also came to recognize the commercial potential of paid-time religious programs. Increasingly other stations began to replace network programs, local programs, and denominational programs with programs that paid for their air-time.

There were accompanying factors which enabled television station managers to live with the obvious inequity caused by these trends. The FCC decision in relation to religious programming provided the structure within which station managers were freed from the obligation of having to distinguish between different expressions of religious faith or the representativeness of religious programming for a particular area. As has been noted also, the audiences for the paid-time programs tended to be more demonstrative in support of their programs than were the audiences of other religious programs. This demonstrativeness easily created the impression that there was greater desire and support for paid-time programs than may actually have been the case.

The paid-time programs have tended also to be more in harmony with the general interests of the television industry than have other types of religious programs. Evangelical programs have tended to be more affirmative toward and supportive of the American broadcasting system than have other religious organizations.[15] The content of the paid-time religious programs has tended also to be more like other television programs—formats have been similar, appeals have been consumer-oriented, guests have been faces familiar to the television audience, production techniques have been those common to the television industry—and this has made possible an easier blending of religious programs with the programming intentions of station managers in general.

Changes in the nature of religious television in the 1960s and 1970s can therefore be seen to have been a function of a historical coincidence of a number of related factors: social conditions, government regulation, audience response, and general trends in religious culture. The adjudication of these factors and how they were to be represented to the public, though, has lain primarily with the television industry, which controls the airwaves and the content communicated through them. Of greatest concern is that the television industry has preferred to present only those aspects of American religious life which are advantageous to their own financial interests. The danger is that as broadcasting becomes increasingly deregulated, the tendencies of the broadcast industry in this direction will intensify.

The power of the television industry has acted in this way to shape the public perception of American religious life and culture, not so much by the creation of a particular phenomenon, but by the selective promotion of one particular expression over another in a way that distorts the factual situation. For while evangelical expressions of Christianity in America have been increasing in strength and influence in recent years, there is still a major, if not majority, segment of the American population whose religious faith does not fall under the evangelical umbrella. Yet these major religious expressions are rarely seen on television in America anymore.

In relation to American religious culture, therefore, television has exercised a major status-conferral effect, not on the basis of a representativeness, nor on a calculated moral-evaluative basis, but solely on the basis of a correspondence of a minority religious ethos with television's own economic, functional, and mythical goals.

It is one of the affirmations of this study that this power exercised by the television industry in relation to religious culture is of greater concern than any individual aspect of religious television. When one attempts to assess the present and future situations in religious television, the power of the commercial television industry over the perception of social reality must be of major consideration.

Notes

1. Linda-Jo Lacey, "The Electric Church: An FCC 'Established' Institution?" *Federal Communication Law Journal* 31 (1978), pp. 252–62.
2. Dean R. Hoge and David A. Roozen, eds., *Understanding Church Growth and Decline, 1950–78*, New York: Pilgrim Press, 1977, pp. 328–30.
3. Ibid., p. 328.
4. Ibid., pp. 329–30.

5. Reginald W. Bibby and Merlin B. Brinkerhoff, "The Circulation of the Saints: A Study of People Who Join Conservative Churches," *Journal for the Scientific Study of Religion*, 12 September 1973, p. 276.
6. Ibid., p. 283.
7. Rodney Stark and Charles Y. Glock, *American Piety: The Nature of Religious Commitment*, Berkeley: University of California Press, 1968, pp. 81–107.
8. See for example, William Kuhns, *The Electronic Gospel*, New York: Herder and Herder, 1969; George Gerbner, "Television as New Religion," *New Catholic World*, May/April 1978, pp. 52–56; and Gregor T. Goethals, *The TV Ritual: Worship at the Video Altar*, Boston: Beacon Press, 1981.
9. See particularly the cultural indicators research centered at the Annenberg School of Communication in Pennsylvania, described in George Gerbner et al., *Violence Profile No. 11: Trends in Network Television Drama and Viewer Conceptions of Social Reality, 1967–79*, Philadelphia: Annenberg School of Communication, University of Pennsylvania, 1980.
10. That is, two percent of the possible national television households. Nielsen, "Report on Syndicated Program Audiences," November 1979, p. R-7.
11. The Roman Catholic program, "Insight," for example, was the third largest-rating religious program in the areas in which it was broadcast. A wider national exposure could easily have made it one of the largest-rating religious programs. Some network religious specials also rate as high as or higher than the syndicated paid-time programs.
12. Eric Barnouw, *Tube of Plenty: The Evolution of American Television*, New York: Oxford University Press, 1975, pp. 163–64.
13. Broadcast Institute of North America, "Religious Programming on Television: An Analysis of a Sample Week," New York, 1973, p. 47.
14. Ibid., pp. 49–52.
15. Compare, for example, the comment by NRB Executive Secretary, Ben Armstrong: "That's the great genius of the American system. There is a choice of radio and TV stations, each working to capture its share of the audience. Broadcasting in this country is unique because it operates as part of the competitive system of private enterprise." *Electric Church*, p. 134.

3

The Electronic Evangelists

All of the electronic evangelists can boast of humble beginnings, a strong element in their testimonies that their present status is a sure indication of God's direct blessing on them. Oral Roberts began life as a stuttering child of destitute parents. He later overcame his stuttering and took to the "sawdust trail," holding revival and healing services in the Southern states before making his first television program in a studio in 1954. Today he has also overcome his destitution, presiding over a multimillion-dollar organization which includes Oral Roberts University and the City of Faith complex in Tulsa, Oklahoma. His television organization still produces one of the highest-rating television programs in America, a variety show with Oral Roberts as the main speaker.

Jerry Falwell was just out of Bible College when he began his church in 1956 with 35 adults and their children meeting in a former Donald Duck bottling company building in Lynchburg, Virginia. Today he is the senior pastor of the church, the large Thomas Road Baptist Church, which in 1978 had a membership of 15,000. His television program, "The Old Time Gospel Hour," is an edited version of one of the morning services from the church. Through the program, Falwell has been able to develop a number of Liberty Baptist Schools and the "Liberty Mountain" project—a college and proposed future projects on a hill in Lynchburg. In 1980 his program also gave him national attention as the head of Moral Majority, a national citizens' movement.

The host of the "700 Club," Pat Robertson, was trained initially as a lawyer but failed to pass the bar exams for New York State and found his law career frustrated. Following this, after residing in the slums of Brooklyn, he purchased a defunct television station in Virginia Beach in 1960 with a view to establishing the first religious television station. His first broadcast in 1961 was a program that lasted one-and-a-half hours.

Today, just 20 short years later, he oversees the Christian Broadcasting Network which, from its $50-million headquarters in Virginia Beach, incorporates four television stations, six radio stations, a missionary radio station, a recording company, a programming service which makes 24-hour-a-day programming available to the more than 3,000 cable systems in the U.S.A. and Canada, a news network, a university, and a satellite earth station.[1] His network has also been responsible for the development of the first Christian soap opera.

Robert Schuller began his ministry in 1955 when the Reformed Church in America sent him to Orange County, California, to begin a new congregation. His first service was held in a drive-in theater with Schuller investing the last of his savings to buy an organ for the occasion and preaching from the roof of the theater snack bar. Today he preaches from the "Crystal Cathedral," the $15-million glass sanctuary of the Garden Grove Community Church. His television program, "Hour of Power," is also an edited broadcast of one of the morning worship services at the church.

The list could go on to include other television evangelists: Rex Humbard, Jim Bakker, Jimmy Swaggart, James Robison, Kenneth Copeland, and others. Though a few of them are ordained ministers of churches and most consider themselves primarily preachers, their daily schedules are more comparable to those of executives of major corporations than of regular clergy. Much of their day is spent in planning meetings, executive conferences, program review and taping sessions, and press and public relations interviews.

There is a strong charisma in these men* which separates them from the thousands of other faithful preachers and aspirants who also have spent long hours in the preparation and planning of material and programs and long hours trying to convince stubborn church bodies of the desirability of purchasing television equipment.

But their charisma alone has not produced these success stories. Their success is also a result of a careful and determined marketing: the product of a unique blending of charisma with personal drive and audacity, accurate social intuition, hard-nosed business advice and judgment, and adoption of modern marketing principles and techniques. It is important to realize that the present major religious broadcasters are just the tip of the iceberg. For those who have succeeded in making it into major national syndication there are many other aspiring broadcasters whose programs have never gone beyond more than local or regional syndication. One account suggests that there are 180 syndicated religious programs produced in America.[2]

The principle of momentum is of great importance in the development of religious television on this level. Once your program begins to move, it

*Katherine Kuhlman, who died in 1975, has been the only woman to make it to the religious television big-time.

is essential to maintain this momentum and expand it as soon and as continuously as possible. This momentum creates an aura of success ("God's blessing") which encourages further audience loyalty and enthusiasm. It also enables the expansion of one's program to other markets which in turn broadens one's potential financial base. The broadcasters who have succeeded in this process have been those who have been willing and competent to ride this roller coaster.

The first hurdle over which one must pass is simply to get the money. Television is a capital-intensive industry and regardless of how much charisma or vocal support one may have, if one does not have the money to produce a program and pay for its syndication one does not succeed in television. While a broadcaster can generally attract some income and support on the basis of the relevance of his message and his personality, if he is to generate the large amount of money which is needed for a national television ministry he needs a precise, effective, and almost exhaustive money-generating organization. What has separated the sheep from the goats in religious broadcasting in America is the effectiveness with which individual evangelists have been able to put together a "message package" and an organization capable of generating and processing mass support.

This distinction is well illustrated by the example of two different producers of television programs within one denomination of Independent Christian Churches. Christian Television Mission produced programs which were aired primarily on sustaining-time provided free by stations around the country. It derived its income mainly from members of the denomination across the country. From 1969 to 1971 its budget was progressively $99,076, $111,382 and $125,081. Its counterpart within the same denomination was Christian Evangelizers Association, which produced the syndicated program, "Revival Fires"; the program received financial support from church members across the country but cultivated audience support in addition. In 1971 Christian Evangelizers Association employed a professional fund-raising organization to develop the solicitation of audience members, that year spending $252,000 or 22.5 percent of its budget on fund-raising activities. The effect, however, was dramatic. While its counterpart in 1970–71 experienced only nominal increases in budget income, the Christian Evangelizers Association budget increased from $571,000 in 1970 to $1,117,000 in 1971, the increase due almost solely to the intensive audience solicitation campaign. The adoption of this intensive audience solicitation within the organization enabled the program to expand to such an extent that in 1971 it was the third most widely syndicated religious program in the country.[3]

The difference in the growth rate of these two programs at this time illustrates also the differences in growth not only between evangelical and mainline programming, but also between different types of evangelical programming, those which purchase their air-time and solicit their audience for support and those which air their programs on sustaining-time and undertake no audience solicitation. These differences are important in understanding the shaping effect that television has on religious programming. What appears to be true is that the greater discrimination is to be found not on the basis of the theological or ecclesiastical tradition from which the program comes, but from the nature of the financial relationship between the broadcaster and the television station. There are more similarities between a mainline sustaining-time program and an evangelical sustaining-time program than there are between an evangelical sustaining-time program and an evangelical paid-time program.

A major part of each religious broadcast organization therefore is its fund-raising section. Fund raising consumes a large part of each organization's regular budget. In 1979, 35 percent of the Rex Humbard organization's budget, or $10.5 million, was spent on the building of audience loyalty and the solicitation of its financial support.[4] For the program "The Old Time Gospel Hour," the figure was $10.99 million or 23.7 percent of the organization's budget.[5]

Such large amounts of money are needed for several reasons. One is simply to meet the costs of processing the large number of individual donations which comprise the backbone of the broadcasters' support. Jerry Falwell's organization in 1976–77, for example, received nearly 80 percent of its $22.2-million income from 762,000 individual contributions.[6] Any organization that does not develop the capability to handle such volume is effectively cutting off the source of its own lifeblood. Thomas Road Baptist Church in 1976–77 used about 60 people daily to sort through the day's mail of around 10,000 envelopes. The Oral Roberts organization is reported to have a similar mailroom, capable of handling 20,000 pieces of mail each day.[7] Each contribution and letter must be accurately recorded and classified for subsequent computerization and recall when the financial planners are calling out lists of names for future mail appeals.

This bulk mail is not only the lifeblood of the broadcasters but it also becomes a type of barometer of the broadcaster's performance in relation to his audience. When faced with the reality of meeting expenses of $1 million each week or else beginning the downward spiral of reducing the syndication of one's program, a broadcaster becomes very sensitive to the audience feedback provided by one's mailroom. The daily report on both income and issues from the mailroom becomes an important item in each broadcaster's daily briefing. Evangelical broadcaster, Tom Bisset, describes some of the pressures under which a broadcaster works:

If a broadcaster touches a "hot" subject even accidentally, he will know about it in a week or even days. Mail, the broadcasters' lifeline, is a built-in polling device that records audience preferences with Gallup-like accuracy. So, unless broadcasters have iron-clad formats, their programs begin to focus on those issues and emphases that bring in the mail—and the money. The necessity of paying for air-time also prompts broadcasters to follow the money.[8]

It is one way in which the economic structures of television shape the nature of the message broadcast by it. While in other ecclesiastical organizations one has greater freedom to reject the desires of one's constituency or at least to evaluate the integrity of their requests on the basis of one's own theological stance, the broadcaster's dependence on his audience income for his very survival removes that theological freedom to a large extent.

It is this reality that contradicts the claim by the paid-time broadcasters that by cultivating audience support they have been able to free themselves from network and local station control over their programs and thus act independently in proclaiming the gospel. It can be seen that audience-supported programs have not achieved economic (and therefore theological) freedom as they claim, but have simply transferred their economic dependence from one source to another: from the television industry management to the television audience. It may be argued that the second master is as constricting as the first.

To be dependent on one's audience for support, particularly in a fickle selective medium such as television, means that the gospel must not only be proclaimed, but it must be proclaimed in such a way that it meets with the approval of a large share of one's audience. If it doesn't, one loses one's base for essential financial support. Further, it is not sufficient simply to offer a message which meets with one's dominant audience support but it must be presented in such a way that it triggers the audience's desire to give.

The dangers in this situation are several. First, it makes popular appreciation and response to the Christian message one of the main criteria for the selection of what is proclaimed, a situation that has been rejected from the earliest beginnings of the Christian faith.[9] In fact, in practice, the paid-time religious broadcasters have subtly reversed these early principles of the Christian faith: whatever evokes a popular response is seen as an indication of the truth of the message and of God's blessing. It becomes a small step to take for the broadcasters to lose any critical distinction between the validity of their intentions, the finance needed to achieve those intentions, and the methods necessary to maintain those finances.

As has been noted, what makes this subtle elision relatively easy and discomfort-free for the paid-time broadcasters is their particular theology of technology. Evangelicals traditionally have rejected organic approaches to the understanding of society and technology in favor of more individualistic approaches. Once one has provided a moral purpose for the use of any particular technology, one is justified in adapting to the requirements inherent in that particular technology.

This approach reflects a strong teleological ethical stance, one where the validity of a particular motivation to a large extent justifies the measures subsequently adopted to achieve the goal. This attitude was strongly reflected in an encounter between one of the broadcasters and a critic at the Consultation on the Electronic Church held in New York in 1980. Broadcaster Pat Robertson of CBN was one of the speakers at the Consultation with theologian Colin Williams as respondent. Robertson's address comprised primarily a statement of his perception of the need for the church to become involved in television and his sincerity in tackling this need. While recognizing the validity of this concern, Williams' criticism in response was directed at the problems inherent in the methods being used by the evangelicals in addressing the problems television posed. Robertson's response totally avoided dialogue on the criticisms which had been made. His handling of subsequent questions by participants reflected the same unwillingness to engage in conceptual debate on the nature of television and the demands it imposes on its users; rather, he placed a strong emphasis on his own personal integrity and good intentions in what he was doing. Such an avoidance of conceptual debate may reflect a definite public-relations strategy by Robertson in relation to the particular situation, but a similar avoidance by other broadcasters in the wider debate on the issue reflects a lack of conceptual grappling with the issue.[10]

Their approach to the use of television has made the paid-time broadcasters very vulnerable to the demands of their financial advisers. This vulnerability is seen not only in their susceptibility to the demands of their audience but also in the more aggressive aspects of their money-raising activities. While their personal sincerity may remain intact,[11] organizationally this sincerity becomes very tenuous because of the overt money-making apparent in all of it.

The first step in the raising of money on such a grand scale is the development of a list of potential contributors. There are several standard strategies used by broadcasters to obtain the names of audience members which can then be used by their fund-raising sections.

Direct on-air solicitation is one of the major strategies used. In one study of people who had become CBN "partners," 67 percent of them indicated that their first action in becoming a partner was to call or send in a contribution.[12] Special programs such as telethons are often a valuable way of highlighting the opportunity for audience members to contribute. The same study of CBN partners indicated that 70 percent of the partners who had seen a CBN telethon had contributed to CBN in response to it.[13] CBN is reported to have raised $10 million in one such telethon.[14]

A second method employed for encouraging audience contributions and the acquisition of names is the offering of "incentives," such as free gifts—records or books. The method works on the basis that if a person makes the effort to send away for a free gift he or she is also more prone to be responsive to a request for a contribution to the organization. This marketing device also taps into the residual guilt felt by a person receiving something for nothing. Rarely a week passes on most paid-time religious programs without the viewer's being offered the opportunity to receive one of these gifts. In addition to the two million "Jesus First" pins offered by "The Old Time Gospel Hour" program, building bricks that are laser-engraved with the donor's name for each $500 given toward a particular building fund have been offered.[15] Popular offerings include records (often the broadcaster's own or one from his family), books (often the broad-caster's own), jewelry, badges, tie-pins, magazines, bibles, and pens. That the method is a profitable one is testified to by its universal usage, and by research. In a study of the congregation of the Irvington Presbyterian Church in Indiana, Clifford Hilton found that one of the reasons given by members for making contributions to a Christian broadcaster was "as a contribution for a gift received."[16]

A third method for obtaining names is the opportunity for viewers to write or call for counseling, prayer, or simply for conversation. While this opportunity ostensibly provides a service to viewers, it also provides a rich source of names for the broadcaster whose audience members have indicated a responsiveness to his program. Telephone conversationalists at the broad-casting center are instructed to obtain the name of each caller, which is then passed on for later fund solicitation. Because of the large response gained in this way, broadcasters have developed a strong emphasis on this contact in their programs. Oral Roberts frequently mentions on his program that he personally answers every letter he receives; other broadcasters have established and developed telephone-call facilities. Eight percent of the regular financial supporters of CBN indicated in one study that their initial contact with the program was by calling a telephone counseling center of CBN.[17]

Though on-air solicitation is often restrained, once a person's name is obtained through one of these methods, intensive direct-mail solicitation of the person is undertaken. These mail solicitations also reveal several common features.

Letters to audience members generally assume a very "personalized" approach. The audience member's name is scattered throughout the text of the letter by specialized computer selection and on-line printer to give the impression that a unique relationship exists between broadcaster and individual, even though the particular letter is one of perhaps millions printed. An intimacy is also frequently suggested in the letter's text. One direct mailing received by the author from Oral Roberts read:

Dear Brother Horsfield,

I must tell you an almost overwhelming feeling has come over me about you. I don't know if there's something I don't know about. It may be something that is happening or is about to happen. But something inside me says you are hurting in some way spiritually . . . or physically . . . or emotionally . . . or financially. I tell you I feel this, there's a problem.

I guess you have a right to say, "Well, Oral, if you don't know what it is you feel I'm hurting with, why write me?" I can't answer that except I'm very sensitive to God and to you as my partner. You see, you have a different relationship with me: I feel closer to you and I believe you feel closer to me.

Such a presumed relationship and intimate understanding of what must be more than tens of thousands of persons on this particular mailing list not only contradicts the sincerity implied in the Christian faith but verges on personal fraud and manipulation.

A second common feature in the mass mailings of paid-time religious broadcasters is the opportunity to participate in supporting the programs as a member of a select group of some sort. Oral Roberts has his "prayer partners"; CBN their "700 Club members"; Rex Humbard his "Prayer Key Family." Membership in these "select" fraternities generally carries with it exclusive privileges in exchange for an ongoing financial commitment. In April 1981 Jim Bakker of the PTL Network offered this opportunity through one of his direct-mail letters:

This month, I want you to do something special. I want you to make a commitment to support God's work at PTL every month. . . . I have a special new gift for you when you mail in your pledge. It's an exciting, full-color book featuring all of your favorite guests on PTL. . . . It's a PTL program in print!

Also, as a monthly member of the PTL Club you will receive your PTL partner card, PTL lapel pin and a special edition of "Action Magazine." Every month, you will receive my letter and either "Action Magazine" or "Action Update" detailing what God is doing through your support.

The only criterion for becoming a member of one of these select clubs is financial: you become a regular supporter for a set amount of money.

The third common characteristic of these direct mailings is a frequent and recurring "emergency" being faced by the broadcaster for which the audience member's support is urgently required. The appeal to the viewer is never presented within the reasonable context of calculated stewardship or responsible use of one's possessions: rather, the approach is designed to catch the viewer's attention with a more desperate and urgent religious horror story. One letter from Rex Humbard in April 1980 began,

Dear Peter,

I've got some very bad news. My heart is broken and I have not been able to eat or sleep. For today I had to do something that wars against every fiber in my being. . . . I had to take the first step to remove our program from the TV stations in your area. . . . Eternal souls are at stake. For if our program goes off the air—there are men, women, boys and girls who will spend eternity in hell. People will miss heaven because I lost God's call to your city.

This recurring image of urgency and impending disaster has had the effect of habituating even responsive supporters. The CBN's research agency, in a study of partners and their giving, reported that as a result of their support of CBN and other religious organizations, partners found that "the volume of Christian mail coming into their homes is at times overwhelming . . . including what is described as a 'redundant theme of financial crisis.'" As a result of this finding, the research group suggested to the management of CBN that "radically new direct mail strategies seem to be in order, both in terms of delivery and content, if CBN is to *stand out* and be *read*."[18]

No contact made by a broadcaster is spared the follow-up solicitation. In response to a $1 donation sent to the Rex Humbard ministry in January 1980, the author received in a four-month period 10 letters, including one thanking him for the contribution, one seeking a special prayer request he may have along with a further contribution, three inviting him to become a member of the Humbard "Prayer Key Family," one advising him that he had been enrolled as a member of the Prayer Key Family (though no indication of willingness had been given), and four seeking urgent financial contributions to prevent cancellation of the program in the area. Altogether 32 mailings were received before I finally asked for my name to be removed from their lists in October 1981—all in response to a $1 donation.

A person making a genuine enquiry about the nature of the Christian faith is hounded in the same way. In January 1981, the author wrote to five broadcasters seeking clarification from them of what it meant to become and live as a Christian. In response to this enquiry, he received a total of 54 mailings in a nine-month period. Of these only six mailings were directed specifically at the original enquiry. The remaining 39 were various forms of fund solicitation. The one exception to this was the Billy Graham organization. In response to the enquiry, the counseling department of the organization sent one mailing of various materials directed at answering the questions asked. In contrast to the other broadcasters, no "personal" letter was received from "Billy Graham himself," and no subsequent financial appeals were forthcoming as a result of his enquiry.

The shaping influence of the economic demands of television can also be seen in the strong consumer approach to religious faith taken on the paid-time programs. While the concept of receiving "God's blessing" as a reward for something well done has always been an element in fundamentalist and evangelical theology, in the practice of the paid-time broadcasters it has been developed to its extreme as a device to motivate viewers to give.

Common to most paid-time religious broadcasters, therefore, is some concept of "seed faith," a principle by which if you give something to God (i.e., to his servant, the broadcaster) you in effect plant a financial seed for which God will reward you with a subsequent harvest of increased financial return. It is promised that everything given by a person will be repaid by God, generally in a multiplied way. The idea appears to have first been popularized by Oral Roberts, but it has now become a theological concept in the public domain, with most broadcasters using it or variations of it.

The problem is, of course, that the concept hovers on the fringe of becoming a simple buying of miracles. While the broadcaster may not have this in mind initially, by promoting the benefits to be gained by a contribution to his organization, he causes the viewer, who perhaps may not perceive all the theological subtleties of the concept, to end up giving simply to get.

This superstitious understanding of consumer religion becomes even more noticeable in other devices used by broadcasters to obtain contributions. The Christian Broadcasting Network, for example, when building their new broadcasting complex in Virginia Beach, made available to viewers something called the "Seven Lifetime Prayer Requests." For a contribution of at least $100, a viewer was able to forward his seven lifetime wishes to CBN; the wishes were then to be microfilmed and interred in a pillar inside the prayer chapel where they would be surrounded by prayer "twenty-four hours a day until Jesus came back."[19] The PTL Network similarly in one letter promised.

As an extra little "thank you" when you send your $120 gift, we are going to put your name or the name of someone you love, inside the altar of the Prayer Chapel (first level of the Upper Room, which we are building a replica of), where thousands will pray each week.[20]

Such methods represent a modern return to the purchasing of indulgences, with the only proviso being one's willingness to pay the required amount in order to set the mechanisms of miracle-working in motion.

The religious broadcaster who is dependent on his audience for financial support always walks on thin ice. His sole contact with his supporters is through his weekly (or in a few cases daily) program and the mail. There is no durability of commitment on the part of his supporter, no personal eye-to-eye contact by which the viewer may perceive the demands of normal interpersonal relationship and support. The whole relationship between broadcaster and his supporters is dependent on the broadcaster and his organization accurately perceiving the mood and desires of the audience, and creating a package to fulfill those moods and desires. In this, he is competing not only with the viewer's other personal realtionships and perhaps his or her relationship to a local church, but also with the other broadcasters who are struggling to gain the loyalty of the same viewer and who are prepared to offer even better "faith products" in order to gain the viewer's support for themselves.

The total effect is the shaping of one's approach and message according to the dictates of one's business advisers rather than by the mandates of traditional theological sources. Most preachers, of course, are faced with the same pressure of their own perceptions of the meaning of faith, the perception of others, the situation of their hearers, and the demands of their church. Most preachers also make adjustments in their message over time in response to these demands. But no other preachers face the overwhelming pressures faced by television preachers, who have no leisure to reflect on the integrity of changes being called for by advisers, and for whom the continued existence of one's whole $1-million-a-week organization virtually hangs on each decision.

It is valid to ask, therefore, whether in their organizational practices and their message, paid-time religious broadcasters have become slaves to their environments and to the demands of their businesses. Does such a mass approach to Christian communication provide a valid option for Christian communication in a mass society, or does it reflect a capitulation of the essential aspects of the Christian faith to the demands of the economic environment, enabling, as Marshall Frady suggests, "one more advance of the front of totalitarian sensibility."[21]

Rather than providing a religious alternative to other television programs, paid-time religious programs appear to have become submerged in the television environment to the extent that they have become an indistinguishable part of it.

Notes

1. Armstrong, *Electric Church*, p. 101.
2. "Some True Beliefs about Religious Programming," *P. D. Cue* (Official Publication of the National Association of Television Program Executives) April 1977, p. 14.
3. David D. Stauffer, "Description and Analysis of the Historical Development and Management Practices of the Independent Christian Church Religious Television Program Syndicators," Ph.D. dissertation, Ohio State University, 1972, pp. 65–70.
4. Budget estimate given by the Rex Humbard organization in personal correspondence to the author, July 9, 1980.
5. Thomas Road Baptist Church and Related Ministries, "Consolidated Statement for the Year Ended June 30, 1979."
6. Jim Montgomery, "The Electric Church," *The Wall Street Journal*, May 19, 1978, p. 1.
7. Jerry Sholes, *Give Me That Prime-Time Religion*, New York: Hawthorn Books, 1979, p. 1.
8. J. Thomas Bisset, "Religious Broadcasting: Assessing the State of the Art," *Christianity Today*, December 12, 1980, p. 29.
9. Compare, for example, Matthew 7: 13–14. "The gate is wide and the road is easy that leads to hell, and there are many who travel it. The gate is narrow and the way is hard that leads to life, and few people find it."

10. Tapes of Robertson's address and Williams' response are available from the National Council of Churches in New York.

11. There have been a number of articles and books that have called into question the personal integrity and sincerity of broadcasters, e.g. Sholes, *Prime-Time Religion*, and Dick Dabney, "God's Own Network," *Harpers*, August 1980, pp. 33–52.

12. Market Research Group, "National CBN Partner Survey," Southfield, 1978, Table 89-A.

13. Ibid., Table 165.

14. "Stars of the Cathode Church," *Time*, February 4, 1980, pp. 64–65.

15. Montgomery, "Electric Church."

16. Clifford T. Hilton, "The Influence of Television Worship Services on the Irvington Presbyterian Church, Indianapolis, Indiana," D.Min. thesis, Drew University, 1980, p. 57.

17. Market Research Group, "National CBN Partner," Table 89-A.

18. Market Research Group, "Report on '700 Club' Finances and Direct Mail Focus Group Panel Discussions, Detroit, Michigan," Southfield, 1978, p. S-12.

19. Dabney, "God's Own Network," p. 46.

20. In a letter of June 1981.

21. Marshall Frady, *Billy Graham: A Parable of American Righteousness*, Boston: Little Brown & Co., 1979, p. 287.

4

Religious Programs and Television Culture

Because it was the weekend of July 4th, the theme of the service being broadcast from the Crystal Cathedral in California was "The American Flag." Robert Schuller opened the service and the program from this church made of glass with his typical staccato affirmation, "This is the day which the Lord has made. . ." Inside the church, among the dancing fountains and potted plants, was an array of American flags of varying sizes. Standing at the front of the church was a military band in full uniform performing before the congregation of thousands who applauded but never sang.

The service itself was a packed and professional presentation of musical items, readings, and prayers around the theme of the day. In capturing the spectacle, the television cameras moved in soft fades between shots of the performers, the visual grandeur of the church, the preacher, and the faces of the attentive but passive congregation.

Schuller's sermon was entitled "I am the American Flag," a nationalistic address in which he adopted the persona of the flag. With exaggerated gestures and abrupt facial expressions that he has developed over the years, and with appropriate strains of strings and brass in the background, Schuller painted word-pictures of America's achievements over the years and her magnanimity toward other nations and their peoples. Briefly he acknowledged but justified America's failings and international mistakes, and then, with a gently rising crescendo of strings in the background he reaffirmed the greatness of the American way of life and the unqualified possibilities of the future.

Following his address, as the military band played, a parade of flags borne by uniformed groups moved along the aisles and a huge American flag was raised from its folded position to stretch completely from the floor to the ceiling of that high sanctuary. It was indeed a visual masterpiece, one which brought obvious "oohs"of surprise and applause from the congregation. The symbol of American nationalism, the flag, when raised to the ceiling also covered the altar—the symbol of God's presence in the church—from the view of the congregation and the television audience, presenting a kind of symbolism that was probably not fully intended.

While the service was produced specifically to celebrate a particular occasion in American cultural life, it was consistent with many other services and programs presented on American religious television. All of the major paid-time religious programs have a central charismatic figure or host such as Robert Schuller, Oral Roberts, Rex Humbard, Pat Robertson, Jimmy Swaggart, Jim Bakker, and so on. Many stage their programs in picturesque or grand locations or contexts such as gardens, large auditoriums, or building complexes, and they present visual displays staged with precision. In all of the programs, the audience remains passive, merely fulfilling a cameo role as representatives of the viewing audience. All the major programs present happy sounds and images of success, with faith acting as the key to this success. They all reflect a harmonious blending of the Christian faith with various aspects of traditional American life and culture.

These characteristics reappear in each program, although the broadcasters have come from a diversity of backgrounds, personal experience, educational advancement, theological stance, and ecclesiastical affiliation. Television has succeeded in narrowing this representative diversity, even among the strongly independent and idiosyncratic evangelical and fundamentalist Christians, to a common television product with very few variations. What is it in television that has effectively moulded the diversity of the Christian faith into such uniformity?

Religion and Culture

Before considering the question of uniformity, it is important to clarify the relationship of religious faith to culture. There is a tendency to criticize religious faith whenever it reflects aspects of the culture in which it is expressed, as if for religious faith to be genuine it must also be culturally aseptic. There are few theologians or serious religious thinkers who would support such a view.

People cannot escape the influence of their culture on how they understand, appropriate, interpret, and express religious faith. Religious faith will always reflect specific cultural attributes. Within religious philosophy, this fact is not regretted, but rather is recognized and affirmed as one of the ways in which the persistent truth of a religious insight or revelation is apprehended and expressed in relation to changing circumstances. John

Macquarrie in his *Principles of Christian Theology* therefore identifies culture as one of the formative factors in theological understanding, along with experience, revelation, scripture, tradition, and reason.[1] Similarly, Paul Tillich suggests that theological thought continually moves in a dialectical tension between two poles: "the eternal truth of its foundation and the temporal situation in which the eternal truth must be received."[2]

The question to be considered in the analysis of any religious phenomenon or expression, therefore, is not whether it reflects any cultural attributes or not, but whether in addressing itself relevantly to the immediate cultural situation it has also effectively retained the essence of its historical and revelatory insights. The history of Christian thought has been a process of continual evaluation of new expressions of traditional faith to determine whether these new expressions adequately preserve the essential aspects of the faith, or whether they have sacrificed essential elements under the pressure and demands of the immediate cultural environment.

Christian theologians have begun to develop an interest in the content of Christian television programs for reasons of evaluation. Broadcasters are among the first, and the most visible Christian communicators to interact actively with the emerging electronic environment. The concern expressed is that current religious programs, in accomodating themselves to the demands of commercial television, have lost the essence of the Christian message and have simply become indistinguishable facsimiles of other commercial television programs.

This concern is directed at the extent to which the content of religious programs on television reflects the dominant values and social functions of commercial television. While this in itself is not a negative attribute, it becomes negative when these values and functions contradict traditional and essential aspects of the Christian religion.

The Influence of Television's Economic Demands

Because television is a capital-intensive industry, economic realities play a major part in determining its policies and content. This same reality applies also to religious television. J. H. Ellens, in a major study of denominational broadcasting, found that there were three major determinants that influenced the particular format adopted by denominational executives for a particular religious program: economics, technology, and theology. Ellens found that the determinants influenced the programs in that order of importance. When adequate money was available, denominational executives programmed in accordance with the theological objectives of the program. Most frequently, however, the format used was the cheapest one, regardless of the theological intention of the program.[3]

Economics play a dominant part in religious television so that religious programs are more easily and accurately identified not by their particular theological background or even ecclesiastical affiliation, but by the dominant mode through which they are financed. The method of financing the program has the capacity to remove otherwise normally distinguishable differences.

Religious television programs therefore can be divided into two main groups: *sustaining-time programs*, where the network or local station meets all or part of the costs of producing and broadcasting the program; and *paid-time programs*, where the broadcaster himself meets all the costs of producing and broadcasting the program, mainly by raising money from viewers. While it is possible for a denomination to meet all costs of producing and broadcasting a program, such types of program are rare. Only one program known to the author is produced in this way: the Seventh Day Adventist program "It Is Written," which is produced by the central communication agency of the church from denominational funds, with local churches of the denomination paying for its broadcast in their local area. This program is an exception, however. Most religious programs that purchase their air-time are supported by funds solicited from their viewing audiences.

The particular way in which a religious program is financed exerts a specific pressure on the nature of that program. When finance is provided by a network or local station, either in the form of direct subsidy, use of facilities, or provision of free air-time, the network or station exerts some pressures on the nature of the program. These pressures are not usually in the form of direct suggestions on content or method, but rather in the form of parameters within which the program must be shaped.

These conditions arise out of the networks' and stations' own industrial needs. As has been noted, networks and stations are careful to avoid program material that could cause them legal problems or sufficiently adverse public reaction, which would negatively affect their image. The CBS network, for example, took total control of its religious programming in 1933 because of the problems caused by the radio programs of Father Charles Coughlin. To this day, the CBS network has only used its own religious programs. Networks are under constant pressure from their affiliate stations to provide programming which is uncontroversial for each affiliate's local viewing area and which will not involve the affiliate station in debates that could involve the provision of expensive answering time under the FCC equal-access requirement. WABC-TV in New York, for example, vetoed several religious programs during the 1960s because they considered them to be more political than religious in content and were afraid that equal time would have to be given for opponents of those views.[4]

The pressure on sustaining-time programs, therefore, is the pressure to be innocuous, or free from objectionable material. In spite of these parameters, it should be noted that many of the sustaining-time programs were of high quality and dealt with substantial issues at a deeper level of analysis than was possible in programs forced to maintain ratings. Many of the sustaining-time programs have won numerous secular awards, including several Emmys, television's most prestigious award.

Theologian Martin Marty has noted, however, that to impose certain restrictions on the broadcast of religious faith is to remove the essence of that faith. The essence of the Christian faith is not general truths that can be contained within respectable parameters, but its particularity: it speaks of the revelation of God in a particular person at a particular time with a particular answer to questions of human meaning and existence. This essential particularity must inevitably bring it into conflict with any demands requiring adherence and presentation of the "broad religious truths" preferred by the networks and stations. Marty questions the extent to which any Christian communicator can accept the demands placed on his message by television stations and still retain the integrity of that message.[5]

It was partly as a result of having to circumvent the restrictions of network and station control that many evangelical and fundamentalist broadcasters developed economic independence from the networks and stations, cultivating their own independent audience support. In this way, they claim, they are able to develop better programs and free themselves from the demands and interference of the television industry.

Freedom from the economic realities of the television industry is not so simple. Even where a local station does not provide direct economic assistance to a program, it still has its own capital investment to protect. The station would be financially responsible for providing equal-access time should a program be sufficiently partisan or controversial that free time for response is demanded by an opposing group. As previously mentioned, this situation happened with station WFAA in Dallas, which was asked for equal time under the FCC Fairness Doctrine when religious broadcaster James Robison attacked homosexuals on one of his programs. In this case the broadcaster had an identifiable cause by which to rally support, but in most cases if a station experiences problems with a program it is easy to replace it with another prepared not to cause trouble. There are plenty of such programs waiting in the wings to purchase that same air-time. Station manager Robert Finnimore of WOR-TV in New York reportedly turns down five evangelistic programs for each one he accepts, so paid-time programs are not as independent as they may think.[6] When station WSOC in Charlotte, North Carolina, experienced trouble with evangelist Charles Sustare, it decided to drop his and all paid-time programs from its schedule. Evangelical broadcasters therefore must still take into account the economic interests of the local television management and produce a program that also reinforces good public relations with the station management.

Paid-time broadcasters are also limited in the air-time made available to them by the local station. Many stations are hesitant to make prime-time

available for religious broadcasts because of the "audience flow" programming principle. Because most religious programs are lower-rating programs,
to place them in prime-time could have a detrimental effect on the audiences
for programs before or after the religious program

It has been noted that paid-time programs have not achieved
economic independence from the industry, as they have claimed, but have
simply transferred their economic dependence from one source to another:
from the television industry to the television audience. Becoming dependent
on one's audience for support ties one into adopting a consumer or
marketing approach to one's message. Broadcasters have become very
skillful in selecting those aspects of a particular religious message that find
favor with their hearers and avoiding those aspects that may be integral to
the same message but unfavorable to the audience. Economic dependence
on the audience also effects a shaping of the message away from long-term
consideration of issues and needs toward a message addressed to the
immediately perceived desires of the audience. Most broadcasters now
conduct regular market research to detect which aspects of the Christian
message will evoke greater response from their audiences, even to the point
of evaluating the acceptability of a particular host's prayers.

Most of the current paid-time broadcasters see no contradiction
between such methods and the traditional Christian faith. Jim Bakker, host
of the "PTL Club" openly adopts marketing analogies: "We have a better
product than soap or automobiles. We have eternal life!"[7] Others disagree.
Television researcher George Gerbner suggests that the commoditization of
the Christian faith in response to the economic demands of television
removes the distinctiveness of the Christian faith and absorbs it as an indistinguishable part of the broader message of television, "the established
religion of the industrial order."[8]

The inescapable influence of the television milieu is one of the most
persistent problems facing religious broadcasters and is one that needs some
clear and systematic articulation if religious broadcasting is to proceed on
a clear foundation.

The Influence of Television's Social Functions

In their comprehensive survey of research into television and its effects,
George Comstock and his associates note that television within American
society principally serves two social functions: that of entertainment and of
killing vacant time. Of these the dominant function is entertainment.

Television's central role as an entertainer holds for both the more and the less
educated, and probably for other segments of the population as well, despite variations in attitudes towards television, amount of viewing, and other factors among
segments.

In relation to the killing of vacant time, Comstock notes, "Viewers typically do not decide to watch a specific program; they make two decisions. The first is *whether* to view, and the second is *what* to view; of these, the first is by far the most important."[9]

These dominant social functions now served by television have been of continuing concern to the Public Broadcasting System, which derives much of its raison d'être from the broadcast of more demanding cultural or educational programming. In one of their studies of audience viewing patterns in relation to their television programming they found that

Many people justify their many hours of television watching as needed because of the effort they expend during their working day. . . . Public television in its adult programming is thought of as demanding and hard work by a good number of viewers and therefore unable to fit in with their need to relax.[10]

The dominant functions of television, combined with the pressure on stations to maximize their audience, has shaped television programming in America in several characteristic ways: it has led away from in-depth, demanding analyses to an oversimplification of issues and their solutions; it has fed the desire for instant gratification of needs rather than disciplined resolution; and it has tended toward the sensationalization of events and experiences. Each of these results has had a marked shaping effect on religious programs as well, particularly those programs that have placed themselves in a situation where their continued existence depends on their successfully competing within this system.

Oversimplification

Because of the emphasis on providing entertainment, most of the television programming avoids in-depth, demanding analyses of issues, events, and human relationships and depends heavily on the adoption of stereotyped characters, plots, and relationships. Former advertising executive Jerry Mander suggests that this process is also a function of the medium.

Most information which would be useful to thorough human understanding of the complexity of existence cannot penetrate the medium at all. The effect is to confine the information field within the very narrow, hard-edged, and objective form which the medium can convey.[11]

The Cultural Indicators Research Program at Annenberg School of Communications suggests that not only does television oversimplify, but also that it oversimplifies in systematic ways. The result is that the central messages across television's various types of programming are remarkably homogenous and repetitive, and in many cases antithetical to what exists in real life.[12]

This is the structured environment into which religious broadcasters must project their message. The result is a strong pressure on these broadcasters to avoid presentations or topics which require concentration, reflective thought, or ambiguity. The shaping of their message in response to this pressure is apparent in most programming, as articulated by Robert Schuller:

Explaining that he sees the purpose of the television sermon as only the first step in leading a person to Christ, the "Hour of Power" speaker purposely emphasizes the benefits the listener can receive. . . . "I've learned that the first step has to be simple and easy. Once they understand that Christians really care about them, they're willing to listen to the deeper, harder parts of the message."[13]

What is not explained is how members of the audience are to understand that there are further steps to be taken when the only presentation of religious faith shown them stresses that the path to Christ is simple and unambiguous. While Schuller may incorporate other opportunities to delve more deeply into the content and implications of the Christian faith through his local church program at Garden Grove, television viewers receive none of this information either through the television program or the direct-mail follow-up. What remains unspoken in all of this is also that the "really caring" of which Schuller speaks is actually a staged, edited program with the preacher developed according to the demands of good television. Should the viewer be inclined to reach out to this person who "really cares," the response will be not a person but a computer with "the range of human woes, struggles and hopes" quantified and mechanized, mockingly tossing out piped answers along with offers of jewelry and appeals for financial support.

It is perhaps no surprise that the theological tradition that has come to succeed in this medium is the fundamentalist–evangelical tradition. This tradition has always tended to be singular-minded in their interpretation of theology, ethics, and socio-personal problems, a stance which has constantly drawn reaction and criticism from more liberal and academic members of the Christian community. The paid-time broadcasters have pushed the simplification of the Christian message to such an extent, however, that in recent years they have also begun to be criticized by leaders of their own traditions. Evangelical Phill Butler, for example, has criticized a large percentage of paid-time programs as "not much more than a glossy pabulum—spiritualized entertainment with little of the tough stuff of discipleship in it."[14] Similarly Carl Henry, the leading, distinguished evangelical theologian, sees the current upsurge in the religious use of mass media as "a destructive trend which neglects a systematic presentation of Christian truth."[15]

Instant Gratification

Eric Barnouw, in his analysis of television's history, suggests that the shaping of television programming into the present form with its easy and immediate answers to easily defined problems was largely due to the demands of the television advertisers. In the 1950s, conflicts emerged between the writers and producers of television drama and the sponsors of the dramas. While the dramatists were producing programs which dealt with complex issues and conflicts, many of which did not end in easy resolution, advertisers were pressing for pleasant programs to provide a good lead-in for their commercials. The conflict was eventually resolved in favor of the advertisers. Barnouw comments,

In the commercials there was always a solution as clear-cut as the snap of a finger. . . . Chayefsky and other anthology writers took these same problems and made them complicated. . . . It made the commercial seem fradulent.[16]

Former FCC commissioner Nicholas Johnson has noted this characteristic of television also.

I have become more and more aware of the extent to which television not only distributes programs and sells products, but also preaches a general philosophy of life . . . that there are instant solutions to life's most pressing personal problems. You don't need to think about your own emotional maturity and development of individuality, your discipline, training and education, your willingness to cooperate and compromise and work with other people; you don't need to think about developing deep and meaningful human relationships and trying to keep them in order.[17]

That the church should be concerned about such a phenomenon has rarely been questioned. What has been questioned and debated is the appropriate manner in which the Christian faith, which stresses such things as self-discipline, sacrifice, and service is to be communicated by a medium which stresses instant personal gratification.

The paid-time religious programmers have rightly sensed that this characteristic exists in television and they have rightly sought to address the Christian faith relevantly to this characteristic. The problem is, though, that by making themselves financially dependent on the very people to whom they are speaking they have removed much of their freedom to challenge this tendency.

Such a tendency has always existed within the church, but in the challenge for individuals to develop self-discipline, to exercise personal sacrifice, and to perform social or community service, the church has always offered a supportive, affirmative group within which these characteristics can be sought without total loss of personal worth or personal disintegration. The television broadcasters do not have this same supportive capability. On the contrary, because of the capital intensiveness of their enterprise, the pressure is on them to avoid any program elements or demands that would antagonize their audience. Lacking the durability of personal relationships with their viewing audience, they must avoid any demands on their audience which would give them cause to change channels to another program or another religious broadcaster.

Paid-time programs therefore stress heavily the benefits one is able to gain from religious faith. This emphasis is usually achieved through interviews of people who have achieved benefits similar to those offered the audience. Little mention is made of corresponding failures, endurance, and hard work, which may also be part of the same experience. In fact, for the broadcasters, it would appear that such efforts as personal sacrifice, service, self-discipline, hard work, setbacks, failures, and endurance are without theological significance. God's presence is to be known only through benefit and gain, toward which the viewer is continually prompted.

Paid-time religious programs are perhaps the finest example of sophisticated, market-researched consumer faith. Rightly perceiving the nature of the television environment and having to succeed financially within it, the broadcasters have allowed their programs to be almost totally shaped by it. By making themselves financially dependent on this environment and its inhabitants, they have removed their capacity to challenge it.

Sensationalism

With the strongly competitive nature of American television and the combined functions it serves as both entertainer and killer of vacant time, there is a strong emphasis on the production of material that will catch and hold the viewer's attention.

Paid-time religious broadcasters face the same pressures because they have chosen to compete with other television programming. Sustaining-time programs, on the other hand, do not face the same pressures. Ben Armstrong sees competitiveness as one of the strengths of the American broadcasting system and considers such competition a good thing for religious programs because it stimulates them to improve their performance.

Competitiveness among religious programs has many ramifications. It means that religious programs must constantly be changing or looking for something novel in order to attract and maintain the viewers' attention. These pressures on religious broadcasters find expression in their tendency to exaggerate reality either by selection, avoidance, or creation of certain incidents over others and the tendency to compromise with the illusion and sensation which television as a whole promotes through its programming. The pressure is to emphasize the miraculous over the mundane, the larger-than-life experiences over those that are meaningful but pedestrian, and suggestions of God's favor through outstanding events rather than assurance of his continuing presence through the day-to-day. The effect of this pressure is suggested by theologian Martin Marty:

Each evangelist is only as good as his or her last act. Each must be more sensational than the other. The success stories must outdo the others. . . . People "down on the charts," down in the ratings, down in the standings, don't make it.[18]

As a consequence of this pressure, there has developed a regular cadre of religious program guests who move in a circuit from one program to another—Pat Boone, Dale Evans and Roy Rogers, Chuck Colson, Efrem Zimbalist, Jr. All of them fulfill admirably the desired qualities of being well-known celebrities who also have experienced something sensational that can be paraded. But the effect of their presence is basically contradictory to the Christian message, which stresses the importance of the anonymous, the outcast, and the value of those who have not been able to make it in social terms. The innate contradiction of this message of paid-time television is highlighted by writer Virginia Stem Owens: "It is with what the camera cannot hope to catch, with what it in fact drives away, that the gospel is concerned."[19]

The Influence of Television's Mythic Structures

Far from being merely a neutral communication medium, television in America has become an integrated symbolic world filling the socially functional role demanded of it both by its viewers and its advertisers. Such integrated mythic structures provide the continuity and stability among the different types of programs, a continuity and stability needed by television's advertisers, used by its creative writers and producers, and sought by its users in their search for relaxation and entertainment.

This situation was first suggested in 1948 by Paul Lazarsfeld and Robert Merton in their classic article, "Mass Communication, Popular Taste and Organized Social Action." In the article, the authors contended that since the mass media are supported by great business concerns which are tied to the present social and economic system, the media contribute to the maintenance of that system. This social maintenance can be seen not just in the advertisements in the mass media but also in story elements and images which in some way express confirmation or approval of the present structures of society. Such confirmation is provided not just by what is said but "more significantly from what is not said."[20]

Most recently, an empirical approach to the study of these myths has been developing in the Cultural Indicators Research Program. The researchers are demonstrating that television promotes consistent values, attitudes, and beliefs which serve the functional needs of those who control and use the medium: "Commercial television, unlike other media, presents an organically composed total world of interrelated stories (both drama and news) produced to the same set of market specifications."[21]

These interrelated myths, created by the selective inclusion or exclusion of particular persons, groups, or power relationships within television's perspective have the capacity to replace the real-life equivalents in people's perception. Television even has the capacity to create pseudo-events which can displace real life in immediacy and importance. Take, for example, the international interest created recently by the question, "Who shot J. R.?" the mean character from the program "Dallas."

The majority of the research at Annenberg School of Communications has been directed toward the portrayal of violence, role stereotypes, and power relationships on television. William Fore, the Assistant Secretary for Communication in the National Council of Churches of Christ, suggests that there are several other dominant myths in television programming that are of direct relevance for religious broadcasters. These myths are:

- The fittest survive
- Happiness consists of limitless material acquisition
- Consumption is inherently good
- Property, wealth, and power are more important than people
- Progress is an inherent good

Fore asserts that "the whole weight of Christian history, thought and teaching stands diametrically opposed to the media world and its values."[22]

When a religious message is broadcast within the television milieu, the broadcaster faces an unavoidable dilemma. He must determine the extent to which the message is to be accommodated to those myths so that it will be perceived as "real" and relevant by the audience for whom the television myths are potent and determinative. If the broadcaster accommodates his message to these myths, he must also decide what the distinctiveness of his message is in relation to them. If he chooses to challenge the myths on the basis of his message, he must decide the extent to which such a challenge is feasible while still preserving the perceived reality of his message by the audience.

Those on opposite sides of the dilemma have inevitably criticized the others. Hence Ben Armstrong, representing the paid-time broadcasters, has criticized the network and mainline denominational religious programs as being too slow and sterile for television. These programs, he suggests are irrelevant to the mass audience of television because they fail to understand and adapt to the true nature of television as it functions in American society.[23] Bill Fore, on the other hand, has criticized the paid-time programmers on the grounds that their programs and message are indistinguishable from other commercial programs. According to Fore, they have been minimally shaped by the central truths of the Christian message and maximally shaped by the media myths expected by the television audience.[24]

Even a casual observation of the paid-time programs reveals their correspondence to the television myths described above. There is a strong emphasis on success and material gain. The programs interpret religious faith primarily as a device for promoting material success. As noted, Oral Roberts advocates the concept of "Seed Faith"; Pat Robertson promotes the "Kingdom Principles"; both state that if you give to God you will receive money in return. Rex Humbard, Jim Bakker, and Jerry Falwell all reflect what has been called a "health and wealth" theology, one which promotes the idea that God blesses those who are faithful to Him by giving them good health and material success. Jerry Falwell reflected this thought when questioned about his wealthy lifestyle. His reply was that "material wealth is God's way of blessing people who put him first."[25]

There is also a strong promotion of celebrities on paid-time religious programs, particularly those celebrities who have acquired fame within the secular world, with the underlying assumption that greater power exists with those granted status by the mass media. "B. J. Thomas endorses Jesus as Bruce Jenner endorses cereal," Virginia Stem Owens observes.[26]

The elements just mentioned have always been present in sections of evangelical and fundamentalist thought. There has always been a tradition which has emphasized the dramatic in religious practice, which has affirmed that God rewards those who acknowledge him, and which has promoted celebrities in an effort to impress. This was a characteristic of the early evangelists who first attracted the attention of newspapers in the last century. What remains significant in relation to religious television, though, is the way in which these strands of religious thought have come to dominate the content of religion on television. There is now little representation on television of other strands of religious thought: the more mystical, practical, apologetic, liturgical, or social-issues approaches to religious faith. Television has succeeded in narrowing the expression of religious thought to that which is most supportive of its own limited view and economic goals.

Thus television has exerted a strong censoring effect on the presentation of religious faith, not by an active censorship of views but by a selection and preference. The covert nature of this influence makes it of greater danger to the future development of religious faith in America. Because the selective nature of television is often overlooked, the diversity of American religious culture is in danger of being narrowed to that particular strand of religious faith which is now being promoted by television largely because of its acceptance and coherence with television's own social and economic goals.

There is a danger, therefore, that television and the television industry have a disproportionate influence in setting the agenda for the churches in their understanding of their mission, the presentation of their message, and the basis of their interaction with each other. For example, in the presence of the advantage held by the paid-time religious programmers, several denominations which had previously cooperated with others in the common production of religious programs have now decided to compete on their own through the purchase of their own television stations, the production of their own programs, and the cultivation of their own audiences. Television has had sufficient power and attraction, it would appear, to move many churches away from an interactive basis of cooperation to one of competition with each other. A further problem is that, in moving to a more competitive stance with the paid-time programs, these denominations are adopting the same techniques and myths already present in the paid-time programs.

While one can never escape the influence of one's culture on one's understanding and communication of religious faith, the power currently exerted by the structures, functions, and characteristics of television on religious faith is so powerful that its subtleties have scarcely begun to be considered. This influence is felt in relation to all types of religious programming, both sustaining-time programming and paid-time programming. It is still present even when a religious group chooses to buy its own television station.

Rarely in its long history has the Christian church been so closely tied to and dependent on an external organization over which it has so little control as it does when communicating through the medium of television. It may be that the power of television will come to be seen as of greater importance than the individual influence of any particular religious program or even religious programs as a whole.

Notes

1. John Macquarrie, *Principles of Christian Theology*, London: SCM, 1966, pp. 4–17.
2. Paul Tillich, *Systematic Theology*, 3 vols., Chicago: University of Chicago Press, 1951–63, p. I:3.
3. J. H. Ellens, "Program Format in Religious Television: A History and Analysis of Program Format in Nationally Distributed Denominational Religious Television Broadcasting in the United States of America," Ph.D. dissertation, Wayne State University, 1970, pp. 284–85.
4. Kahle, "Religion and Network Television," p. III:4.
5. Martin Marty, *The Improper Opinion: Mass Media and the Christian Faith*, Philadelphia: The Westminster Press, 1961, p. 66.
6. Quoted in Louis Gorfain, "Pray TV," *New York*, October 6, 1980, p. 49.
7. Quoted in Armstrong, *Electric Church*, p. 108.
8. George Gerbner, with Kathleen Connoly, "Television as New Religion," *New Catholic World*, May/April 1978, p. 56.

9. George Comstock et al., *Television and Human Behavior*, New York: Columbia University Press, 1978, p. 172.
10. Communication Research, Corporation for Public Broadcasting, *A Qualitative Study: The Effect of Television on People's Lives*, Washington: Corporation for Public Broadcasting, 1978, pp. 22–25.
11. Jerry Mander, "Four Arguments for the Elimination of Television," *The Co-Evolution Quarterly*, Winter 1977/78, p. 40.
12. See for example, George Gerbner et al., "Cultural Indicators: Violence Profile No. 9," *Journal of Communication*, Summer 1978, pp. 176–207.
13. In Armstrong, *Electric Church*, p. 113.
14. Phill Butler, "The Christian Use of Radio and Television," *Interlit*, December 1977, pp. 2–15.
15. Carl F. H. Henry, "Evangelicals: Out of the Closet but Going Nowhere?" *Christianity Today*, January 1980, pp. 16–22.
16. Eric Barnouw, *Tube of Plenty: The Evolution of American Television*, New York: Oxford University Press, 1975, pp. 163–64.
17. Nicholas Johnson, "The Careening of America," *The Humanist*, July/August 1972, p. 11.
18. Martin Marty, "The Invisible Religion," *Presbyterian Survey*, May 1979, p. 13.
19. Virginia Stem Owens, *The Total Image, or Selling Jesus in the Modern Age*, Grand Rapids: W. B. Eerdmans, 1980, p. 4.
20. Paul F. Lazarsfeld and Robert K. Merton, "Mass Communication, Popular Taste and Organized Social Action," in *Process and Effects of Mass Communications*, rev. ed., edited by Wilbur Schramm and Donald F. Roberts, Urbana: University of Illinois Press, 1971, pp. 554–78.
21. George Gerbner et al., "The Demonstration of Power: Violence Profile No. 10," *Journal of Communication*, Summer 1979, p. 180.
22. William F. Fore, "Mass Media's Mythic World: At Odds with Christian Values," *Christian Century*, January 19, 1977, pp. 34–35.
23. Armstrong, *Electric Church*, p. 134.
24. William F. Fore, "There is No Such Thing as a TV Pastor," *TV Guide*, July 19, 1980, p. 18.
25. Kenneth L. Woodward, "A $1 Million Habit,"*Newsweek*, September 15, 1980, p. 35.
26. Owens, *Total Image*, p. 34.

5

The Struggle
within the Churches

At the Electronic Church Consultation held in New York in 1980, one of the speakers—psychologist and television researcher Robert Liebert—suggested that the growth of religious television in America had created a holy war within U.S. Christendom.

The situation I will describe has every hallmark of an intensifying war of survival among battling Christian groups . . . one between liberalism and fundamentalism and the other between local community churches and broadcast ministries.[1]

While Liebert's comments may have been oversimplified and deliberately overstated, he was accurate in highlighting the conflict which the growth of evangelical and fundamentalist television over the past decade has caused within different American church groups and leaders. In analyzing the social implications of religious television, it is essential to understand something of this conflict, for it illuminates the challenge which paid-time television programs have posed to established religious culture within the country.

As one analyzes the debate that has taken place in the churches over the use of television, one tendency becomes apparent: the major conceptualization of issues has come from the critics of the paid-time broadcasters rather than from the broadcasters themselves. The major energies of the paid-time broadcasters have been directed toward the practical exigencies of program and organizational development, increasing their technical competence, and fund raising. The broadcasters' strength has been in their capability as technicians of the medium rather than as theologians or philosophers. Consequently there has been little systematic "apologia" given by the broadcasters. This fact in itself has been one of the criticisms levelled at the paid-time broadcast organizations: that the development of religious television in recent years has been the result of opportunism and cut-throat free enterprise rather than soundly based theological strategy.

Any defense offered by the broadcasters is to be found scattered throughout journals and magazines, mostly in interviews where someone else is doing the questioning and the writing. Few articles have been written by the broadcasters themselves—they are practitioners of the image, not the word. The most substantial raison d'être for the broadcasters is provided by Ben Armstrong in his book *The Electric Church*. Yet even this book is light in conceptual development and strong in image creation.

The avoidance of sound defense of their activities, particularly in their relations with the church, is beginning to have an effect. The persistent criticisms made by thinkers within the church along with a growing body of adverse research is creating an increasing questioning of paid-time programming, even from people within similar theological traditions as the broadcasters themselves.

The debate in the church over the growth of paid-time religious programs has centered on several major issues.

The Nature of the Church

The growth of paid-time religious television and its many affiliated religious services, industries, and practices presents a radical challenge to established ideas about the nature of the Christian church. It proposes through suggestion and practice the possibility of a new type of church based on electronic connection, frequently referred to as the "electric" or "electronic" church.

Credit for the coining of the term "electric church" to describe this phenomenon has been claimed by Ben Armstrong. The term came to him on a plane flight to Chicago. Impressed by the lights of the city as the plane circled overhead, Armstrong saw them as an image of the "millions of religious broadcasting listeners and viewers" whom he identified as "the members of a great and new manifestation of the church created by God for this age—the electric church."[2]

Armstrong's actual concept of the nature of such a church is ambiguous. On the one hand he suggests that religious broadcasting is a radically different structure of the traditional church: "a revolutionary new form of the worshipping, witnessing church that existed twenty centuries ago." As in New Testament times, worship again takes place in the home, with the new apostles of the air waves visiting these home-Christians through the radio and television. Through the electric church, power is once again removed from the church hierarchy and returned to the people.[3]

On the other hand, Armstrong suggests that the electric church must be understood only as an expression of one aspect of the wider structure and work of the church. "This electric church is not a replacement for the local assembly of believers but a complement to it." The element of corporate fellowship, according to Armstrong, must "never be eclipsed by the electric church."[4]

Before proceeding, it is necessary to clarify what is meant by the term "church," for the term is used in many different ways, both to describe the church universal and to describe a local gathering. The church in its broadest sense is used to describe the community of people, across the ages, across denominational and national lines, which recognizes Jesus Christ as Lord and responds to his mission and message in worship, sacraments, fellowship, witness, and service. In particular historical situations, however, the church may take particular forms. It may be organized hierarchically or congregationally, it may be strongly liturgical or loosely charismatic, it may be clearly defined in name and identity or loosely defined.

Roman Catholic theologian Richard McBrien suggests that a group of persons can be called a church when the following theological and pastoral conditions are fulfilled:

1. there is a corporate confession of the Lordship of Jesus;
2. this confession is ratified in the sacraments, particularly Baptism and the Lord's Supper;
3. there is a regular use of the scriptures in developing the life of the community;
4. there is a sense of fellowship within the group, i.e., a common awareness of the call to become an interactive community;
5. there is an acceptance of the Gospel of Jesus Christ as the conscious motivation for the community's values and ethical commitment; and
6. there exist certain formal ministries which are designed and exercised to enable the community to exercise and remain faithful to its mission and to provide order, coherence and stability to its internal life.[5]

McBrien notes that each of these ecclesial elements admits of degrees: the reality of "church" is not equally realized in every place and in every community. But where such conditions are present to some degree, the reality of "church" is present to that degree.

It is doubtful that Armstrong, if pressed, would really want to defend the thesis that religious television could be classified as a new type of legitimate church, despite his theological meanderings in that direction. Many other broadcasters on different occasions have avowed that they are primarily "evangelistic" organizations, fulfilling some functions of the church's mission in complement to the church, but not replacing it. Their relationship to the church, it is frequently claimed, is not that of a substitute but of a specialized service function.

Theologically, such television organizations, in their relationship with their audiences, are deficient in two characteristics that have traditionally been seen as essential to identifying a body as a church: they have no sacramental dimension to their worship and there is no meaningful sense of their audiences being a particular community in Christ.

While an organization may function as a Christian organization without possessing all attributes of the church, theologically it is held that such bodies do not contain all the conditions required for a full and competent expression of the depth of the Gospel, and require the correction of the church in its fullness. In Protestant practice, such groups have come to be known as "parachurch organizations," groups which exist as a service function to the church without becoming a substitute for it. Members of these groups usually hold membership in a church. Whereas a church is seen as essential to the continuing work of Christ, these parachurch organizations have validity only insofar as their services are still needed.

The major criticism of the religious broadcast organizations is that while they may claim not to be a new type of church, in pratice they are acting as self-sufficient churches and thus threatening the life of the church by displacing the functions and role of the church with their own inadequate expressions of the Gospel. This functional displacement of the church by the religious broadcasters is identified in several ways.

First, religious programs and broadcast groups are diverting people's attention, loyalty, and financial support away from the local church toward the television organization. While criticisms of this nature have come primarily from mainline churches, which have experienced decreases in membership and financial giving in the past 15 years, in recent years criticism has also come from evangelicals.

In defense, broadcasters claim that their programs reinforce the local church. They claim that people's donations to their programs are "above and beyond" what is normally given to local churches, though it is difficult to envisage how church people can begin to give upwards of $500 million each year to broadcast ministries without having it affect their giving elsewhere. Broadcasters suggest that their programs actually boost the local church by channelling converts to their membership and by developing the commitment and giving of church members. The persistent problem has been that little concrete research has been done to verify either these claims or the criticisms, so that the conflict between broadcasters and the church has remained largely speculative, circumstantial, and finally very subjective. Some research on these issues is beginning to emerge and will be considered later in this work.

The second criticism levelled at the broadcasters is that their programs undercut the corporate functions of the church. Religious programs act as a functional alternative to the local church, thus decreasing attendance and involvement by reinforcing the social tendency toward the individualizing of religious experience at the expense of its corporate expressions, and placing a burden on the religious broadcasting organizations which they are not equipped to handle. Phillip Yancey, in an analysis of the work of the PTL Network, has noted

PTL is not the church; it is only a mouthpiece. But by appealing to the needs in humanity that can only be met on local, corporate-body level, PTL fosters exactly the kind of situation it is not set up to handle.[6]

The concerns expressed about religious television promoting the individualization of religious experience have strong empirical support. General research has demonstrated that television viewing increases the "privatization of experience," and has led to a decrease in social interactive activity.[7] More specific research has identified a similar trend in religious belief, with a developing attitude in America that sees religious faith as a private, personal affair.[8] This attitude reflects the emergence of what Carl Dudley calls "the new believers—those who believe without belonging."[9]

Religious broadcasters certainly have not created this effect, but they have capitalized on it, and in acquiescing to it they have reinforced its application to religious faith and practice as well. Their programs reflect little of the idea that there is a wider church in which viewers should be involved. The programs have become self-sufficient churches in themselves, providing all services to viewers to maintain viewer loyalty. Once a year Rex Humbard even presents a televised communion service, "inviting all believers who are watching at home to gather around their televison sets." Humbard also visits foreign countries in which his programs are broadcast, occasions which Ben Armstrong refers to as "pastoral visits on a jet-age scale to a large but scattered congregation." Humbard frequently refers to himself as "your television pastor."[10] These broadcasters do not claim to replace the local church, but the images used and activities engaged in indicate an effort to present themselves as equivalent to the local church.

The paid-time religious broadcasters may reject the concept of an electric church, but functionally they appear to be promoting the concept. In doing so, they are removing the important aspects of the Christian faith which can only be communicated through an interactive, person-to-person community: personal challenge to change within a supportive community, individualized teaching, and personal-care functions such as counseling, support, and continuity of relationship. In their place is a one-way program viewed in isolation. Sustaining-time programs generally do not fall into the same trap. Not being dependent on their audience for financial support, they do not need to cultivate audience loyalty by the provision of centralized images, services, and emotional satisfaction.

The Mission of the Church

When the paid-time religious broadcasters do make the effort to defend themselves and their enterprise against their detractors, they do so by demonstrating how their programs further the mission of the church. In particular, they focus on three major areas of the church's traditional activity: evangelism, pastoral care, and social and political influence.

Evangelism

Evangelicals and fundamentalists have traditionally been heavily oriented toward evangelism—the communication of the Christian message to those who are ignorant or unconvinced of its validity. Paid-time religious broadcasters are almost totally unrestrained in their praise of the potential of radio and television to contribute to the task of evangelism. Jerry Falwell, for example, has commented: "We have not yet touched the hem of the garment with respect to the great opportunities we as Christians have to spread the gospel."[11] Similarly, Ben Armstrong asserts that "broadcast religion touches more people than all the churches combined."[12]

Most of the religious broadcasters make available in-house statistics on the number of people who have been converted through their programs. These figures are frequently couched in comparative terms, highlighting the effectiveness of these programs in comparison to the more modest efforts of local churches. For example, a recent PTL leaflet noted that "PTL Counselors in 1979 prayed with some 28,143 people to receive Christ as Saviour. These new converts would represent a new church of over 500 people every week started by PTL."[13]

Critics have long suspected that such figures are exaggerated, but it is only in recent years that research statistics have appeared to confirm some of these suspicions. These findings will be dealt with in detail in the research chapter on religious broadcasting and the local church. It is sufficient to say here that studies call into question the validity of the figures given by the broadcasters to justify their evangelistic activities. Many of those who are claimed to have been converted through the programs turn out to be people who were already Christian or who have been confused about why they were calling a broadcaster, or who called seeking help of some other kind.[14] Other studies also raise questions about the durability of the changes effected on people through these programs, even when the programs seek to work in close conjunction with a local church.[15] Though people may be genuine at the time of contact with a religious broadcaster, research studies indicate that very few continue this change in a local church or Christian community.[16]

In spite of these findings, religious broadcasters continue to affirm the great contribution they are making to the evangelistic outreach of the church. Ben Armstrong still states that "penny for penny, per capita studies indicate there is no better way to reach the largest number of people with the life-changing news of Jesus Christ than through radio and television."[17] Others are beginning to question not only the accuracy but the honesty of such claims, even suggesting that by raising millions of dollars each year in the name of evangelism the broadcasters are perpetuating a massive fraud among well-meaning but naive religious supporters. Falwell's claim that his program was viewed regularly by an audience of 20 million people, a figure widely quoted during the preelection period in 1980, is totally without substantiation: in November 1980, according to Nielsen figures, the audience was 1.2 million, a figure of which Falwell would have been well aware. Similarly, Armstrong's claim that "religious broadcasters are reaching more people than all of the nation's churches combined" has doubtful statistical validity. The study on which Armstrong's claim is based indicated that only 20 percent of a national sample listened to a radio broadcast often and 28 percent listened occasionally.[18] Armstrong combined these two figures to conclude that in an average week 47 percent of the America population turn on radio or television for at least one religious program, a rather doubtful conclusion. These figures certainly do not tally with other research, such as the Nielsen surveys which list the combined audience for all syndicated religious programs on television in November 1980 as 19.1 million adults and children. Nor do the figures describe the limited outreach these programs have among non-church goers, a characteristic that will be considered in more detail in chapter 9.

Awareness of the limitations of television in evangelism is now beginning to permeate the thinking of evangelicals as well, people who have traditionally been supportive of the programs. Evangelical radio broadcaster Tom Bisset, in an article uncharacteristically honest for an evangelical broadcaster in its self-analysis, reviewed the research of evangelical Christianity in the U.S. commissioned by *Christianity Today* and felt forced to question the composition of the religious programs' audience:

Does this mean we are talking to ourselves? Has religious broadcasting simply become another form of institutionalized Christianity, comfortably settled down in the delusion that we are reaching the world for Christ through the mass media? And if so, can we justify the money spent?[19]

Similarly James Engel, Professor of Communication at the evangelical Wheaton Graduate School, and responsible for the training of evangelical communicators, places himself among a "large and growing group within this industry that are calling for some rethinking of basic assumptions and a restoration of a ministry cutting edge that seems to have been lost in some quarters."[20]

Pastoral Care and Counseling

Paid-time religious broadcasters argue strongly that their programs are meeting needs among people who are not being touched by the traditional church. There can be no doubt that the broadcasters have the capacity to stir a response in certain of their viewers. The immediacy and intimacy of communication by television and the host's presence in the viewer's home has meant that Christian television programs have been able to tap human needs and concerns which would otherwise go untouched by the church or other social agencies. The effectiveness of the medium in touching these needs and establishing an evocative relationship between the viewer and broadcaster had led to a shaping of many of the religious programs toward this aspect of the market by cultivating a strong emphasis on and appeal to personal concerns such as well being, personal contentedness, satisfactory relationships, and physical health and healing.

By establishing opportunities for viewers to contact them with their problems, either by phone or mail, broadcasters have uncovered a mass of social unsettledness. The PTL Network's claim that in 1979 over 478,000 calls were received on their "prayer lines" is one indicator of this response.[21] WXNE–Channel 25, the CBN station in Boston, in the first two years of its operation from 1977–79, logged 36,225 "counseling" calls, the majority of which were simply "prayer requests," people calling in to express a concern and to request a prayer for themselves or someone else.[22]

Critics of paid-time religious television programs certainly do not attempt to deny the fact that a need for counseling exists or that something needs to be done about this need. Their criticisms center on the methods used by religious broadcasters to uncover these problems and their effectiveness in addressing the problems they encounter.

Because of the lack of personal interaction and support resources and the demands of dealing with mass requests for help, the counseling and care offered can be little more than hasty advice based on quick judgments, a criticism also levelled at media psychology programs.[23] Further pressure is added to the counseling situation by the financial pressures on the programs' counseling services and their secondary role as name-getters for subsequent mailings and financial solicitations. The danger, as broadcaster Tom Bisset suggests, is that the broadcasters are offering a "band-aid salvation: fast-talk and quick cure in the era of feeling."[24]

Evangelical writer Phillip Yancey elucidates this problem with a case he encountered while serving as a telephone counselor at PTL; at the time, he was doing research on the organization for an article. In the center at North Carolina, he received a call for help from a woman in California who was struggling on her own to raise two troubled children on welfare. The call, for Yancey, illustrated the dilemma faced in dealing with problems under such conditions:

This lady, eager to do right, but unable to cope with the pressures of her world, represents millions with great human needs. PTL and other programs like it tap into these needs, awakening a thirst for justice and hope and joy. Yet television is limited; it is not the church, and so its help is incomplete. What the Californian woman needs is some old-fashioned, sacrificial Christian love—someone to be her friend, to keep her sons sometimes, perhaps to help out financially. I can't help wondering how many of her Christian neighbors are too busy watching TV to give her that love.[25]

Yancey suggests that the broadcasters' limited ability to meet the needs they arouse may result in leaving persons bitterly unsatisfied rather than convinced of the church's concern.

This inadequacy is even more unacceptable when one considers that, as a recognized part of the church, religious broadcasters have access to one of the most widely dispersed and pervasive networks of pastoral care in the country—the local church. Yet broadcasters rarely use the facilities available through these local churches. Several personal experiences of this author suggest this lack of follow-up. As a local clergyman working in the Boston area, the author gave his name to CBN Boston and was accepted as one of their local referral pastors to whom cases that needed extended follow-up were referred. In the two years of acting in this capacity, however, he received only five referrals from the CBN station in the area. In-house figures from the station indicate that from the 36,225 calls received by the station during the years 1977–79, only 1,118 referrals were made to a local church or clergyman in the area.[26] The author also wrote to five of the broadcasters seeking their advice on living as a Christian. Only one broadcaster included the name of a local church from which he could gain further information, and no local church made contact with him as a result of his enquiry, even though two churches of the same affiliation as the broadcasters' existed on the block where he was living.

If the paid-time broadcasters see themselves as being complementary to the local church, as they claim to do, there is little evidence of a genuine effort on their part to develop a working relationship with the churches, particularly in the area of ongoing care. This unwillingness is strange, for the local church offers many of the pastoral-care facilities lacking in the broadcast organizations: continuity of interpersonal relationship, group support, the possibility of extended personal counseling, and the sacramental and interactive aspects of worship.

The lack of continuity in the counseling relationship and the lack of genuine individual responsiveness created by the mass-counseling methods employed by broadcasters make a mockery of genuine pastoral care and religious compassion. The intimacy of communication claimed by the broadcasters falls very short as an acceptable model of Christian concern and communication for several reasons.

First, the implied intimacy of the relationship is basically dishonest. The presentation of the broadcaster as a compassionate friend is actually a selective, edited, and cultivated image neatly honed by market research and designed to evoke a particular response. The host may individually be a compassionate person at times (there are several accounts suggesting the opposite for some broadcasters) but such intimacy and compassion lack plausibility when not expressed in specific, spontaneous, interpersonal situations free of the watchful, editorially corrective eye of the camera.

Second, the broadcasters' intimacy and compassion are not interactive. A television host cannot respond specifically to a person's situation. Yet for many Christians this mutuality, responsiveness, and vulnerability of one person to the other is the essence of the Christian message of the incarnation (i.e., "in the flesh"). As theologian Harvey Cox has noted: "God's message to humanity was not emblazoned across the sky (but) was written in the life and suffering of a man who was willing to open himself to the abuse and contempt of those who rejected him."[27] In removing this aspect of vulnerability, one removes the essence of the Christian concept of love.

Third, a one-way, electronic relationship lacks the creative challenge and demands which a loving relationship brings. Not only is the viewer unable to share his or her reactions in the immediacy of a person-to-person encounter with the broadcaster, but the viewer does not have to expose himself or herself personally to the judgment and demands of the message as it is embodied in the actual presence of another person, with the incongruities and decisions that the presence of another person involves. In the artificial relationship of broadcaster to viewer, the broadcaster becomes the lackey of the viewer, forced continually to provide what is explicitly or implicitly demanded under the threat of being discarded and replaced by another when he no longer fulfills the desires of his viewer.

Because paid-time religious broadcasters refuse to recognize these inherent limitations of the medium and thus refuse to compensate for them in the presentation of their message, they are in constant danger of removing the nonverbal, experiential, and interpersonal dimensions of religious faith and substituting in their place a passive observation of pseudo-religious spectacle. James Taylor has suggested that if the early church had had the use of mass media more people would have known about Christianity but far fewer people would have been converted to become Christians themselves.[28] Increasingly, church leaders are questioning how a demanding gospel can be communicated on a medium such as television, which is characterized by the peculiar qualities of being entertaining, relaxing, and undemanding of personal effort or exertion by its viewers.

Social and Political Impact

Jerry Falwell is one broadcaster who has justified his broadcasting activities on the basis of the political visibility and impact they have given to the church: "Television and radio are enabling the Christian community to reach a level of public exposure and contacts never before possible."[29] Falwell is one obvious example of an otherwise unknown preacher who gained national publicity through his broadcasting efforts. Other religious television personalities have achieved similar fame, particularly during the recent presidential elections.

It is difficult to assess objectively the actual impact which these programs have had. The number of articles which appeared in the newsweekly magazines at the time does give some indication of the perceived potential of these movements during the 1980 presidential election.[30]

While these programs may have given religious spokespersons greater publicity than they had had for some time, there has been substantial criticism within the church of the paid-time broadcasters' political activities. Though there were a few social commentators who challenged the right of the broadcasters to influence the elections, most religious critics did not deny the right of the broadcasters to exercise power in this arena: it is the business of religious faith to attempt to influence society in the direction of greater good, and many of the critics were themselves veterans of the social rights activities of the 1960s. The criticisms were directed rather at the nature of the changes being sought and the methods used to achieve these changes.

Central to the criticisms has been the conviction shared by many religious leaders that the exercise of social power should be directed by a concern for justice on a representative basis rather than a concern to impose one's own particular standards and beliefs on others. The criticism of Christian broadcasters by others within the church was that they were using the inordinate power they had gained through the unrepresentative mass media to promote their own preferred and highly selective causes rather than to encourage the exercise of responsible representation.

The continual focus on several select moral issues to the avoidance of others at times caught the broadcasters in embarrassing contradictions. One method by which they attempted to rally support for politicians who supported their particular causes was by endorsing a "rating" system which collated scores for each individual legislator according to how that legislator voted on several issues considered by the broadcasters to be "Christian" issues of the election. When the scores were tallied, however, several recognized and highly respected Christian legislators, including Jesuit

Robert Drinan of Massachusetts, evangelical Mark Hatfield of Oregon, and Paul Simon of Illinois received extremely low ratings on their legislative behavior as it reflected their "Christian" commitment. At the same time two congressmen who received the top score for their "Christian" legislative activity were shortly to be convicted for criminal activity: one for accepting a bribe of $25,000 in the Abscam scandal and the other for homosexual solicitation of boys in Washington.

The paid-time religious broadcasters claimed to represent the biblical position on political issues, but the biblical basis of their policies was seen to be rather suspect. Spurious biblical warrant was quoted for increased military spending and the development of American nuclear capability. Other issues upon which they focused attention, such as abortion, homosexuality, pornography, and prayer in public schools were found to be of minor biblical concern compared to other issues which they avoided, such as justice and God's concern for the poor.

Television certainly offers the potential for social and political impact by religious broadcasters who seek to use it in that way, and yet, the example set by broadcasters in the 1980 election year left much to be desired in the eyes of many Christian leaders and adherents.

The Methods of the Paid-Time Broadcasters

Considerable criticism was directed toward the conservative broadcasters because of the highly competitive nature of their methods in attracting viewers and in promoting their own cause. Their willingness to compete against other religious broadcasters in the open market blended nicely with the spirit of free enterprise and gave the television industry an unexpected financial blessing by enabling it to sell time for religious broadcasts rather than provide time without charge. In the process, however, the paid-time broadcasters undercut cooperative ventures among the different churches and frustrated the efforts of other religious leaders to encourage justice and an attitude of social responsibility within the television industry.

This competitiveness of the paid-time broadcasters has its basis in conservative theology, which is strongly competitive in concept. Salvation is conceived of as a struggle between God and the devil for the soul of the individual. With the alternatives being eternal blissful heaven or everlasting punitive hell, this battle frequently is intense. Christian discipleship is understood largely as competition against negative forces, either within oneself or within one's environment. Providence is seen as God's working on the side of the believer or the faithful to promote his or her cause and to frustrate the opposition. The resolution of these conflicting forces, achieved through divine competition, is seen as the dynamic by which the divine will works out its purpose.

When the struggle is understood in these eternal dimensions, the more mundane consequences of competitiveness, such as lack of representativeness in the presentation of religious culture on television can be seen as almost inconsequential. The competitiveness tends to minimize cooperation with other religious groups not within the close parameters of one's own theological tradition. In fact, competitiveness between Christian groups is seen as more desirable than cooperation because competitiveness acts as a stimulus to better performance whereas cooperation becomes time consuming and modifying.

Mainline churches, on the other hand, without this strong emphasis on snatching people from the threat of hell, have tended to interpret mission less as competition and more as nurture, cooperation, and action for social justice. In relation to television, this mission has expressed itself as attempts to be responsible in their approach to and use of television by stressing cooperative ventures, justice in programming through the representation of the variety of community beliefs and aspirations, and social responsibility through encouraging humanizing programs and television's responsiveness to the needs of society.

This approach has run counter to the evangelical approach. Because the paid-time broadcasters' emphasis on competitiveness has coincided with the same stress in the television industry as a whole, they have been favored. Mainline groups have been critical of this advantage taken by the paid-time broadcasters because it has frustrated their efforts to encourage stations to act responsibly in the public interest. In accepting their advantage, paid-time broadcasters have also acted selfishly, ignoring the interests of the community as a whole in favor of their own particular interests. Such power, according to the mainline churches, should be used not to further one's own advantage exclusively but also to further the interests of the community through advocacy functions and a general critique of the broadcast system. These functions, they claim, are not being fulfilled by the paid-time broadcasters.

The Church and Culture

Many of the differences between the paid-time broadcasters and the sustaining-time broadcasters have come about because of their different understandings of the relationship among the church, the Christian message, and American culture. In the two decades of rapid change in religious broadcasting, it has been the evangelicals who have become most affirmative of American culture.

Evangelical and fundamentalist theology has continually stressed the individual as the foundational unit of society. Morality is understood as the behavior of the individual and limited in its definition largely to personal morality in such issues as sexual attitudes and conduct, honesty and integrity of intentions, and fidelity in relation to one's marital commitments. Social morality is to a large extent viewed as this personal morality writ large: there is little understanding in evangelical ethics of group morality, corporate ethics or social behavior. Christian discipleship has tended therefore to be interpreted mainly in terms of individual morality and witness rather than in action for change in other dimensions such as social structures or political systems.

Evangelical social philosophy, therefore, became attractive to many during the 1960s, when it helped masses of people conceptualize and handle the traumatic social changes which were taking place in American society. By personalizing all issues, evangelical theology provided the means by which people could integrate these major social changes. In the process, however, it has tended to be strong in its affirmation of the social and political status quo. With its special emphasis on individual conversion, it reassured people that whatever social change was necessary could be achieved by changing individuals within the system. This attitude was strongly coupled with biblical warrant for the Christian's obedient acceptance of appropriate political authorities.

This attitude was well expressed by Billy Graham, one of the major spokespersons of the evangelical tradition. In the midst of the social turmoil of the 1960s, he wrote,

We have been trying to solve every ill of society as though society were made up of regenerate men to whom we had an obligation to speak with Christian advice . . . Thus the government may try to legislate Christian behavior, but it soon finds that men remain unchanged. The changing of men is the primary mission of the church. The only way to change men is to get them converted to Jesus Christ. Then they will have the capacity to live up to the Christian command to "Love thy neighbor."[31]

Coming out of the 1960s, therefore, conservative Protestant theology including that of the evangelical broadcasters was strong in its affirmation of traditional American culture, including the values of free-enterprise capitalism and the validity of capitalism's monetary rewards. For many this included a renewed emphasis on the divine destiny of American democracy. Any shortcomings in the American system tended to be understood in the context of individuals' failures within the system rather than faults in the system itself.

Vernon Grounds, former President of Conservative Baptist Theological Seminary, noted at the time that the dominant social attitudes that had come to characterize evangelical churches (and these same attitudes can be detected in the major evangelical television programs) are (1) an overriding social and political conservatism; (2) a distinct otherworldliness that nevertheless allows for material success; (3) a strong individualism and bourgeois mentality; and (4) an unprophetic acquiescence to prevailing social norms.[32]

This combination of social attitudes made blending into the general television milieu relatively friction-free for the paid-time broadcasters. In moving into this milieu, however, they also adopted other characteristics of it
with little question: glamour, pageantry, style, sensationalism, and exaggeration. Yet by identifying morality in personal terms, they could do so
with little challenge to their basic message.

Mainline theology and social philosophy, on the other hand, allow for a
concept of corporate or social morality as well as individual or personal
morality. Mainline ethicists stress that structures and societies themselves
are moral agents which in their adoption must be evaluated for their coherence with one's basic message and stance. Their ethicists' criticism of paid-
time broadcasters has been that in their unquestioning acquiescence to the
exploitative images and structures of television and their uncritical endorsement of television's functioning within American society, paid-time broadcasters have caught themselves in a moral contradiction: the identification
of the Christian message of justice, love, and community with television's
structural characteristics of injustice, inhumanity, and exploitation.

Not only these characteristics of television have been of concern to religious writers. They point to other destructive aspects of television that
have been stressed by television researchers and theorists: the privatization
of experience at the expense of family and social interaction and relationships;[33] the promotion of fear as the appropriate attitude to life;[34]
television's cultural levelling effects which blur local, regional, and national
differences and impose a distorted and primarily free-enterprise, competitive
and capitalistic picture of events and their significance;[35] television's sup-
pression of social dialogue;[36] its distorted and exploitative presentation of
certain social groups;[37] the increasing alienation felt by most viewers in relation to this central means of social communication;[38] and its negative effects
on the development of the full range of human potential.[39]

This medium, mainline critics suggest, should not be one of the primary
means of achieving the church's mission, as it is for the paid-time broadcasters: it should be one of the primary targets of the church's mission.

This debate between different religious broadcasters and church leaders
reflects differing attitudes towards technology, involving again the differences that have been noted between emphasis on personal morality and
corporate morality. For most evangelicals, television is a tool to be used and
if the end is justified, then so also are the means required by the tool in
achieving those ends. The effect of the demands of television on the paid-
time broadcasters is apparent: similar images, formats, and production techniques as those used by successful secular programs; attention-grabbing
devices such as constant references to miracles; dramatic incidents and spectacle; and the use of celebrities are all justified by the broadcasters as essential to using television effectively. "What are they asking us to do?" asks
Mike Nason, executive producer of Robert Schuller's "Hour of Power"

program. "Get black and white, adjust our glasses before we read a scripture, shuffle up to the camera? By that time we've lost our viewer. He's gone to watch Bugs Bunny."[39] Similarly, Pat Robertson has noted,

To maintain professional standards in our industry and to be effective in the marketplace, a degree of entertainment and showmanship is sometimes necessary. Communication by mass media is not the same as the direct personal contact between pulpit and pew.[40]

That is the dilemma and there are many thinkers, including evangelicals, who feel that the broadcasters have identified themselves too closely with this television culture and in the process have cheapened the message of the Christian faith and reduced it to an unacceptable form of spiritual entertainment or "superbowl Christianity." This reservation is expressed by one evangelical writer as follows:

Of course there is nothing wrong with a person giving his Christian witness. Even Paul told his story on two or three occasions. But according to the record he didn't send out a direct-mail piece urging Christians to see him in person at the sports arena flanked by the recently born-again coach and halfback of the Super Bowl champions. Nor did he go coast to coast on color television where his testimony was scheduled to follow right behind a country music star singing her latest country gospel hit. It's hard to picture Paul promoting tapes of his latest crusade in Athens . . .[41]

What is interesting is that evangelicals have been the religious figures to make such full adaptations to the demands of television. In the past, the fundamentalist and evangelical traditions within Christianity have tended to stand in a counterculture relationship with American society while the mainline churches have been more identified as a culture-affirming religious tradition. As television is coming to dictate the mainstream of American culture, the evangelical and fundamentalist traditions have become the affirmers and mainline churches have become the mavericks, resisting the imposition of this culture through such means as media advocacy on behalf of powerless social groups, media criticism, and media-awareness programs.

A review of the revivalist tradition in America, however, reveals the similarities of modern television preachers and the earlier manifestations of revivalist preaching during the nineteenth and early twentieth centuries. As William McLoughlin competently points out in his book *Revivals, Awakenings and Reform*, the American revivalist tradition came into existence in the early nineteenth century at the same time as the mass market and popular media such as the penny newspaper. Revivalist preachers used every trick of the popular media of the time: advertisements, billboards, posters, and news stories to draw attention to themselves and to promote their cause. The program formats and styles now seen on paid-time television programs to a large extent can be seen in the meetings of earlier revivalists such as Moody and Sunday: the charismatic preacher, the emphasis on quick, dramatic conversions, popular gospel singing, and the witnessing of prominent personalities.

Similarly, the reaction of the established churches to those theological mavericks and the conflicts the evangelicals caused within the churches then are not unlike the reaction and conflicts they have caused today. The difference, however, is that now they have been able to gain exposure on a more universal and nationally apprehended medium.

Their stance, though, has caught the paid-time broadcasters in an interesting theological paradox. For, while their message contains a strong element of social doom, calling people to flee from confidence in society to a belief in the imminent coming of Jesus, their actions are very affirmative of the durability and worth of this society. In denouncing American society, the broadcasters use figures who are distinguished by their success in this society: Pat Boone, Efrem Zimbalist, Jr., Charles Colson, plus the endless parade of successful authors, recording stars, actors, and so on. The message of imminent doom is conveyed through a program which features pleasant faces, happy sound, and upbeat music. The continual reminder that Jesus is coming soon is interspersed with appeals and documentaries reminding viewers to contribute to the building of new centers, colleges, holiday villages, churches, and hospitals. Calls to flee from the imminent destruction are accompanied by demonstrations of how viewers may find happiness in this life and material wealth which is God's blessing to those who trust him. Edward Berckman suggests that the success of the evangelical and fundamentalist broadcasters lies in their ability to hold to and present this paradox: "The appeal lies in (their) ability to maintain a precarious balance: to communicate a sense of a threatened world while, at the same time, vigorously presenting an image of success."[42]

The Religious Use of Mass Media

Each time a new mass medium has emerged, the church has been there and adapted the medium's use to the church's purpose. The first mass printing of a text was of the bible in 1456; a regularly scheduled religious service appeared on radio only two months after regular radio programming began in 1920; and religious programs were among the first year's offerings on television in 1940. Within the church, there have always been the enthusiastic communicators who have tried to raise the church's sights to see the potential of mass communication.

But also within the church there have always been the critics who have cautioned against the hazards of greeting any new advance with unquestioning praise. These critics have not always been conservatives seeking to preserve an established domain nor the jealous attacking a successful project. In relation to the mass media, some of the strongest criticisms within the church have come from people actively involved not only in the mission of the church but in seeking the vision to encompass new developments in society. It is not accurate to seek to pass off such criticisms simply on the basis that other religious leaders "feel threatened" or that they express "resentment for another's success."[43]

Criticisms of the use of mass media for religious communication center on two main arguments, the first based on philosophical and theological grounds, and the second based on the structural implications of the television industry itself.

There has been a persistent body of people who question the use of mass media in religious communication as an inherent contradiction in terms. The essence of Christian communication according to many is its responsiveness, its service of human need, and its affirmation of the individual. To speak of "mass" communication is an impossibility. Theologian Harvey Cox has made the point that "you cannot communicate a message about love and reciprocity when you are telling someone with no opportunity of him/her talking back."[44] What results in this case is a reduction of the gospel message to information and often carefully hidden coercive information. Such one-way communication of a religious message eventually strips the message of its interactive, existential dimensions. Writer Virginia Stem Owens challenges this basic presumption underlying current religious mass media:

Theologically (a Radio Church) is a contradiction in terms. In our rush to support modern man's spirituality in the style to which he had become accustomed, we had forgotten the one thing necessary for worship—total presence.... There are very few experiences where one must still be physically present to participate in them, so far has technology extended our nerve-endings. Birth and death, sex and liturgy, remain the holdouts. None of these can be performed satisfactorily by proxy or long distance.[45]

These criticisms suggest that the problem facing religious communicators is not just a matter of content but a questioning of the nature of the whole medium itself. The particular contents of television, however, aggravate the problem and make it an especially pernicious antagonist to the Christian message. Television's highly centralized, capital-intensive, hard-edged conceptualizations make it virtually impossible even for Christian content to remain intact. One of the most ascerbic critics in this regard has been the experienced mass-media practitioner, Malcolm Muggeridge. In his challenge of the use of mass media for religious communication, Muggeridge focuses on the question of the *illusion* created and presented by the mass media, particularly that of television: "Not only *can* the camera lie, it always lies. . . . The ostensibly serious offerings of the media, on the other hand, represent a different menace precisely because they are liable to pass for being objective and authentic, whereas actually they, too, belong to the realm of fantasy."[46] Muggeridge who, late in life, became an active Christian, considers that the fantasy image of the television screen stands in direct contrast to the reality of Christ and therefore is totally unadaptable to the proclamation of the Christian message.

Now we, the legatees of Christendom, are in our turn succumbing to fantasy, of which the media are an outward and visible manifestation. Thus the effect of the media at all levels is to draw people away from reality, which means away from Christ, and into fantasy.[47]

One defense against such criticisms offered by the paid-time broadcasters is that these critics have failed to realize the significant difference between print media and electronic media. The critics, in McLuhan's terms, are bound by the linear logic of the written page. It is the electronic communicators who have perceived the gestaltic logic of the electronic media and have applied that logic to the explication of the Christian message. It is significant in this regard that most discussion about religious uses of television takes place in print, while the actual practice continues in electronics. Editor James Taylor of the United Church of Canada suggests that today the church is in a new Reformation, the significance of which for the life of the church may be as dramatic as the Reformation in the sixteenth century, which derived much of its momentum from the development of print. This new Reformation will bring ways of thinking as foreign to religious thinkers today as did the Reformation then. Taylor acquiesces to what he views as the inevitable: "We might as well face the fact that more and more people who would otherwise have belonged to our churches are going to be born again out of television's experiential womb."[48] Whether Taylor is right or not may be proven only by the historical perspective to be gained by the passage of time. It is possible that, as audience figures suggest, this new Reformation may already have reached a plateau. In the meantime, however, religious communicators must address the problem as clearly and logically as possible, weighing the issues involved even if they are forced, again in McLuhan's terms, to use a logic gained from a rear-vision view.

The second objection to the religious use of mass media from within the church arises out of concern for the implications of the organization of the mass media themselves. Harvey Cox has highlighted this problem:

The problem with the mass media is not their content—though God knows that is bad enough. The trouble is their structure and the pattern of their control. They are massive one way signalling systems that allow for virtually no response. They are controlled by the rich and the powerful. . . . They are run for profit, for controlling people and selling them things.

This context, according to Cox, cuts right across the message of the gospel, rendering it totally ineffective—"A gospel presented in a context which contradicts the gospel is no longer the gospel at all."[49] This is a problem particularly with those who receive the messages of American broadcasting outside the American system. Jesuit communicator Stefan Bamberger notes,

Latin American Christians have very realistically brought to our attention the fact that the mass media in many countries are commercially and politically dominated. . . . How can one identify with a set-up which, in most parts of its program, flatly promotes the consumer society and often obeys political dictatorship?[50]

This apparent conflict has never been a problem for the paid-time broadcasters, who consider it beyond the scope of Christian concern to effect social change except through the conversion of individuals, a process which can take place regardless of contexts and suggested identifications. Their task, as they see it, is not to change social structures but to use what tools are available for the purpose of spreading the gospel. This limited evangelical understanding of "spreading the gospel," understood largely as verbal content, lies at the base of much of the debate over religious uses of mass media. Other religious communicators feel that spreading the gospel also involves action on behalf of the poor, the oppressed, and those suffering because of powerlessness to resist exploitation.

The alternatives suggested by the critics of current religious broadcasting reflect this broader concern to embody the gospel in action not only through television but also against television. Harvey Cox suggests that the proper function of the American religious communicator should not be a personally beneficial one but a surrogate one: "to be the voice of the powerless and poor of the world . . . to use the media to allow people to give expression to their fear, to let people cry out, and to make media accessible."[51] Many mainline broadcasters assert that one of the major objects of their broadcasting is producing programs which raise issues of social concern and which give expression to minority groups and causes.

Theologian Robert McAfee Brown suggests that the most appropriate stance for the church to take in regard to the mass media is to use its facilities to counter the depersonalizing and privatizing effect of the media in society. In this case the church's mission to television may represent a massive clash of institutions, with the church becoming a paradigm of a counterculture or antienvironment organization in which human values are preserved and restored to their foremost position in society.

If depersonalization turns out to be the greatest single threat in the future, it can be strongly argued that the church has the special role of warning about this and safeguarding the personal dimension against encroachment in the name of efficiency, progress, or technological necessity.[52]

Various churches and church leaders have been following this approach. The media awareness program, *Television Awareness Training*, was developed by a group of churches to develop social awareness of the influence of television on social attitudes and values. The program is now being used internationally, with adaptations made for particular national contexts. The United Church of Christ has continually played an active part in media advocacy, devoting much of the time of their Office of Communication to media criticism, lobbying, and organizing community and legal-action groups against the television industry on behalf of disenfranchised groups.

At the moment, however, it is unlikely that such action will become a universal strategy of the churches. Not only are there major theological differences between the groups which lead them to conceive the problem of media differently, but there is now major capital investment to be protected and justified, not only in television but in the large, related fields of religious music, publishing, entertainment, and alternate education. These gain their distinctiveness not from their rejection of the marketing approach in the name of religious faith but from their almost total integration of modern consumer marketing with religion, producing what Virginia Stem Owens identifies as a range of prepackaged, certified Christian lifestyles to meet one's particular demands and aspirations, with appropriate seminars available to show a person how to fit into that life-style.

The answer, according to one group, is to be the mouthpiece for the poor and disenfranchised, to resist the imposition of the media, to be the counterculture in which human values are preserved. The answer, according to the other group, is for religious faith to ride the technological roller coaster wherever it goes, with a strong confidence in the capabilities of technology to contribute to the furthering of the Christian cause. The only potential limitation would be the money to enable the church to do it. "The church won't be able to do much if (the world) can keep it poor and underfinanced. The billion dollar category is what is needed to be truly effective," says paid-time religious broadcaster Pat Robertson.[53]

It is apparent that the conflict within the church caused by the growth of evangelical broadcasting in recent years is more than just a case of "sour grapes" or "ego-defensiveness." It represents a marked difference in approaches to religious faith and practice arising out of theological, philosophical, social, and practical differences.

These differences within the church have made it as a whole vulnerable to manipulation by the powerful television industry which in the past two decades has permitted and encouraged the growth of paid-time broadcasting because that approach is most in harmony with its own economic goals and methods. The paid-time religious broadcasters in general have not yet been able to perceive or acknowledge the use that has been made of them, or the power of the television industry to shape their message and their organizations. Nor have they acknowledged their vulnerability to possible future changes in broadcast policy according to the inclinations of the television industry. By undercutting the moral basis of representativeness in religious programming on television, the paid-time religious broadcasters have removed one of the major contributions that religious groups could have made in influencing television in America: that of acting as agents in challenging the television industry to act within its moral responsibility as a utility for genuine social communication.

Notes

1. Robert M. Liebert, "The Electronic Church: A Psychological Perspective," paper presented at the Electronic Church Consultation, New York University, February 6–7, 1980, p. 1.
2. Armstrong, *Electric Church*, p. 8.
3. Ibid., pp. 8–9, 149.
4. Ibid., pp. 9–10.
5. See Richard McBrien, "The Electronic Church: A Catholic Theologian's Perspective," paper presented at the Electronic Church Consultation, New York University, February 6–7, 1980, p. 3. Also Lesslie Newbigin, *The Household of God: Lectures on the Nature of the Church*, London: SCM Press, 1953, p. 21; and Emil Brunner, *The Divine Imperative*, Philadelphia: Westminster, 1947, pp. 300–301.
6. Philip Yancey, "The Ironies and Impact of PTL," *Christianity Today*, September 21, 1979, p. 33. See also other conservative criticisms such as D. G. Kehl, "Peddling the Power and the Promises," *Christianity Today*, March 1980, pp. 16–19; and Russ Williams, "Heavenly Message, Earthly Designs," *Sojourners*, September 1979, pp. 12–28.
7. George Comstock, "The Impact of Television on American Institutions," *Journal of Communication*, Spring 1978, pp. 12–28.
8. The Gallup Organization, *The Unchurched American*, p. 1.
9. Carl S. Dudley, *Where Have All Our People Gone: New Choices for Old Churches*, New York: Pilgrim Press, 1979, p. 11.
10. Armstrong, *Electric Church*, p. 84.
11. In Bisset, "Religious Broadcasting," p. 31.
12. Armstrong, *Electric Church*, p. 7.
13. "PTL Counseling," a leaflet of the PTL Network. No date.
14. James F. Engel, "Pilot Research Study," pp. 23–33.
15. Win Arn, "Mass Evangelism—The Bottom Line," *Church Growth: America*, January/February, 1978, pp. 6–9.
16. Win Arn, "A Church Growth Look at 'Here's Life, America,'" *Church Growth: America*, January/February, 1977, pp. 8–9.
17. Armstrong, *Electric Church*, p. 135.
18. Ronald L. Johnstone, "Who Listens to Religious Radio Broadcasts Anymore?" *Journal of Broadcasting*, Winter 1971–72, p. 92.
19. Bisset, "Religious Broadcasting," p. 29.
20. Engel, *Contemporary Christian Communications*, p. 258.

21. "PTL Counseling."
22. CBN Boston, "Monthly Statistical and Activity Reports," October 1977 to September 1979.
23. See Berkeley Rice, "Call-In Therapy: Reach Out and Shrink Someone," *Psychology Today*, December 1981, p. 88.
24. Bisset, "Religious Broadcasting," p. 33.
25. Yancey, "Ironies and Impact," p. 33.
26. CBN Boston, "Monthly Statistical and Activity Report."
27. Harvey Cox, "Bad News for the Good News," *The American Baptist*, January 1979, pp. 2–3.
28. James A. Taylor, "No Miracles from the Media," *Christian Century*, May 30, 1979, p. 614.
29. Quoted in Bisset, "Religious Broadcasting," p. 31.
30. See for example, James Mann with Sarah Petersen, "Preachers in Politics: Decisive Force in '80?" *U.S. News and World Report*, September 15, 1980, pp. 24–26; and Allan J. Mayer, "A Tide of Born Again Politics?" *Newsweek*, September 15, 1980, pp. 28–36.
31. Billy Graham, *World Aflame*, Garden City: Doubleday, 1965, p. 181.
32. Vernon Grounds, *Revolution and the Christian Faith*, Philadelphia: Lippincott, 1971.
33. Comstock, "The Impact of Television," p. 14.
34. Gerbner, "Television as New Religion," pp. 54–55. It is interesting to note how Christian broadcasters use this same fear-creation by highlighting threats to common values, by stressing crises in society or in the program, and by interpreting criticism or investigation of their programs as personal persecution by adversaries.
35. See for example Emile G. McAnany, "Television: Mass Communication and Elite Controls," *Society*, September/October 1975, pp. 41–46; and Ithiel de Sola Pool, "Direct-Broadcast Satellites and Cultural Integrity," *Society*, September/October 1975, pp. 47–56.
36. Everett C. Parker, "Christian Communication and Secular Man," New York, 1966. (Mimeographed)
37. Gerbner et al., "The Demonstration of Power," pp. 177–96.
38. Comstock et al., *Television and Human Behavior*, pp. 128–35.
39. See particularly Mander, "Four Arguments," p. 40; and *Children and Television: Senate Standing Committee on Education and the Arts Inquiry into the Impact of Television on the Development and Learning Behaviour of Children*, Canberra: Australian Government Publishing Service, 1978, pp. 28–51.
40. Quoted in Hadden and Swann, *Prime-Time Preachers*, pp. 108–9.
41. In Bisset, "Religious Broadcasting," p. 31.
42. B. Russel Holt, "Superbowl Christianity," *Ministry*, May 1980, p. 19.
43. Edward M. Berckman, "The Old-Time Gospel Hour and Fundamentalist Paradox," *Christian Century*, March 29, 1978, p. 337.
44. Armstrong, *Electric Church*, pp. 144–45.
45. Cox, "Bad News for the Good News."
46. Owens, *The Total Image*, pp. 63–64.
47. Malcolm Muggeridge, *Christ and the Media*, Grand Rapids: Wm B. Erdmans, 1977, pp. 30, 61–62.

48. Ibid., p. 60.
49. James Taylor, "Progeny of Programmers: Evangelical Religion and the Television Age," *Christian Century*, April 20, 1977, p. 382.
50. Cox, "Bad News for the Good News."
51. Stefan Bamberger, "Reflections on the Ecclesiological Aspect of Group Media," in *Multimedia International Yearbook, 1978*, Rome: Multimedia International, 1978, pp. 5–18.
52. Sharon Mielke, "Press Told to Aid Powerless," *United Methodist Reporter*, May 23, 1980, p. 3.
53. Robert McAfee Brown, *Frontiers for the Church Today*, New York: Oxford University Press, 1973, p. 78.
54. Phyllis Mather Rice, "Interview with Pat Robertson," *Your Church*, May/June 1979, pp. 5–15.

PART II

Research in
Religious Television

6

Research and
Religious Television

One of the curious aspects of the recent public concern about the growth and influence of religious television programs and broadcasters has been the virtual absence of any factual verification of rumors and speculation. It is curious both because of the importance of the political positions that religious television was said to be influencing, particularly the presidency of the United States (positions normally subjected to precise scrutiny and analysis); and because of the magnitude of the influence that religious broadcasters were believed to be exerting on these positions. *U.S. News and World Report*, for example, subheaded a December 15, 1980, article on preachers in politics by asking the question of them, "Decisive Force in '80?" Even the otherwise astute *Wall Street Journal* dropped its guard on July 11, 1980, and reported that the television evangelists were reaching an estimated 128 million viewers every week, a figure which we will come to see is grossly overestimated. Some religious journals were even drawn into the mild hysteria and were debating whether the religious broadcasters intended or would be able to establish America as a religious republic.

It was not until 1981, after much of the election furor had passed and the country was settling down to a new president that writers began to challenge publicly the empirical validity of many of the claims which had been made about the size and influence of the religious broadcasters. One of these articles was appropriately called, "The Making of a Media Myth."[1] Had this empirical evaluation been done earlier, much of the explosiveness that the paid-time religious broadcasters brought to the political climate may have been defused.

It is instructive to consider why the situation developed the way it did: why so much of what was said about the size, extent, and influence of religious television has not been subjected to sound empirical analysis.

To a large extent the situation was exaggerated by the social conditions in which it arose. The ambiguity of the preelection atmosphere provided an environment in which reports on the possible influence of religious broadcasters on the election outcome were able to grow.[2] This perception was backed by a widespread public feeling that conservative religious practice and influence in America were in the ascendancy. The previous election of Jimmy Carter as president raised the public consciousness of evangelical Christianity, leading pollster George Gallup to proclaim 1976 as "the year of the evangelical." Once raised to the status of a social trend, obvious examples of evangelicalism's existence and influence were frequently featured as news items, thus reinforcing the public perception and lowering the barriers of skepticism which usually accompany new movements. Though some social commentators questioned the public's perception of the size of the evangelical movement and the validity of some of the measures used, few of them could match the status granted the movement by the general media as a whole.

Journalists and editors also failed to authenticate the empirical validity of the data they were using. To a certain extent this failure reflects their own belief in the existence of a major evangelical revival. To a certain extent it reflects the pressures on them to meet deadlines, maintain dramatic appeal, and sustain attention for their readers. Their failure to check the information was also caused by the lack of readily available data on the subject of religious broadcasting. Though there is a substantial amount of empirical information accumulated over the past 25 years on religious broadcasting and of relevance to religious broadcasting, this research has not been collated into a comprehensive statement and therefore has not been readily available for reference concerning specific aspects of religious broadcasting's extent and influence.

One of the purposes of this book, and particularly this second section, is to collate all the research available on the subject of religious broadcasting, so that issues which have been raised may be reexamined on an empirical basis rather than on the basis of a biased expectation or speculation. By laying such an empirical foundation, it is hoped also that future efforts and directions in religious broadcasting may be more realistic in their goals and objectives.

Some particular issues have already been identified as central to the debate over religious television and its influence. These issues will be reexamined in the light of what has been demonstrated empirically. The issues identified in this regard are:

1. *The nature of changes in the structure of religious television.*   Chapter 7 will examine the research relevant to this issue, particularly as it addresses the questions: Have paid-time religious programs really displaced other types of religious programs? What effects have they had on the struc-

ture of religious television in general? Have paid-time religious programs been able to break through the programming restrictions experienced by other types of religious programs?

2. *The size of the religious television audience.*   In chapter 8 the research concerning the following questions will be examined: How large is the religious television audience? What have been the historical trends in the audience? Which programs attract the largest audiences?

3. *The characteristics of the religious television audience.*   Chapter 9 will examine the research pertaining to the questions, What kind of people watch religious programs? Are religious programs watched by people not otherwise in contact with a church? Why do people watch particular religious television programs?

4. *Attitudinal effects of religious television programs.*   Chapter 10 will cover research of the following issues: Do religious television programs effect attitudinal and behavioral changes in viewers? What is the expected nature of this change? Is there evidence of people's being "converted" by religious programs?

5. *The local church and its relationship to religious television.*   Chapter 11 will discuss research on the following questions: Are religious television programs having a positive or negative effect on local churches? Are they diverting money away from the local church? Are they increasing or decreasing local church membership?

6. *Cultural effects of religious television.*   Chapter 12 will examine the following questions in the light of the available research: To what extent did religious broadcasters influence the outcome of the 1980 elections? To what extent are religious television programs affecting American culture?

The Nature of Research in Religious Television

Before examining the specific research that can clarify many of these questions, it will be valuable to consider in overview the extent to which religious television has been subjected to empirical analysis and evaluation.

The subject of religious television was given an early research impetus. One of the most significant and comprehensive research projects on religious television was conducted only a few years after regular religious television series had begun. The study, published in 1955 under the title *The Television–Radio Audience and Religion*, was developed by the National Council of Churches in association with Yale University. Using a sample of 3,559 households, the study examined the radio and television viewing habits of both secular and religious programs by residents of the community of New Haven, Connecticut. The study correlated a range of relevant social and personal variables, utilized a variety of research methodologies and statistical tests, and brought forward a series of conclusions and proposals which will be referred to throughout this section. Many of these proposals have been demonstrated by subsequent research and experience to have been prophetic.

Despite this impressive beginning, little research impetus was retained as religious television developed. The amount of subsequent research conducted on religious television in America has been relatively small in comparison to the large number of people and agencies which have been producing religious programs over the past 35 years. Of the 176 religious program producers, agencies, and television stations approached by the author in 1981, for example, only six indicated that they had undertaken independent research into their program audiences or program effectiveness.

This scarcity of ongoing research into the effectiveness of religious television programs reflects to a large extent the costs involved in such research. Until recently, religious broadcasting has been the Cinderella of church mission. Producers of religious programs within churches have consistently had to fight to convince church hierarchies of the value of mass-media communication. The producers have generally been able to procure only minimal funding from the church for programming and have been heavily dependent on public-service grants of time and facilities by stations and networks in order to continue their programming. Little money was available for promotion, let alone for research into program effectiveness. What evaluation took place was usually based on informal feedback, mostly in the form of viewer-mail response.

Religious television has not been successful in attracting public funding for research either, as have other areas of mass media such as television violence and children's programming. Because public research funds are often allocated on a strongly socially functional basis, it has only been recently when religious broadcasting had risen to the level of social and political controversy that funds have begun to be allocated for social research into the phenomenon.

The broadcasters who have had money available for research into religious television's effectiveness, namely the evangelical and fundamentalist organizations, do not have a tradition of using empirical research for evaluating effectiveness. While for the social scientist empirical data form the major source for his or her understanding and evaluation of a phenomenon, for the religious practitioner empirical data are just one source of determinative information, and often fill a secondary role behind other sources such as personal experience, intuition, and religious tradition. This is particularly true for the evangelical tradition of Christianity, which is strongly revelation-centered. Most of the large evangelical broadcast organizations do use statistical research, but that use is limited largely to market research for the purpose of syndication and program planning. The effectiveness of programming in reaching theological goals tends to be assessed on the basis of mail response and its theological implications rather than by consistent statistical analysis.

For these reasons, research into religious television has been scattered and piecemeal. The major source of the research has been academic dissertations: these have been the most substantial in terms of empirical methodology and usable information for critical purposes. The other major source of research information comes from that research which has been privately commissioned by religious agencies for their own in-house use. Because of the "hidden" nature of the research, little of it has been known or publicly available.

The majority of the research undertaken on religious television has been directed toward understanding the nature of the audience of the programs. The emphasis that has been placed on this area of research reflects the concern to measure the extent of a program's outreach, as well as the desire to define research parameters clearly in such an area of study, and the ease of access to primary data. The major studies in this area are the following:

1955. E. C. Parker; D. W. Barry; and D. W. Smythe, *The Television–Radio Audience and Religion*, New York: Harper and Row.

1962. J. L. Dennis, "An Analysis of the Audience of Religious Radio and Television Programs in the Detroit Metropolitan Area," Ph.D. dissertation, University of Michigan.

1965. H. W. Robinson, "A Study of the Audience for Religious Radio and Television Broadcasts in Seven Cities throughout the United States," Ph.D. dissertation, University of Illinois. (The two studies by Dennis and Robinson parallel each other to a large extent and reach similar conclusions with regard to the audiences of religious programs in these locations and in this period.)

1969. R. Ringe, "An Analysis of Selected Personality and Behavioral Characteristics which Affect Receptivity to Religious Broadcasting," Ph.D. dissertation, Ohio State University. (One of the first attempts to study empirically the correspondence between personality characteristics and program preference.)

1971. D. C. Solt, "A Study of the Audience Profile of Religious Broadcasts in Onondaga County," Ph.D. dissertation, Syracuse University.

1978. The Gallup Organization and the Princeton Religion Research Center, "Evangelical Christianity in the United States: National Parallel Surveys of General Public and Clergy," Princeton. (This is one of several studies conducted by this group. This one was commissioned by the evangelical journal, *Christianity Today*, and in its multivariate analyses provides useful information on differences between users and nonusers of religious television.

1978. Market Research Group, "National CBN Partner Survey," Southfield; and "National Former '700 Club' Partner Survey," Southfield.

(Two of a larger number of market-research studies commissioned by the Christian Broadcasting Network for in-house use. The first is the larger, providing statistical analyses on specific characteristics, preferences, and habits of a sample of CBN supporters.)

1979. J. M. Buddenbaum, "The Audience for Religious Programs," M.A. thesis, Indiana University. (Using data from another study of media usage, this is one of the first studies of religious television to incorporate theoretical directions of the uses-and-gratifications school, and provides some insights into how people use religious television programs.)

Findings of these studies have been remarkably consistent in relation to major demographic characteristics of the religious television audience. Along with other research studies, they provide the material for development of a relatively clear profile of the religious television audience.

There have been only limited studies concerning other areas of religious television. There have been no substantial analyses of the content of religious programs, for example, to indicate objectively the presence or nature of common content forms or patterns in religious programs, how these may have changed over time, or how they relate to other variables influential in the process such as the sponsoring tradition or the method by which the program acquires its funding. Such an absence of objective data on program content is surprising, considering that intense discussion on the message of religious programs has been taking place for almost a decade. While there have been limited surveys, none have employed a transferable statistical analysis.

Similarly, there are only limited major statistical studies in the vast area of uses and effects of religious broadcasts. These are:

1966. W. H. Rockenstein, "Children and Religious Television: An Experimental Study of the Reactions of Children in the 5th, 6th, 7th and 8th Grades in Monogalia County, West Virginia, to Children's Television Programming," Ph.D. dissertation, Northwestern University. (The first of only two known studies of religious television to employ an experimental laboratory setting.)

1975. G. S. Thompson, "The Effect of the Use of Mass Media to Establish a Local Church: A Study of the Pilot Church Project of the Christian and Missionary Alliance in Tallahassee, Florida," Ph.D. dissertation, Florida State University. (Despite some methodological inadequacies, this study is useful for the data it provides on the use of various media of communication in a practical church situation. To date it has not been duplicated.)

1979. F. Klos, "A Study of the Origin, Utilization, and Impact of the 'Davey and Goliath' Series, 1959–77, and Its Present Effectiveness in

Teaching Religious Values to Children," Ed.D. dissertation, Temple University. (The second study to employ an experimental laboratory method to study specific attitudinal change produced by religious television programs.)

1980. R. E. Frank and M. G. Greenberg, *The Public's Use of Television: Who Watches and Why*, Beverly Hills: Sage. (As part of a much larger study, this work provides useful information on characteristics of the audience and non-audience of religious programs, particularly in regard to how the use of religious programs corresponds to other personality characteristics and social stances.)

The above studies do not exhaust the statistical research available for clarification of issues in religious broadcasting. There are a large number of minor studies which contribute some relevant research information on one or more aspects of religious television. Not all of these are concerned exclusively with the subject of religious television, but they provide information on religious television as part of a larger study into a broader area of mass communication. When linked with other information, though, these smaller studies make a significant contribution to the overall picture.

Substantial data on religious television is also obtained by the rating services, Nielsen and Arbitron. These services are able to derive on a regular and comparable basis a large body of information on different aspects of the audiences of religious television programs. The Nielsen Company, for example, each November produces a "Report on Syndicated Program Audiences" which lists not only audience sizes for the various syndicated religious programs, but also age and sex variables, national and DMA ratings, and syndication information.

Not all research that has been conducted on the audiences and effects of religious television is available for scholarly use. The competitive nature of religious television that has developed in recent years has resulted in some broadcasters becoming secretive about such things as privately commissioned market research, finances, and developmental intentions. Of the four large paid-time religious broadcast organizations that responded to the author's search for research, three indicated that they had conducted private research but that they did not make it available to "outsiders." Even the fourth, which eventually made some of its research available, required numerous letters, phone calls, and the author's personally cornering the broadcaster himself in a New York elevator before research data from the organization was finally obtained. It is likely, therefore, that substantial research is being held by the major religious broadcasters which could be of value in addressing some of the persistent questions in religious broadcasting, if it were made available for wider use.

The nature of the research conducted over the past three decades appears to suggest that one of the major aims of religious broadcasters has been simply to acquire a particular audience. Research has been concerned primarily with evaluating whether this was being done. There has been little persistent research designed to evaluate the extent to which particular goals were achieved once the audience was attracted.

It may be argued that the lack of research into the effects of religious programs is compensated by broadcasters' use of research from other areas of mass-media effects to form opinions on the effects which may be expected from their programs. Certainly the religious broadcaster has access to the much larger body of general communication research on associated topics such as audience patterns and viewing behavior, attitude and value change, and communication uses and effects. There is evidence in various religious communication textbooks to indicate that religious broadcasters have drawn heavily on communication theory in formulating goals for religious broadcasting. However, it becomes apparent in these textbooks that the selection of broadcast theory used as a basis for broadcast planning is heavily influenced by the broadcaster's theological stance. Quite obviously the theoretical perspective from which one views the data determines to a large extent the influences one derives from it.

The attitude of the present paid-time religious broadcasters, for example, is indicative of what Schramm referred to as the "hypodermic" approach to mass-communication effect (i.e., where the message of the broadcaster acts as a powerful and direct stimulus to action on the part of the receiver). A close parallel is observable between a comment by an early protagonist of the theory, Dorwin Cartwright, who in 1949 suggested that, "it is conceivable that one persuasive person could, through the use of mass media, bend the world's population to his will,"[3] and the 1979 affirmation by NRB Executive Secretary Ben Armstrong, "I believe that God has raised up this powerful technology of radio and television expressly to reach every man, woman, boy, and girl on earth with the even more powerful message of the gospel."[4] This very dramatic and direct theory of mass-communication effect blends easily with the evangelicals' well-defined theology and their predilection for unambiguous concepts of preaching and behavior. The mail they receive from viewers for them is adequate verification of the influence they believe they are having. Appeals to viewers for support by these broadcasters are continually couched in terms that reflect their conceptualization of a dramatic and powerful mass-communication effect.

Mainline broadcasters, on the other hand, usually hold an understanding of mass-communication effects as being less dramatic and more indirect than do the evangelicals. Their programming, consequently, has consistently been low-key and nonurgent in tone and content compared to the intense, urgent, and sensational evangelical programs.

In evaluating the influence religious television has or may have on its audience and society, one needs to be aware, therefore, of the perspective from which the subject is being viewed. The previous lack of available research into the effects of religious broadcasting has contributed to the ambiguous situation in which different Christian broadcasters presented very different views on the issues arising from religious broadcasting, each claiming an empirical basis for their assertions. It is hoped that the following analysis of research, as it relates to the issues which have been raised, will advance substantially a sound and impartial evaluation of the effects and effectiveness of religious broadcasting, and lay a foundation for future research and planning.

Notes

1. The first to do so were William Martin's article, "The Birth of a Media Myth" and Hadden and Swann's book *Prime-Time Preachers*.
2. It is interesting to note the extent to which the process that emerged in the reporting of the influence of the paid-time religious broadcasters parallels that of development of rumors, as described in G. W. Allport and L. Postman, *The Psychology of Rumor*, New York: Henry Holy, 1947.
3. Dorwin Cartwright, "Some Principles of Mass Persuasion: Selected Findings of Research on the Sale of U.S. War Bonds," *Human Relations* 2, July 1949, pp. 253–67.
4. Armstrong, *Electric Church*, p. 7.

7

The Effects of Paid-Time Religious Programs on the Structure of Religious Television

In chapter 1 it was noted that rapid changes in the structure of religious television occurred during the 1960s and 1970s. This chapter will consider the nature of these changes in more detail, focusing especially on whether the growth of paid-time religious programs has furthered the presentation of religious faith on television, and whether the paid-time broadcasters have been successful in breaking through some of the restrictions faced by religious broadcasters in communicating by television.

The Effects of the Growth of Paid-Time Religious Programming

Research supports the observation that there has been a marked increase in both the size and number of paid-time religious programs during the 1960s and 1970s. However, the research calls into question some of the claims that have been made about the extent and universality of this increase.

It is wrong to conclude that the growth in the number and size of paid-time religious programs has simply increased the amount of religious programming on American television, and thus advanced the general cause of religious faith. The growth in paid-time religious programs has taken place primarily through the displacement of other types of programming. When the Broadcast Institute of North America surveyed religious programming in the country in 1971, they found that stations which had begun to sell time for religious programs averaged fewer network and locally produced religious programs than did those stations which did not sell time for religious programming.[1] The study identified what they called a "water table of religious programming nationwide." The researchers found that station managers tended to look at each other's behavior rather than at community interest and response in determining how much religious programming to broadcast. The growth of paid-time religious programs had

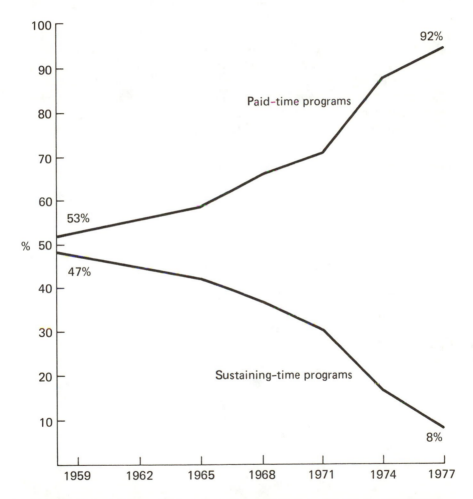

SOURCE: Federal Communications Commission, Submission by the Communications Committee of the United States Catholic Conference and others in the matter of *Amendment of the Commission's Rules Concerning Program Definitions for Commercial Broadcast Stations, etc..* (BC Docket No. 78-355, RM-2709, 1979), Table II.

Figure 7.1 **Proportion of Time Devoted to Sustaining and Paid-Time Religious Programs—Nationwide, 1959–1977.**

not raised this level of programming, but had simply changed the nature of the programming. Station managers have tended during the 1960s and 1970s to substitute religious programming previously aired on public-service time by the more profitable programming that paid for its air-time. Figure 7.1 illustrates the changing proportions of time occupied by paid-time religious programs and time occupied by sustaining-time programs nationally since 1959. As can be seen, there has been a steady growth in the amount of time occupied by paid-time religious programs versus sustaining-time programs since 1959, with particularly rapid changes occurring from 1971 on.

This characteristic is illustrated further by comparing the syndication patterns of three of the major paid-time religious programs with three major sustaining-time syndicated programs during the Nielsen sweeps period in November of each year. As seen in Table 7.1, in the period from 1973 to 1981 each of these major paid-time syndicated programs increased in syndication while each of the three major sustaining-time syndicated programs decreased in syndication.

Table 7.1   Syndication Patterns of Major Syndicated Programs

	Number of Stations on which the Programs Were Aired								
	1973	1974	1975	1976	1977	1978	1979	1980	1981
Paid-time Programs									
Oral Roberts	151	157	168	172	174	176	170	177	185
Rex Humbard	155	168	189	203	213	205	206	209	201
Robert Schuller	29	28	60	85	123	117	144	161	165
Sustaining-time Programs									
Davey & Goliath	27	19	30	26	34	20	15	12	14
This Is the Life	87	92	88	75	55	58	53	45	41
Faith for Today	57	62	57	52	19	35	38	35	—

SOURCE: Nielsen, "Report on Syndicated Program Audience."

Note that two of the sustaining-time programs which suffered a decrease because of the increased syndication of the paid-time religious programs were programs from recognized evangelical denominations. Theologically these denominations, the Lutheran Church–Missouri Synod ("This Is the Life") and the Seventh-Day Adventist Church ("Faith for Today") are very similar to the paid-time religious broadcast organizations. The primary factor leading to their decreased syndication was the method by which their programs were funded and aired.

The effect of the growth in paid-time religious programs was felt not only by other syndicated religious programs but also by network religious programs. Table 7.2 presents the average number of stations which aired the network religious programs during the 1970s. The decrease in acceptance

Table 7.2   Average Number of Stations Broadcasting Network Religious
Programs, 1970–82

	ABC "Directions"	CBS* "Look Up and Live" "For Our Times"	NBC "Specials"
1970	101	93	118
1971	109	89	136
1972	105	85	107
1973	104	85	144
1974	108	94	114
1975	114	71	134
1976	99	?	125
1977	92	?	88
1978	69	?	98
1979	62	39	91
1980	67	33	73
1981	74	33	59
1982	67	33	52 (Jan–Jul)

SOURCE: NCC Communication Commission Annual Reports, based on Network Research.
* "Look Up and Live" continued till 1979. After 1979 it was replaced by "For Our Times."

of network religious programs during the 1970s occurred primarily once
again because the networks found it more profitable to air those programs
that paid for their air-time than those programs for which air-time had to
be provided.

As a consequence of the displacement of these other types of religious
programs, the growth of paid-time religious programming in the 1960s and
1970s has resulted in a marked movement in religious television away from
representating a range of U.S. cultures and traditions toward representing
mainly the Protestant evangelical and fundamentalist traditions, particularly
the independent broadcast organizations. This narrowing of the range of
traditions is shown by an examination of the sources represented by the 12
leading religious syndicated programs. While no figures are available to
indicate the representativeness of the total fare on religious television, an
analysis of the Broadcast Institute study and Nielsen figures indicates that
these 12 top syndicated programs alone account for a large proportion of
the total households reached by religious programs on television.

Table 7.3 indicates that independent evangelical groups in 1981
accounted for 83.3 percent of the top of syndicated religious programs on
television. In comparison, the Roman Catholic Church, the membership of
which in 1979 represented 37.1 percent of the U.S. church population,
produced only one major syndicated television program, the sustaining-time
program "Insight." The National Council of Churches, its affiliated

Table 7.3   Comparative Sources for the 12 Leading Syndicated Religious Programs, 1971–81.

	1971	1975	1979	1981
Independent Evangelical Groups	41.7%	75.0%	83.3%	83.3%
Evangelical Denominations	25.0%	16.7%	8.3%	8.3%
Roman Catholic	16.7%	...	8.3%	8.3%
Other Protestant Denominations	8.3%	8.3%	...	...

SOURCES: Broadcast Institute, *Religious Programming*, p. 58; Nielsen, "Ranking of Syndicated Programs," November 1975, 1979, 1981.

NOTE: "Hour of Power" is identified as an independent evangelical program, even though Robert Schuller is an ordained Reformed Church of America clergyman, because the denomination has no association with the program. Similarly, other television hosts may have associations with a particular denomination but the programs have no denominational identification or accountability.

churches accounting for 30 percent of the U.S. church population, in 1979 and 1981 had no major syndicated religious program.[2]

These figures give concrete support to the suggestion noted earlier that *one of the major consequences of the growth of paid-time religious programming has been a marked narrowing in the representation of American religious life and culture on television.* This consequence parallels a major characteristic of television noted in relation to general communication patterns: one of the major social effects of television lies in its cultural narrowing and its levelling effect on the presentation of cultural diversity. This appears to have been the case with religious programming also.

Another effect of the growth of paid-time religious programs is *the steady increase in the number of stations that now see religion primarily as a commercial venture* and for which payment for air-time has become the dominant principle in the broadcasting of religion.

Since 1960, when the Federal Communications Commission changed its policy ruling on broadcasting in the public interest, there has been a steady increase in the number of stations willing to sell air-time for religious programming. The Broadcast Institute study in 1971 found that 65.7 percent of responding stations had a policy of selling time for religious broadcasts. In 1977, another survey of station managers found that 80.3 percent of television stations found the selling of air-time for religious broadcasts acceptable. There are as yet no more recent figures.[3]

This trend becomes significant in the light of other research suggesting that once a station adopts a policy of selling time for religious broadcasts, paid-time religious programming becomes the dominant type of religious programming broadcast on the station. There appears to be a dynamic within the programming policies of a station whereby once it is decided to

Table 7.4 Distribution of Religious Programs by Station Affiliation, 1971.

	Stations which sell time for religious programs	Stations which do not sell time for religious programs
Nonaffiliated Stations	72.2%	27.8%
Paid-time programs	58.4%	24.3%
Sustaining syndicated programs	22.5%	40.5%
Local programs	19.1%	35.2%
ABC Affiliated Stations	70.4%	29.6%
Paid-time programs	42.1%	7.9%
Sustaining syndicated programs	36.6%	48.9%
Local programs	12.8%	34.8%
Network programs	8.5%	8.4%
CBS Affiliated Stations	63.5%	36.5%
Paid-time programs	40.6%	6.9%
Sustaining syndicated programs	34.0%	39.5%
Local programs	12.8%	25.7%
Network programs	12.6%	27.9%
NBC Affiliated Stations	60.9%	39.1%
Paid-time programs	32.3%	10.6%
Sustaining syndicated programs	46.3%	56.0%
Local programs	21.4%	33.4%
Network programs*		

SOURCE: Broadcast Institute, *Religious Programming*, pp. 49–52.

NOTE: Those stations which stated they had a policy of not selling time for religious broadcasts still reflect a level of paid-time religious programming. The survey notes but does not explain this phenomenon.

* NBC did not broadcast any network religious programs during the week of the survey. NBC affiliates can be seen to have compensated with a greater than normal amount of syndicated programming.

sell air-time for religious programs, other types of religious programming are deemphasized. Though there is no substantial research to support this affirmation, it is suggested by the overall changes that emerged from the Broadcast Institute study in 1971. Table 7.4 provides a breakdown of the types of religious programs which were broadcast on affiliated and nonaffiliated stations in 1971 according to whether the stations sold time for religious broadcasts or not.

While stations which sold time for religious programs in 1971 still broadcast other types of religious programming, there is a distinct narrowing of programming to favor paid-time religious programs. With the exception of the NBC affiliates, whose regular schedules had been disrupted during the survey week, all other stations that sold time for religious broadcasts showed a dominance of paid-time programming. Programs dependent on provided air-time had decreased as a consequence. In particular, local programming was the hardest hit by the increase in paid-time religious programs. This trend is likely to have been more accentuated since 1971 with the increase in the number of stations finding paid-time religious programs acceptable: a significant consequence of the economic motivation of the general television industry.

Has the Growth in Paid-Time Religious Programs Increased the Amount of Religion on Television?

Contrary to what paid-time broadcasters maintain, research suggests that in addition to the displacement of other types of programming, the recent growth of paid-time religious programming may have resulted in less rather than more religious programming on television. While the evidence for such a proposition remains tentative, its tentativeness calls into question the certainty with which paid-time religious broadcasters assert that their efforts in competing on the basis recognized by the television industry (i.e., financial competence) have been responsible for increasing the amount of religious programming on television.

There have been no studies yet which draw specific comparisons between the total amount of religious programming on television in different historical periods. Certainly there has been a marked growth in the amount of syndicated religious programming, but there has also been a corresponding decrease in other types of religious programming which previously filled a substantial block in station schedules.

We have noted already that the Broadcast Institute study in 1971 identified a fairly even level of religious programming across the country, indicating that station managers were not only influenced by the demand for air-time for religious programs, but also by peer example. This study found also that stations which provided only free air-time for religious programs tended to broadcast more religious programs during the week of the survey than did stations which sold air-time for programs (an average of 6.08 programs per station compared to 4.51 programs per station).[4] The reasons for this difference were not given in the study. It is possible that stations which did not accept payment for air-time for religious programs reflected a greater concern for public-service programming and therefore presented a wider representation of other programming such as network and local programs. It is possible also that once a station began to sell air-time for religious programs, it became unwilling to provide the same time free for other sustaining-time programs.

It is possible, therefore, that while there has been a large and rapid growth in paid-time religious programs, there has been an even greater corresponding decline in other types of religious programs: sustaining-time syndicated programming, local programming, and network programming. The increase since 1971 in the number of stations now selling time for religious broadcasts suggests the possibility that by removing the moral basis on which station managers have broadcast religious programs, the paid-time religious broadcasters have decreased the total presentation of religious faith on television. Audience figures presented in detail in the next chapter suggest that these syndicated programs have displaced higher-rating network programs, which may also result in a smaller audience for religious programming on television.

Arbitron figures suggest that in 1981 and 1982 there was a further marked increase in the number of syndicated religious programs over 1980 and even over the previous high points of 1976. Given the saturation of broadcast time which appears to have been reached, it is possible that these increases are accounted for by the relatively low marginal increases for production and distribution of these programs through the cable market. Because of the lack of comprehensive information about the effects of cable development on the total television industry, it is difficult to tell what effects these new programs will have on religious broadcasting in general.

Have Paid-Time Religious Programs Broken Out of the Religious Ghetto?

One of the justifications the paid-time religious broadcasters have given for their monopolizing of the airwaves, their displacement of other religious programs on television, and their commercializing of religion on television is that through such an approach they have been able to overcome the barriers that have restricted religious broadcasters who have been dependent on the goodwill of stations and networks. A review of the research, however, suggests that this justification does not stand up to close empirical analysis.

A large majority of religious programs have traditionally been aired and continue to be aired on Sundays, particularly in the "religious-ghetto" hours of early Sunday morning. It takes only a cursory survey of a local television guide to become aware of this fact. The Broadcast Institute study in 1971 found that 82 percent of religious broadcast time was on Sundays, with only 5.5 percent on Saturdays and 12.5 percent on weekdays.[5]

There appear to be three main reasons for the concentration of religious programs on Sundays: (1) Sunday is the traditional day of Christian worship and therefore seemed most appropriate for Christian broadcasts; (2) Christian broadcasts on the networks were originally conceived as alternatives for those, such as shut-ins, who could not attend regular services at a church;[6] (3) Sunday morning was the period of lowest audience for broadcasters and therefore was the least commercially damaging for stations in fulfilling their FCC obligations by providing free air-time for religious broadcasts. This low-audience period also made time less expensive for paid-time religious broadcasters to purchase.

The perennial problem faced by religious broadcasters is that the size of the potential audience on Sunday mornings limits the audience potential for their broadcasts. Research on the "Frontiers of Faith" series, for example, found that in 1961 only 10 percent of the sets were in use at the hour the programs were broadcast. More recently, George Comstock has noted that on Sunday mornings in 1976 the potential national audience averaged only 13 million adults, compared to 70 million in prime-time.[7]

This limited opportunity to reach a large audience has stimulated religious broadcasters, like other programmers, to seek ways by which to gain access to time periods that have a greater potential audience.[8] Paid-time religious programs, by accumulating the financial resources to pay for their air-time, were conceived as one possible way of securing more favorable air-time for religious broadcasts.

Despite the large amounts of money invested in paid-time religious programs and the purchase of air-time for these programs, the available research suggests that with only a few exceptions *paid-time religious programs have not succeeded in breaking out of the religious ghetto period.* In fact the inverse appears to be true: *the growth of paid-time religious programs appears to have resulted in a greater concentration of religious programs on Sundays in general and Sunday mornings in particular.* The primary source of data on this issue again comes from the Broadcast Institute study of 1971. The study found that in 1971, 88.9 percent of all paid-time religious programs were broadcast on Sundays, compared to 77.3 percent of sustaining syndicated programs and 73.5 percent of local religious programs. Furthermore, in 1971, 70 percent of all paid-time religious programs appeared between the hours of 8:00 a.m. and noon on Sundays, compared to 46 percent of syndicated programs aired on sustaining-time.[9]

These figures, while only tentative, suggest that paid-time religious programs are more concentrated in the religious-ghetto hours of Sunday morning because *broadcasters who purchase time for their programs actively seek out the Sunday morning time-slot.* There may be several reasons for this phenomenon. One is that air-time is generally cheaper to purchase in the low-audience period of Sunday morning. Another is that by broadcasting on Sunday mornings, the paid-time religious broadcaster is more likely to be seen by those for whom Sunday morning is a recognized worship period, the sympathetic viewer whose viewing and support is essential for paid-time programs. Still another reason is that television stations would prefer the consistently low-rating paid-time religious programs to remain in that period. For example, when questioned in 1968 about their placement of religious programs, stations' owners gave very low priority to "the desires of the program's sponsor" when scheduling programs.[10]

On the other hand, the mainline programs, particularly those produced in association with the networks, have been able to maintain a more favorable audience period. The CBS series, "For Our Times," airs late on Sunday morning in the favorable period following "Sunday Morning." Some denominational groups such as the United Methodist Church ("Six American Families") and the Episcopal Church ("The Lion, the Witch, and the Wardrobe") have participated in the production of specials aired on prime-time.

There are two exceptions to this restriction on paid-time religious broadcasters. One is for those paid-time religious broadcasters who are able to produce occasional specials which are broadcast during or near prime-time, particularly on the independent UHF stations. Oral Roberts and Billy Graham are two of the paid-time religious broadcasters who have been able to purchase desirable air-time for their occasional specials.

The other exception to this proposition exists where a religious broadcaster or group owns a station or network of stations. These stations tend to be less rigorously competitive than other commercial stations because they are able to compensate for lost audience and advertising revenue by direct viewer contributions. Religious ownership of stations would not have been a major factor in 1971 at the time of the Broadcast Institute's study, but it may be a more significant factor in recent years because of the growth in the number of religious television stations across the country. There has been no research as yet to indicate the extent to which stations using a religious format present more religious programming outside the Sunday period than other stations. Increasingly, however, these stations are facing the economic pressures of the strongly competitive television industry. For example, WXNE-25 in Boston, a CBN-owned station, has decreased the amount of religious programming over the past two years and increased general programming designed to attract greater commercial sponsorship and income. Competition in the industry is bound to reduce the amount of time made available on weekdays to traditionally low-rating religious programs, even on religious stations.

There are several other syndication characteristics in religious programming which indicate that though the commercial emphasis of paid-time religious programs was designed to help them buy their way out of the ghetto, it may have forced them more deeply into it. For example, *religious television programs are aired more frequently in those regions of the country which are already high in average church attendance.* This pattern is apparent *even in evangelical programs* which are supposedly aimed at the unchurched and unconvinced. In 1971 the highest "average airings per station" of religious programs were found to be in a sequence of regions in the south-east, east-central, mid-central, and north-west regions of the country. This area roughly parallels that found to be highest in average church attendance in the nation.[11]

The reasons for this tendency are self-apparent. Broadcasters recognize that it is easier to gain an interested and sympathetic audience for religious programs in those regions and among those groups who are already interested in religion and for whom religious practice is an important element in their lives. This factor, however, catches "evangelical" programs in a curious paradox. Evangelical programs derive their raison d'être from their intent to spread the gospel to those who are beyond the current reach of the church, yet their syndication patterns reflect the practice of aiming for those areas of the country already high in church attendance and religious interest. The chief reason for this appears again to be financial: to continue to exist, paid-time evangelical programs must continually develop a supportive audience. Support is unlikely to come from antagonists, even though they may ostensibly be the target of the program. Therefore, the paid-time religious broadcasters are forced into the paradox of broadcasting a program for outsiders primarily to insiders in order to ensure continuing financial support: further evidence of the power of television's demands to shape the message of the program. This is not true, however, for the larger paid-time religious broadcasters. Five of the top six paid-time evangelical programs achieve better than 90 percent coverage of the nation's television households. But their audiences demonstrate the same trends as in the syndication patterns of all programs.[12]

The pressure that economic considerations exert on religious broadcasters once the latter accept the principle of purchasing time for programs is seen in another characteristic of religious program syndication. *Once a station which operates on a "religious" format opens in an area, there is a tendency for religious programs in that area to appear on that station* rather than for the new station to supplement existing programming on other stations.

While the research in this area is still only suggestive and probably does not apply to the high-demand markets, it corresponds to what has been noted in relation to the lack of growth in overall religious programming as a consequence of paid-time programming and other syndication characteristics for religious programming. Robinson in 1964 found no significant differences in the percentage of listeners and nonlisteners to religious radio broadcasts in a city with a religious radio station and a similar city without a religious radio station.[13] Stuart Johnson, in a study of the distribution patterns of evangelical radio programs, found that when a station with a "religious" format opens in an area, there is a tendency for religious programs in the area to begin to appear on these stations.[14] Though such studies have not been completed for television, similar characteristics between the financing of religious radio and television programs and between the syndication patterns of paid-time religious radio and television programs indicate that similar trends may be found for religious television stations.

It appears that while paid-time religious television programs have achieved a measure of financial independence from networks and stations, their financial dependence on their audience exerts a comparable influence. It forces them to be aired in places and at times where the audience is more likely to be supportive of and sympathetic to their program. It has created the anomaly where programs considered to be "evangelical" in content appear more frequently in areas already high in religious interest, commitment, and activity: on Sunday mornings, in geographical areas of already high church attendance, and on stations recognized as being "religious" in content and format.

Research suggests that, far from being a justification for their monopoly of religious programming on American television, the claim made by paid-time religious broadcasters that they have been able to overcome many of the traditional barriers faced by religious broadcasters and improve the presentation of religious faith on television is largely unfounded. The adoption of purchasing of air-time and audience solicitation as the basis for religious programming on television does not necessarily result in the breaking out of the religious ghetto, but has mainly resulted in religion's becoming more firmly ensconced in it.

Notes

1. Broadcast Institute, "Religious Programming," pp. 49–52.
2. Constant H. Jacquet, Jr., ed., *Yearbook of American and Canadian Churches, 1980*, Nashville: Abingdon, 1980, pp. 231–33.
3. Broadcast Institute, "Religious Programming," p. 52; "Some True Beliefs about Religious Programming," *P. D. Cue*, April 1977, p. 12.
4. Broadcast Institute, "Religious Programming," pp. 49–52.
5. Ibid, pp. 5–6.
6. Ralph M. Jennings, "Policies and Practices of Selected National Religious Bodies as Related to Broadcasting in the Public Interest," Ph. D. dissertation, New York University, 1968, p. 117.
7. Broadcast and Film Commission, "Frontiers of Faith—Report of Research," New York, 1966 (Mimeographed); George Comstock, "The Impact of Television," p. 17.
8. See for example, Ronn Spargur, "Can Churches Break the Prime-Time Barrier?" *Christianity Today*, January 16, 1970, pp. 3–4.
9. Broadcast Institute, "Religious Programming," p. 56.
10. A. William Bluem, *Religious Television Programs: A Study of Relevance*, New York: Hastings House, 1969, pp. 25–26.
11. Broadcast Institute, "Religious Programming," p. 48; Dean R. Hoge and David Roozen, *Understanding Church Growth*, pp. 47–48.
12. Hadden and Swann, *Prime-Time Preachers*, pp. 60–61.

13. Haddon W. Robinson, "A Study of the Audience for Religious Radio and Television Broadcasts in Seven Cities throughout the U.S.," Ph. D. dissertation, University of Illinois, 1964, p. 130.
14. Stuart Johnson, "Contemporary Communications Theory and the Distribution Patterns of Evangelical Radio Programs," Ph. D. dissertation, Northwestern University, 1978.

8

The Size of the Religious Television Audience

Images of success have always been important to the fundamentalist and evangelical traditions. Success in one's endeavors, indicated by followers, finances, or miraculous occurrences, is frequently understood and promoted as an indication that God is blessing one's enterprise. Under this theological and practical pressure and under the influence of religious fervor and anticipation, the facts on which such success are based can often become distorted, producing the numerically descriptive phrase, "evangelastically speaking."

When certain evangelical preachers moved into the public medium of television, this same emphasis on success came with them. It reflected also a practical need to justify themselves socially after having lived for decades on the periphery of American culture. This need has created the interesting paradox already noted: while in their messages the paid-time religious preachers strongly criticize and even condemn secular society, in the staging and promotion of their programs they use criteria and celebrities from this same society to demonstrate their validity.

One of the dominant expressions of evangelistic success within the broadcasting field is audience size, and the paid-time religious broadcasters in particular lean heavily on this indicator. Much of the media attention attracted by religious broadcasters in the 1980 elections was caused by the popularly held belief that the broadcasters were being watched by a major portion of the American public. A consideration of impartial audience figures indicates that actual audience sizes for a religious broadcasting are much more modest than has been generally believed. In fact, when one considers the consistent exaggeration which took place in the light of audience surveys available at the time, one wonders whether such overstatement was purely accidental. It reflects both the "success–God's blessing" attitude as well as an opportunistic strategy by broadcasters to increase their own influence and promote their own cause in the presence of general public gullibility and naivety.

The recent media attention has also created questions about the historical trends in the followings of religious broadcasters. It is these questions that are to be considered in this chapter, in view of the available research.

The most commonly used figures for estimating audience sizes for television programs are those provided by the large survey companies, Nielsen and Arbitron. These two companies conduct continuous research on a carefully calculated, statistically representative basis into audiences of most broadcast programs on a local, regional, and national level. These audience figures are widely used by broadcasters and advertisers for the determination of a program's popularity and subsequent advertising rates. While there has been occasional criticism of the limitations of the surveys in measuring public reaction to programs, the surveys' reliability and validity in measuring audience sizes is generally accepted. Both survey companies include syndicated religious programs in their regular audience research and many of the large religious organizations subscribe to one or both of these services as an aid in the syndication and marketing of their programs.

How Large Are the Audiences of Religious Television Programs?

The research figures indicate that religious television programs are consistently viewed by only a small percentage of the American population. The most substantial information available is on syndicated programs, that is, by Nielsen definition, those programs that appear in five or more markets across the country. These programs now represent the large majority of religious programs on television. Nielsen survey figures show that in 1981 there were only five syndicated religious programs that had a national rating of one or better. This means that only five religious programs attracted more than one percent of the possible national viewing audience per average telecast during the four-week survey. As shown in Table 8.1, these programs were: Oral Roberts, Hour of Power, Rex Humbard, Insight, and Jimmy Swaggart. These low ratings are not simply the result of limited distribution of these programs. As can be seen in column (5), the major broadcasters have been able to syndicate their programs into most of the television markets in the country, providing in most cases better than 90 per cent coverage of the nation's television households.

Some programs have much more limited syndication but are as popular as the larger programs in the markets in which they are broadcast. The Ro-

TABLE 8.1   Syndication and Ratings of Major Religious Programs, November 1981

(1) Program	(2) National Rating	(3) DMA Rating	(4) Number of Stations	(5) Percent Coverage
Oral Roberts	1.6	1.6	185	96
Hour of Power	1.3	1.4	165	92
Rex Humbard	1.3	1.3	201	95
Insight	1.2	2.4	59	51
Jimmy Swaggart	1.0	1.0	244	96
Day of Discovery	.8	.9	167	84
Old Time Gospel Hour	.7	.7	248	93
Gospel Singing Jubilee	.4	4.2	33	9
Ken Copeland	.4	.5	128	58

SOURCE: Nielsen, "Report on Syndicated Program Audience."

man Catholic sustaining-time program "Insight," for example, has a smaller syndication than the larger programs: 59 stations for 51 percent coverage of the country. But in the markets where it is seen, or Designated Market Areas (column 3), it draws a greater percentage of viewers than most of the other programs. Similarly the smaller program "Gospel Singing Jubilee" is syndicated over 33 stations, but in those markets where it does appear it has a rating of 4.2, greater than any other religious program.

Religious programs are low in the overall rating of syndicated programs in the country. Of 339 syndicated programs ranked by Nielsen in November 1980 according to DMA ratings, the highest rating religious program, "Insight," was only 174th on the list. The next, "Hour of Power," was 223rd. In terms of actual audience numbers, in November 1980 only two of the programs had audiences of over two million. Another four had audiences of between one and two million. (See Table 8.2.)

These figures certainly belie the claims made by some of the paid-time religious broadcasters during the preelection period of 1980. The figures are nowhere near the 20-million mark claimed by Jerry Falwell for his "Old Time Gospel Hour"; the 20 million claimed by Jim Bakker of "PTL Club"; the 60-million potential audience claimed by James Robison or the ten million homes which "are reached and helped each week by our TV program."[1] While such extravagant claims may be seen by some as unfortunate overstatements stimulated by the enthusiasm of the preachers and the controversial mood at the time, others see such exaggerations as deliberate deception by the broadcasters, designed to increase their influence dis-

TABLE 8.2   Sizes of Audiences for Syndicated
Religious Programs, November 1980

Program	Audience (Persons)
Oral Roberts	2,275,110
Hour of Power	2,088,980
Rex Humbard	1,923,900
Jimmy Swaggart	1,651,860
Day of Discovery	1,243,920
Old Time Gospel Hour	1,219,520
Insight	780,767
PTL Club	621,000
700 Club	447,640

SOURCE: Derived from Nielsen, "Report on Syndicated
Program Audience."

proportionately and to further their own cause. Such overstatements have
done little to allay fears about the dependability of the broadcasters in using
any power they may acquire and in acting as responsible representatives in
the use of the public airwaves.

There are, of course, many variables which affect a program's popularity as measured by audience size; finding the right combination of these
variables is one of the arts of the broadcast programming industry. Given
the present uses made of television in the United States, much of a program's
audience is drawn, not from people who intentionally watch television to
see a particular program at a particular time, but from people who have
committed themselves to watching *something* at that particular time.[2] It
follows, therefore, that if a program can be placed in a time-slot with a
greater audience potential, its chances of gaining a larger audience even by
accident is greatly increased.

Many past and present religious programs are of comparable quality to
other general television programs. Many of them, for example, have won
significant awards for quality and production. For reasons already noted,
however, most religious programs have aired on Sunday mornings when the
potential audience is lowest. Network religious programs are frequently
aired in more favorable time-slots than the paid-time religious programs and
have usually drawn comparable or larger audiences than even the most
popular of the paid-time religious programs. The ABC network program
"Directions" in February 1980 and 1982 had an audience of 596,000 and
616,000, respectively, which places it on a par with the major paid-time
programs "PTL Club" and "700 Club." In February 1970, the NBC special
"Tell It Like It Is" had an audience share of 13 with a viewing audience of
almost five million. Though their audience dropped in the late 1970s, in
1981 the NBC one-hour specials still had an average audience per program

of 1,674,000.[3] The weekly audience for the three network religious programs in mid-1982 was still close to three million, a fact which is frequently overlooked because of their lack of flamboyance, and the controversy that has surrounded the paid-time religious programs.

When religious programs have appeared in prime-time either as an occasional series or as specials they have drawn a much larger audience than regular religious programs. The outstanding example was Bishop Fulton Sheen's series, "Life is Worth Living," which, in the 1950s, drew a sufficiently large audience to enable it to compete and retain commercial sponsorship in prime-time for several years. A study of the program audience in New Haven in 1952 found that Sheen's series was maintaining an audience share of greater than 30 percent, a substantial share for any program, let alone a religious one.[4] Similarly, Oral Roberts' Thanksgiving Special, which was syndicated in prime-time in 1970 reportedly reached over 27 million viewers.[5]

One of the frustrations felt by religious broadcasters has been the difficulty in finding both the finances and the opportunity to sustain a prime-time religious series. The American television industry does not believe that the American public wants such a series as it did when Fulton Sheen was approached in 1950. Unless the industry's attitude changes, it is unlikely that any religious broadcaster will be able to break out of the religious-ghetto slot on a sustained basis.

Trends in Religious Program Audience

The research indicates that after a decade of steady growth, audience sizes for most major paid-time religious programs reached a plateau in 1977 and have been fluctuating since then. Table 8.3 presents the audience figures for the major syndicated programs for the past seven years. This period follows an earlier period of rapid growth in both the number and size of syndicated religious programs. A change occurred in these programs around the years 1977–78. Seven of the 10 major programs listed reached the peak of their growth in those years and since then have been either fluctuating below

TABLE 8.3   Audience Sizes for Leading Syndicated Religious Programs 1975–1981

| | Total Audience (Persons)—000s | | | | | | |
	1975	1976	1977	1978	1979	1980	1981
Oral Roberts	3,490	3,597	3,903	3,198	2,681	2,275	2,452
Hour of Power	759	1,212	1,608	1,813	1,893	2,089	2,069
Rex Humbard	2,265	2,598	2,647	2,375	2,137	1,924	1,968
Jimmy Swaggart	780	1,278	1,523	1,735	1,545	1,652	1,493
Day of Discovery	1,320	1,471	1,740	1,551	1,428	1,244	1,223

TABLE 8.3   (continued)

	1975	1976	1977	1978	1979	1980	1981
	Total Audience (Persons)—000s						
Old Time Gospel Hour	716	1,069	1,265	1,290	1,222	1,220	1,043
Gospel Singing Jubilee	1,015	1,095	1,253	1,041	894	856	630
Insight	187	497	575	528	589	781	990
PTL Club			562	672	608	621	530
James Robison	280	403	423	467	522	533	376

SOURCE: Derived from Nielsen, "Report on Syndicated Program Audience."
NOTE: The figures for 1975 do not include Teens and Children viewers, which are included in the figures for 1976–81.

those levels or declining. With two of the others, "Hour of Power" and "James Robison," that characteristic appears to have been postponed till 1980.

This change in the patterns of growth for the major syndicated programs is reflected also in the patterns for combined audience both for the top 10 programs and for all syndicated programs, as shown in Table 8.4. Again, the growth in the combined audience for syndicated religious programs appears to have reached a peak in 1977 and has been fluctuating

TABLE 8.4   Audience Sizes for Syndicated Programs

	1975	1976	1977	1978	1979	1980	1981
Number of Syndicated Programs	56	56	59	56	52	59	64
Combined viewers for Top Ten Programs (000s)*	11,594	14,107	15,700	14,751	13,519	13,226	13,997
Combined viewers for All Programs (000s)*	15,725	19,890	22,329	20,781	18,612	19,176	21,751
Average viewers per program (000s)	272	355	378	371	358	325	340

SOURCE: These author's computations are derived from Nielsen, "Report on Syndicated Program Audience."

NOTE: The figures for 1975 do not include Teens and Children viewers, which are included in the figures for 1976–1981.

*Combined audience figures are "gross" totals, i.e., may include duplications between program audiences.

since then. Though there was an upturn in combined audience in 1980 and 1981, the total still remains below the peak of 22.3 million for 1977. Recent Arbitron figures for February 1982 suggest that this swing may have returned the combined audience to the level of 1977, and that there has been a continued growth in the number of syndicated programs, placing a greater competitive pressure on the larger programs.

A longer historical period will determine whether these trends will continue. From the present perspective, however, the audience patterns for the past decade are indicative of growth to the point of market saturation (i.e., it appears that in 1977 the paid-time religious broadcasters reached the peak of their growth with the audience segment they can reach with their present program formats and contents). While there has been some restoration toward the peak of 1977 in recent years, and some movement of audience with the emergence of new programs, the overall picture indicates a marked levelling off of the rapid growth of the early 1970s.

One interesting observation to be gained from these figures is that the paid-time religious programs had reached the peak of their influence, numerically at least, almost three years before most public attention was given to them in the election year of 1980. In spite of the amount of public attention focused on them around the time of the election, the figures for November 1980 show no marked difference in the audience of their programs. It may have been this realization among the paid-time broadcasters which caused them to exaggerate the audience figures given to supporters and the news media.

TABLE 8.5   Average Stations, Ratings, and Audience Sizes for NBC One-Hour Religious Specials

Year	Average Number of Stations	Average Rating per Program	Average Audience per Program
1970	118	3.38	4,015,000
1971	136	2.9	3,445,000
1972	107	2.56	3,064,000
1973	144	3.06	3,690,000
1974	114	2.32	2,818,000
1975	134	2.3	2,836,000
1976	125	3.66	4,510,000
1977	88	3.0	3,927,000
1978	98	1.95	2,559,000
1979	91	.98	1,295,000
1980	73	1.43	1,902,000
1981	59	1.25	1,674,000

SOURCE: NCC Communication Commission Reports, based on Nielsen and NBC research.
NOTE: The drop in number of stations in 1977 is attributed primarily to substitution of these programs with paid-time religious programs by network affiliates.

This saturation characteristic is of considerable importance when we consider the future impact of such broadcasters. It removes much of the aura from the paid-time broadcasters as a universally accepted and influential social force and suggests instead that the phenonemon of paid-time religious broadcasting is demographically much more localized. This characteristic becomes clearer when one considers the demographic specifics of the audience of these programs.

The increases in the audience for the paid-time religious programs in the early 1970s initially affected locally produced religious programs. Their displacement of network programs on affiliate stations began to be felt around 1976–77 as can be seen in NBC religious specials (see Table 8.5). Before this decline, many of these network programs were regularly attracting a larger audience than most of the paid-time religious programs. The figures illustrate the drop in acceptance of network programs by affiliates beginning in 1976–77, and the effect which this has had on audience sizes for these programs.

How Large Is the Total Audience of Religious Television Programs?

It is difficult to calculate accurately the total number of people who regularly or occasionally watch religious programs on American television, because of the confusion in some of the available data. In clarifying these data, however, it is useful to distinguish between the audiences for syndicated religious programs and the audiences for the total slate of religious programming. Substantial information about the audiences of *syndicated programs* is provided by the Nielsen figures. These figures indicate that the combined audience for all syndicated religious programs in November 1981, for example, was 21,751,000. While this is a useful guide for calculation, there are some limitations in its accuracy as an absolute measure of the number of individual viewers of syndicated programs.

On the one hand, there are factors which suggest that this figure is too low as an estimate of the total audience for syndicated programs. The Nielsen figures represent the average quarter-hour audience for each program. It is possible that some viewers tune out in one quarter-hour, to be replaced by different viewers in the next quarter-hour. The average audience figures given by Nielsen therefore may be lower than the total number of people who see a particular syndicated religious program during the time of its broadcast. Some authorities suggest that there is about two-thirds more "total audience" for a given program than there is "average audience" at any given quarter hour. If this is accepted as a valid attribute, the total audience of syndicated programs increases to roughly 36 million people.

On the other hand, in the figure for the combined audience for all programs there is considerable duplication of viewers. Research by the

Christian Broadcasting Network indicates that most of their viewers regularly watch other religious programs as well. The extent of this "other viewing" is quite high. CBN found that, depending on the other program, from 44 per cent to 69 per cent of their "700 Club" members are in the audience of the other programs. In some cases they found that some of their members viewed other programs as much as 25 or more times per month.[6] Assuming that there is a similar viewing pattern among viewers of other programs, this duplication could drop the total number of individuals who watch syndicated programs by as much as 50 percent, or down to as low as 15 million. The number of *regular* viewers would most likely be even smaller.

The further inadequacy of the Nielsen figures lies in the fact that they do not measure the audience for cable programs. The audience of cable programs in the United States is still a relatively unknown factor, and with an increase in the number of religious syndicators moving into cable the claim is made that a large number of additional viewers are attracted by cable religious programs. However, while the cable audience may add some viewers to this total number, it is unlikely that it would increase the overall size of the syndicated program audience substantially. By 1981 fewer than 30 percent of the television households in the United States were cable-connected. Even if the addition of cable doubled a household's viewing of religious programming, cable would add only an additional million viewers to the total number. Given the increased diversity, selectivity, and competitiveness which cable brings in the choice of programs, it is unlikely that the movement of syndicated programming into cable will bring about a radical increase in the audience of religious programs. It is more likely to segment ever further the present specialized audience among a larger range of religious programs.

While the picture is far from precise, what is apparent is that the audience claimed by paid-time religious programs is far smaller than has generally been thought. It is unlikely that the regular weekly audience for paid-time religious programs exceeds 20 million people. A more realistic estimate is between 10 and 15 million individual viewers, many of whom watch several different programs each week to produce a higher combined audience figure. The figure of 15 million was the estimate given by Ben Armstrong in private correspondence with the author for the total audience of paid-time religious programs.

To attempt to estimate the total audience for all religious programs is even more difficult. In addition to the audiences for syndicated religious programs, the audience for all religious programs also includes the audiences for other programs such as local religious programs (which increasingly are turning to cable), network religious programs, religious specials, and those programs broadcast outside the regular sweeps period. Some network programs such as "Directions" have average audiences beyond the half-million mark, while some specials can attract an audience greater than one-and-a-half million viewers.

Some general community surveys have established approximate figures. A Gallup Poll in November 1978 found that 24 percent of a representative U.S. adult sample normally spent at least one hour each week watching religious shows on television, a number equal to approximately 36 million adults. An additional 5 percent or 7.5 million adults, indicated that they watched for less than one hour each week.[7] A similar poll conducted in 1980 for the American Research Corporation in Irvine, California, and published in a report titled "Profile of the Christian Marketplace," found that as many as 40 million adults watch some religious programs on a reasonably regular basis.[8]

It is apparent that much more research is needed before the size of the total audience of religious programs and its breakdown into categories of programs can be accurately evaluated. Certainly the picture is sufficiently clear to call into question the figures of over 100 million which have occasionally been quoted, and to assert that not all viewers of religious programs are viewers of the paid-time programs. The picture is also sufficiently ambiguous to question the certainty with which some broadcasters and commentators assert the extent of their outreach and influence.

In establishing the size of the audience for religious programs, one must always distinguish between occasional viewers and regular viewers. There may be a substantial number of viewers who watch religious programs on an occasional basis. This applies particularly to religious "specials," which are frequently seasonal in nature and have the added attraction of extravaganzas and of appearing in more favorable audience periods. The regular and supportive audience of religious programs is much smaller.

Notes

1. William Martin, "The Birth of a Media Myth," pp. 9–16.
2. Comstock et al., *Television and Human Behavior*, p. 172.
3. ABC audience research and Nielsen Research quoted in personal correspondence with W. Fore of the National Council of Churches Communication Commission.
4. Parker et al., *Television–Radio Audience*, p. 210.
5. Ellens, *Models of Religious Broadcasting*, p. 87.
6. Market Research Group, *National CBN Partner*.
7. Gallup, "Evangelical Christianity," p. 43.
8. Quoted in Martin, "Birth of a Media Myth," p. 10.

9

Characteristics of the Religious Television Audience

While the broadcast evangelists envisage television as a God-given tool by which to reach "the world" with their message, research on religious television programs indicates that the actual audience of most religious programs is highly segmented and that those who watch usually do so for very specific reasons. Far from being a broad medium of communication, religious programs on television appear to be a specialized programming service for a specialized audience.

The recent eruption of paid-time religious programs on the modern scene has raised many questions about the audience of these programs. In this chapter, emphasis will be placed on analyzing the available research in relation to three key questions: Who watches religious television programs? Are the programs viewed by people who are otherwise nonreligious or unchurched? Why do people watch these programs?

Who Watches Religious Television Programs?

Much of the information on the demographic characteristics of the regular audience of religious programs again comes from the surveys of the Nielsen Company. A sufficient number of other studies also exists to form a fairly comprehensive picture of the audience of religious programs. The characteristics that emerge from research follow.

1. Women watch religious programs more than men.

In the case of syndicated programs, the proportion of women to men viewers is approximately two to one. Nielsen audience data for November 1979 indicate that the average number of women viewers per household for all syndicated religious programs was .74 compared to .42 men viewers. It is sometimes suggested that the main reason for this disparity is most programs are broadcast at times when women are the major part of the audience. However, Comstock has noted that on Sunday mornings, when most religious programs are broadcast, composition of the national audience is equally male and female, compared to prime-time when the audience comprises 25% more females than males.[1]

The Nielsen figures for November 1979 indicate only three (out of 52) syndicated religious programs in which men equal or outnumber women as viewers. These three are comparatively small programs: "What Does the Bible say?" whose audience of 20,100 is 45 percent men and 45 percent women; "Treehouse Club," a children's program, whose audience of 20,100 is 19 percent men and 9 percent women; and "Missionaries in Action," whose audience of 16,060 is 44 percent men and 38 percent women. Comparative percentages for the major syndicated programs are as follows:

	% Women	% Men
Oral Roberts	59.8%	29.8%
Rex Humbard	55.3	30.3
Hour of Power	60.9	29.5
Jimmy Swaggart	54.6	31.6
Day of Discovery	59.2	30.3
Old Time Gospel Hour	55.3	32.0
Gospel Singing Jubilee	51.6	34.9
PTL Club	61.4	28.8
Insight	41.3	33.1
James Robison	52.5	30.8

Each program shows a significant difference between men and women as viewers, with some programs having as high as 61 percent of their audience composed of women viewers.

These trends have been found in other studies of religious programming also. Dennis, in a 1962 study of the radio and television audience in Detroit, and Robinson, in a 1964 study of the radio and television audience in seven cities, found that women were greater consumers of religious programs than men.[2] Buddenbaum, in 1979, found that regular viewers of religious television programs are twice as likely to be female as male.[3]

2. Viewing of religious programs generally increases with age.

Increasing age has consistently been found to be one of the strongest distinguishing variables between the audience and nonaudience of religious television programs. As age increases, so does viewing of religious television programs. Dramatic differences are noticeable in those who are aged 50 or over. Older women watch more than do older men. Younger men appear to watch less than any other adult group, watching only slightly more adult religious programs than do children.

This characteristic has been demonstrated also in studies as far back as 1962. Dennis found that while increasing age was not directly proportional to increased listening or viewing, significant differences occurred once the person reached the age of 60.[4] Robinson found in his study of the radio and television audience in seven cities that as age increased, the percentage of irregular listeners and viewers decreased and the percentage of regular listeners and viewers increased, to the point where half of all respondents over the age of 60 listened to or watched religious broadcasts regularly.[5] Solt, in a study of religious program audience in a New York county, found significant differences occurring at age 44,[6] while Buddenbaum found that frequent viewers of religious television were most likely to be over the age of 62, while those who never watch are more likely to be under age 34. Among adolescents and young adults, 67.2 percent and 70.3 percent, respectively, reported that they never watched religious programs compared to 25.7% of older adults who said they never watched.[7]

These trends are reflected also in the audience for current paid-time religious programs. The general trend is for women over 50 to be the largest viewing group in the audience of the syndicated programs. In 1979 they represented 45.8 percent of the audience for "Day of Discovery" and 44.2 percent of the audience for "Oral Roberts." Women 18–49 and men over 50 formed approximately equal proportions of the audience for most of the major paid-time religious programs. Men in the age group 18–49 were the smallest adult group of viewers, representing only 8.8 percent of the audience for "Oral Roberts." The pattern changed for only one major syndicated program, the sustaining-time program "Insight." This program is the only one among the top 10 syndicated programs which employs a dramatic format. "Insight" shows a more even distribution of age groups among its audience, with women 18–49 forming 26.3 percent of the audience, the largest age grouping.

This dominant age grouping reflected in most religious programs corresponds to general television viewing patterns. In 1976, for example, women over 50 watched an average of 35.0 hours of television a week, significantly more than men over 50 who watched 31.9 hours and women 18–49 who watched 31.5 hours a week. Men 18–49 watched almost seven hours less per week. In 1978 the figures increased to almost 33 hours a week for men over 50 and 37 hours a week for women over 50.[8]

3. People of lower income, lower education, and in blue-collar occupations watch significantly more religious programs than do those of higher income, higher education, and in white-collar occupations.

These variables are, of course, interrelated. Though not an absolute rule, people with higher education tend to be found in white-collar occupations which pay a larger salary or provide a higher income. The distinction between these two groups has been demonstrated in several studies of religious broadcasting. Dennis, in 1962, found no significant difference between the audience and nonaudience of religious programs up to the high-school level of education. For educational levels beyond high school, however, listening and viewing of religious programs decreased rapidly. He found that even significant differences between the listening and viewing behavior of Reformed compared to Pietistic Protestants levelled as the amount of education increased. He also found that as family income increased, men especially were less likely to view religious programs.[9]

Robinson, in his study of the audience of religious programs in seven cities in the United States in 1964, found that the lowest levels of formal education were much more likely to listen to or view religious programs regularly. He found that only 30 percent of those whose income was less than $13,000 were nonviewers of religious programs compared to 67 percent of those whose income was greater than $16,000.[10]

Solt in 1971 and Buddenbaum in 1979 had similar findings. Both found that increasing formal education correlated statistically with decreasing viewership of religious television programs. Buddenbaum found that the regular audience for religious television programs comprised mainly blue-collar workers and "others," which included housewives and nonclassifiable employed persons. Only 5.3 percent of the professionals identified by the study reported that they watched religious programs regularly compared to 30.4 percent of blue-collar workers and 25.3 percent of "others." Solt found particularly dramatic changes occurring with retirement, a factor that corresponds with the previously identified relevant variable of increasing age. Of those who were retired, Solt found that 40.4 percent were regular viewers, a significantly greater proportion than retired persons who never viewed or occasionally viewed.[11]

These findings relate to trends which have been noted in general television viewing also. If the head of the household has finished four or more years of college, the household in the fall of 1976 watched an average of seven hours of television less per week than households where the head had less than four years of college.[12] This trend has been found among the elderly as well;[13] persons in lower-income households also watch considerably more television—an additional half-hour a day in the fall of 1976—than the average for all individuals. Those in households with an income under $10,000 watched an average of 32.3 hours a week in the fall of 1976 compared with 25.2 hours a week for those with income over $15,000.[14]

Various research findings also suggest that there may be variations in this pattern of relationships in relation to religious television viewing. The nature of the program can effect the nature of the audience. Research on the "Frontiers of Faith" program series found that the better-educated made up the majority of the audience though the less-educated found the program more helpful.[15] Ringe found that those with a twelfth-grade education or less preferred traditional religious programs, while those with more than a twelfth-grade education preferred more novel programs.[16] Dennis found that the effect of education on viewing preferences was not as pronounced on women as on men,[17] while Parker et al. in 1955 found that occupation was not a significant variable in Catholic, Jewish, or mixed-religion households but was significant in distinguishing the audience from nonaudience in Protestant households.[18]

The research suggests, therefore, that while the overall trend is for the viewing of religious programs to decrease as educational and income level increases, changes in the composition of the audience can be effected through the particular format and content adopted.

4. There are geographical patterns identifiable in the audience and nonaudience of religious television programs.

The most detailed figures in support of this finding are those assembled by Arbitron and presented by Hadden and Swann in their book *Prime-Time Preachers*. Though all the major religious programs are broadcast in every major market in the country, the make-up of their audiences shows a distinct bias towards the southern and midwestern states, regions which are highest in church attendance in the country.

All of the major broadcasters except for Robert Schuller are underrepresented in proportion to audience in the eastern states. While the eastern states contain 22.5 percent of the total population of the country, the major broadcasters draw between 10.3 percent and 14.7 percent of their audiences from the area. Robert Schuller, the exception, draws 24 percent of his audience from the eastern states. Similarly, all major broadcasters are underrepresented in the western states, even Robert Schuller, whose home base is in California.

All broadcasters except Schuller are overrepresented in the percentage of their audiences drawn from the southern states. The area contains 32.4 percent of the population of the total country, and Oral Roberts draws 53.9

percent of his audience from the region. This bias is most outstanding with the program "Gospel Singing Jubilee," which draws 97 percent of its just-under-a-million audience from the southern states.[19] This tendency was identified in earlier studies also. Dennis in 1962 found that having one's birthplace in one of the southern states was a significant factor in distinguishing audience from nonaudience of religious programs.[20]

5. The strongest discriminating variables between the audience and nonaudience of religious television programs are religious interest and church affiliation.

As may be expected, religious affiliation and interest are consistently strong differentiating variables between the audience and nonaudience of religious television programs. The major proportion of the audience of religious programs is people who already indicate a high interest in religion. The research provides some elucidation of the various elements of these characteristics.

Protestants are significantly heavier viewers of religious programs in general than are either Catholics or Jews. Robinson found that 90 percent of the regular listeners and viewers of religious programs were Protestants, while greater than 50 percent of Roman Catholics and Jews were non-listeners or nonviewers.[21] It should be noted, however, that the greatest number of religious programs have been Protestant programs. This denominational factor changes when there is a program distinctly aimed at a particular tradition. Bishop Sheen's program "Life Is Worth Living" in 1952 drew 75.5 percent of its New Haven audience from the Roman Catholic community, even though it represented only 52.8 percent of the total population.[22] Similarly, the emphases of the different Protestant programs largely determine the nature of their audiences. Dennis found that General Protestants and Reformed Protestants as groups viewed religious programs significantly less than did Pietistic Protestants, though this may reflect the influence of other common variables such as occupation, education, and income.[23] Solt found that Baptists, Pentecostals, and Independent Protestant groups in 1964 were twice as strong in the regular category of viewing as were Episcopalians and Lutherans. The reverse held for the "never" category.[24] The CBN organization in 1978 was drawing more than 55 percent of its partners from the conservative and evangelical denominations, even though as a group they formed a much smaller percentage of the general population.[25]

While intense religiosity has always been a factor in religious television viewing,[26] this characteristic has come to reflect more of the evangelical ethos as evangelical programs have replaced other types of religious programming on television. The characteristic has most recently been demonstrated by the 1978 Gallup Poll on Evangelical Christianity. From a national population sample, the poll found that those who watch religious television programs compared to those who don't watch religious television programs are more likely to have had a conversion experience, to believe that the bible is free of mistakes, to believe in a personal devil, to read the bible more often, to talk to others about their faith more often, to attend church services more frequently, and to hold to or engage in beliefs and practices characteristic of evangelicals as a whole. The poll also identified characteristics among evangelicals which correspond to other characteristics already noted as significant in distinguishing the religious television audience from the nonaudience: the typical U.S. evangelical was characterized as a white female Southerner, aged 50 or over, with a high-school education and a modest income.[27]

This Gallup poll calls into question the claims made, particularly by some news weeklies prior to the 1980 election, that the evangelical broadcasters had the capacity to sway the opinion of all evangelicals. The poll makes it clear that not all evangelicals watch religious television, not even a majority of evangelicals do. This finding is supported by the actual sizes of the audiences drawn by these programs. The poll indicates that for the three evangelical subgroups identified by the survey, 47 percent, 46 percent, and 45 percent, respectively, indicated that they either didn't watch or didn't know how much time they spent watching religious programs on television each week, and another 9 percent, 6 percent, and 5 percent indicated they watched for less than one hour each week.

In the light of these findings and the statistics on audience sizes for these programs, the paid-time religious programs appear not as a major thrust fully supported and influential on the evangelical movement as a whole, but as a rather small subculture within evangelicalism. Had these factors been recognized previously, their impact on American politics may have been viewed in a more realistic light.

Are Religious Programs Watched by Nonchurched or Nonreligious People?

While the characteristics mentioned in the previous section dominate in the audience of religious television programs, evidence suggests that these programs are watched on occasion and in some cases regularly by non-Protestants, nonevangelicals, those of higher income and education, those in white-collar occupations, and those who claim no religious interest or church affiliation.

In Onondaga County in 1971 Solt found that 18 percent of all regular listeners or viewers of religious radio and television programs were people who claimed they rarely or never went to church.[28] In the Gallup poll of the unchurched in 1978, 28 percent of those considered by the poll to be unchurched people said they had heard or watched a religious program on radio or television in the past 30 days.[29] The Gallup Poll of Evangelical Christianity in 1978 found that 27 percent of those who watched religious programs claimed not to be a member of a church or synagogue, 18 percent claimed not to attend church, and another 18 percent claimed they attended less than once a month.[30] Frank and Greenberg in their study *The Public's Use of Television* found that several of their specified interest groups in the community had a higher-than-average use of religious television programs even though their interest in religion was below average.[31]

While in most audiences of religious programs there is a percentage of people who are unchurched or who indicate little interest in religion in general, it needs to be noted that this percentage is consistently small. It is useful, however, to ask why people who otherwise express little interest in religion spend time watching religious television programs.

Why Do People Watch Particular Religious Television Programs?

The research on the audience of religious broadcasting indicates that there is a correspondence between the nature and content of a program and the dominant characteristics of the audience it attracts. Changes in the nature of one's audience can be brought about, therefore, by appropriate changes in program content and broadcast time.

One of the most valuable theoretical approaches for understanding the connection between the content of a specific program and the nature of the audience it attracts is that of the uses-and-gratifications approach to mass-communication effect. The appropriateness of this approach to religious television was intimated by Parker et al. in their research project in 1955. Arising out of their research into the audience of religious television they noted,

There are logical reasons for listening or non-listening that go deep into the personal and personal–social situation of audience members, far deeper than their simple identification as Catholics or Presbyterians, or non-participants in any church.[32]

In recent years this perception has been given fuller theoretical and research development in relation to general mass communication. The uses-and-gratifications approach has served to emphasize two research perspectives: (1) that the audience has prior social and psychological needs which are brought to the communication experience, and (2) that these prior needs force the individual actively to seek communications which will gratify these needs. The approach stresses that in understanding communication effect one must consider not only the influence of the message being communicated but also the use being made of the message by members of the audience as they actively seek, select, and interpret communications necessary for the satisfactory management of their lives.

In spite of the fact that this approach was reported several decades ago and lies at the base of earlier communication research, little serious theoretical or empirical development of it was made until recently. Central to the recent formulation of the theory have been two books, both published in 1974: *The Uses of Mass Communication* and *Mass Communication Research*.[33] In the former book Katz, Blumler, and Gurevitch outline the uses-and-gratifications approach as being "concerned with (1) the social and psychological origins of (2) needs, which generate (3) expectations of (4) the mass media and other sources, which lead to (5) differential patterns of media exposure (or engagement in other activities) resulting in (6) need gratification and (7) other consequences, perhaps mostly unintended ones."[34]

Several of the findings from this uses-and-gratifications approach are of direct importance for understanding the nature of the audience of religious television programs and the reasons for viewing. One is that because of the active part played by people in the audience in seeking out gratifying communications to meet their personal and social needs, the dominant uses being made of a religious program may be quite different from the stated aims of the program itself.

The major reasons given by the paid-time religious broadcasters for their programs is that of evangelism: that is, of reaching outsiders with the message of the Christian faith with a view to converting them. It is apparent, however, from the dominant characteristics of the audience that, for the most part, the broadcasters are not reaching outsiders, but insiders. Such a correspondence is not inevitable, however. Research has demonstrated that the characteristics of one's audience are shaped by the nature of the program. The differences have been noted, for example, between the audience of the dramatic series "Insight" and the audiences of the commercial religious programs that employ a preaching format. "Insight" was the only top syndicated program to attract a representative audience in relation to age and sex variables. While it may be more effective in reaching a more representative audience, a dramatic format is not suitable for the purpose of building a personal relationship between broadcaster and audience, which for the paid-time broadcasters is essential for maintaining fund raising.

Research suggests other aspects of preferences among different audience groups. Dennis in 1962 found that blacks and blue-collar workers watch all religious programs but prefer evangelistic ones; older persons prefer worship programs, discussion programs, and evangelistic programs; and persons with higher education prefer discussion and dramatic formats.[35] Ringe found that those with a twelfth-grade education or less preferred traditional religious programs, while those with greater than a twelfth-grade education preferred more novel programs. He found also that closed-mindedness and doctrinal orthodoxy were significant variables in determining a preference for traditional religious programs.[36]

The research shows that to a large extent religious broadcasters choose their audience by the content, format, and marketing of their programs. The pressure on the paid-time religious broadcasters to maintain the specific structure of their audience because it is the most financially supportive for them has had the effect of shaping the character of their programs away from their original intention of evangelism, even though they keep the intent of evangelism as a masthead. The dominant needs being met by their programs are now quite different from those that would be consistent with genuine evangelism. The research indicates that the dominant functions now being served by Christian programs for the major segments of its audience appear to be personal inspiration, companionship, and support. When Engel surveyed those who had called Channel 38 in Chicago he found that for the majority of the respondents the most helpful role of the station and its programs had been to help them grow spiritually as Christians.[37] When Hilton surveyed the use of television worship services by members of the Irvington Presbyterian Church, he found also that the major uses made of the programs were for personal inspiration and uplift. The most helpful aspect of the programs mentioned in this regard were the music and singing, mentioned in 55 percent of the responses. Only 4 percent of the members indicated that the television programs had influenced their understanding of what the most important things are about being a Christian, an important part of evangelism.[38]

It appears, therefore, that the paid-time broadcasters have adapted their programs to this dominant use made of the programs by those members of their audiences who are supportive. This adaptation is seen in the development of facilities for personal counseling. Research shows that the dominant use made of these facilities is also for personal support and inspiration, expressed mainly through prayer requests for oneself or another. The CBN Counselling Center in Boston, for example, in its first two years of operation (1977–79) received 36,225 telephone calls. These included only 2,724 calls for salvation but 36,497 requests for prayer. (One call could include more than one prayer request.)[39]

In spite of this dominant use now being made of religious programs by church people, the paid-time broadcasters still maintain that the dominant intention of their programs is evangelism (i.e., reaching outsiders). This is also the basis on which they solicit money from their audience and the basic reason why viewers support the program. In one CBN survey, the single most important reason given by those surveyed for supporting the work of CBN was to "to get the Gospel out."[40] This illusion of evangelism in many ways reflects the central ethos of the evangelical tradition. Because of the importance placed on evangelism, appeals are most effective if they are couched in terms of their evangelical effectiveness, even though that may not be their primary or dominant function. The realization of this contradiction led one evangelical broadcaster to question what was being done: "Does this mean we are talking to ourselves. . . . And if so, can we justify the money spent and the strategies employed?"[41]

A second implication of the uses-and-gratifications research for understanding why people watch religious programs on television is the insight that uses made of the media and gratifications derived from these uses change over an individual's life span.[42] This insight suggests that television communication should not be considered universally attention-gaining, but is effective only with certain population groups. This characteristic may explain the majority of older persons in the religious television audience. Television fulfills a more important role in the lives of older people than it does in the lives of younger people. It is the predominant leisure-time activity of older adults and older adults may watch more religious programs simply by reason of the greater frequency of their viewing. Studies have also found that as viewer age increases there is a corresponding increase in the serious content of programs watched. Religious programs in this context appear to fill some of the needs demonstrated by older viewers: the programs act as a source of information, as a substitute for lost social activity, and as a source of companionship and support. This research insight may imply that religious programs on television will be limited in their effectiveness with those age groups which do not use television as a source of gratification for serious content, and therefore that television should exist as only one element in a much broader strategy for ministry and evangelism.

A third implication for religious television arising out of the uses-and-gratifications research is that the gratifications found from particular programs and the uses made of them differ with different population groups. It is wrong to assume that because a person is watching a particular religious program he or she is doing so for the reasons for which the program was devised. There are a number of studies which indicate that there are other gratifications being sought and gained from religious programs than specifically "religious" ones. In 1962 Dennis found that people viewed religious programs for other than religious reasons. He identified moral, information, entertainment, and substitution motives for viewing also, and though they were clearly subservient to religious motives, they were present in the audiences' motivation to some degree.[43]

Buddenbaum in 1979 correlated frequency of religious television viewing with nine personal needs. She found only two of the needs to be positively correlated with frequency of religious viewing: the need to know onself better and the need to avoid feelings of loneliness. She found a weak correlation between the frequency of viewing and the need to be entertained. The other needs studied—the need to have influence, to plan one's day, to kill time, to relax and release tension, to hear what others say, and to keep tabs on what is going on—were negatively related to frequency of religious television viewing but not at the level of significance.[44] In commenting on these correlations, Buddenbaum noted that the religious television audience reports quite different needs from those of the general television audience. Television viewing as a whole has been found to be most useful in satisfying the needs to be entertained, to kill time, to relax and release tension, and to avoid feelings of loneliness. While religious television viewing correlates positively with the need to know oneself better and also correlates positively with the need to avoid feelings of loneliness, it corresponds negatively with the need to be entertained. It has been noted already that religious television viewing increases significantly with age and that older viewers demonstrate an increased interest in serious content on television, especially news and public-affairs programming, as compensation for losses of more social sources of information and engagement.

One of the most in-depth studies of the reasons why people may view religious programs on television is that of Frank and Greenberg, published under the title *The Public's Use of Television: Who Watches and Why*. As part of the larger study, Frank and Greenberg also studied the viewing of religious programs on television. Their suggestion is that different population groups watch religious programs for very different reasons.

Frank and Greenberg divided the U.S. population in 1978 into 14 groups or interest segments according to clustered interest factors. Of these 14 interest segments they found six to be above the average for the entire population in the viewing of religious programs. Frank and Greenberg's descriptions of these interest segments and the functions they suggest religious television plays for the groups are as follows.[45]

1. Male: Money and Nature's Product. This group is made up of older males with a high proportion rural and retired. They are interested primarily in passive activities that obtain some form of tangible return on their product. Their rate of religious program viewing is 136 percent (based on 100 percent as average for the entire population). Frank and Greenberg suggest that their heavy viewing of religious programs probably helps to satisfy their needs for support and contact and reinforcement of the more traditional values associated with American life.

2. Male: Family and Community-Centered. This group is employed, blue-collar/white-collar adult males. They are married, living in non-metropolitan areas. They have a broad range of interests, including home and community-centered activities and religion. They are usually light television viewers. Their above-average religious viewing rate of 133 percent is probably reflective of their religious, community, and family interests.

3. Female: Elderly Concerns. This is the older segment, with a high percentage of retirees, widows, and with few children. Their few interests include religion and news and information. Their focus is on maintaining a sense of social integration and belonging in the absence of direct inter-personal contact. Their rate of religious program viewing is high, 191 percent. This high rate of religious program viewing matches their expressed interests and their needs to overcome loneliness and to lift their spirits. It corresponds also to the low need within this group for intellectual stimulation.[46]

4. Female: Home and Community-Centered.   This group is made up of adult females with a relatively high percentage of homemakers. Their highest needs are for family ties and understanding others. Their lowest needs are for intellectual stimulation and unique/creative accomplishment. Frank and Greenberg suggest that their high rate of religious program viewing of 164 percent satisfies their need for social integration because of separation from other adult companionship.

5. Mixed: News and Information.   The interests of this group are related to keeping informed on a broad range of subjects and activities. Their needs are focused on being socially stimulating and maintaining family ties. Their rate of religious program viewing is 154 percent, although they are heavy users of television in general both for entertainment and as a means of keeping informed about the world in which they live.

6. Mixed: Highly Diversified.   This group is comprised of southern black adults with children. They have a broad range of interests, especially those permitting personal participation with family and/or other informal small group settings. They have a high need for intellectual stimulation. This segment is the highest segment for amount of in-home time used watching television. Television viewing appears to be a family affair, with a diversity of programs being watched. Their rate of religious program viewing is 164 percent.

The lightest viewing of religious programs takes place by the following interest segments: Males: Mechanics and Outdoor Life, 13 percent; Youth: Competitive Sports and Science/Engineering, 39 percent; Mixed: Cosmo-politan Self-Enrichment, 31 percent; and Female: Family-Integrated Activi-ties, 48 percent.

Not all the groups that indicated high viewing of religious programs correlated with having religion as a general interest factor. Males: Money and Nature's Product, which had a religious program viewing rate of 136 percent had an average interest factor for religion of −.26. The group Mixed: News and Information, which had a religious program viewing rate of 154 percent had an average interest factor for religion of −.29. Similarly, Mixed: Highly Diversified, which had a religious program viewing rate of 164 percent, had an average interest factor for religion of −.07. Conversely, not every nonviewing segment correlated negatively with religion as a general interest factor. The group Female: Arts and Cultural Activities was 6 percent below average for religious television viewing but had an average interest factor score for religion of .21. Youth: Indoor Games and Social Activities had an average interest factor score for religion of .46 but was 36 percent below average for religious television viewing.

This segmentation into group characteristics and situational needs provides an alternative approach to understanding the reasons why some groups are heavy viewers of religious programs while others are not. It also provides an alternative method apart from the heavy-handed shotgun approach of the present paid-time religious broadcasters by which religious communicators may plan a more comprehensive and effective television programming approach. It suggests that religious broadcasters in general would gain by identifying the specific characteristics of their audiences and the uses made of their programs, and working to develop their effectiveness in that area. Their adherence to a universal impact and outreach model can only distract from a more comprehensive and realistic strategy of ministry by the whole church in which television may play its appropriate part.

Notes

1. Comstock, "The Impact of Television," p. 17.
2. Dennis, "Analysis of the Audience," p. 56; Robinson, "Study of the Audience," p. 127.
3. Buddenbaum, "Audience for Religious Television," p. 55.
4. Dennis, "Analysis of the Audience," p. 56.
5. Robinson, "Study of the Audience," p. 127.
6. Solt, "Study of the Audience," pp. 57–59.
7. Buddenbaum, "Audience for Religious Programs," p. 54.
8. Comstock, *Television and Human Behavior*, pp. 91–93; *Nielsen Television 78*, Northbrook: A. C. Nielsen Co, 1978.
9. Dennis, "Analysis of the Audience," pp. 61–67.
10. Robinson, "Study of the Audience," p. 127.
11. Solt, "Study of the Audience," pp. 56–61; Buddenbaum, "Audience for Religious Programs," pp. 56–67.
12. Comstock, *Television and Human Behavior*, pp. 61–62.
13. Elliott S. Schreiber and Douglas A. Boyd, "How the Elderly Perceive TV Commercials," *Journal of Communication*, Winter 1980, pp. 62–70.
14. Comstock, *Television and Human Behavior*, p. 94.
15. Broadcast and Film Commission, "Frontiers of Faith," p. 8.
16. Ringe, "Analysis of Selected Personality," p. 125.
17. Dennis, "Analysis of the Audience," pp. 61–62.
18. Parker et al., *Television–Radio Audience*, p. 202.
19. Hadden and Swann, *Prime-Time Preachers*, pp. 60–61.
20. Dennis, "Analysis of the Audience," pp. 68–70.
21. Robinson, "Study of the Audience," p. 128.

22. Parker et al., *Television-Radio Audience*, Chapter 11.
23. Dennis, "Analysis of the Audience," pp. 71–72.
24. Solt, "Study of the Audience," p. 69.
25. Market Research Group, "National CBN Partner," Table 182.
26. See Dennis, Robinson, and Solt.
27. Gallup, "Evangelical Christianity in the U.S."
28. Solt, "Study of the Audience," pp. 70–76.
29. Gallup, "Unchurched Americans," p. 57.
30. Gallup, "Evangelical Christianity," pp. 109, 125.
31. Frank and Greenberg, *Public's Use of Television*, pp. 55–127.
32. Parker et al., *Television–Radio Audience*, p. 408.
33. Jay G. Blumler and Elihu Katz, eds, *The Uses of Mass Communication: Current Perspectives on Gratification Research*, Beverly Hills: Sage Publications, 1974; W. Phillips Davison and F.T.C. Yu, eds., *Mass Communication Research: Major Issues and Future Directions*, New York: Praeger, 1974.
34. E. Katz; J. G. Blumler and M. Gurevitch, "Utilization of Mass Communication by the Individual," in Blumler and Katz, *Uses of Mass Communication*, p. 20.
35. Dennis, "Analysis of the Audience," p. 180.
36. Ringe, "Analysis of Selected Personality," pp. 106–114, 125.
37. Engel, "Pilot Research Study," pp. 38–39.
38. Hilton, "Influence of Television," pp. 55–56.
39. CBN Boston, "Monthly Statistical Reports."
40. Market Research Group, "Report on 700 Club Finances," p. S-1.
41. Bisset, "Religious Broadcasting," p. 28.
42. See Andrew Morrison, "Mass Media Use by Adults," *American Behavioral Scientist*, September/October 1979, pp. 71–93; Frederick Williams, Herbert Dordick, and Frederick Horstmann, "Where Citizens Go for Information," *Journal of Communication*, Winter 1977, pp. 95–99.
43. Dennis, "Analysis of the Audience," p. 175.
44. Buddenbaum, "Audience for Religious Programs," pp. 60–85.
45. Frank and Greenberg, *Public's Use of Television*, pp. 55–127.
46. The high rate of viewing in this group is reflected in their dominance in the overall religious program audience. This group has also been found to be one of the major users of the paid-time broadcasters' telephone counseling services, expressing their need for companionship and inspiration.

10
Religious Television and Attitude Change

The main reason why most religious broadcasters begin broadcasting is they see it as an effective means to influence people toward their particular religious stance and outlook. Though criticisms occasionally have been made suggesting that the paid-time religious broadcasters are concerned primarily with raising money, there can, perhaps, be little doubt that the essential reason why religious broadcasters are in the business is for the purpose of changing people's attitudes toward religious faith.

The question which has been asked from the beginning of television, however, is how effective are the religious broadcasters and television itself in achieving this purpose? It is apparent from the increase in the number of religious programs and the growth of the paid-time religious organizations that television is able to achieve some effects. Such effects, however, could result mostly from people whose attitude toward religion is already favorable. What is not as clear is the extent to which religious programs on television are able to change people's attitudes toward religious faith. This chapter will examine the empirical evidence available in relation to this question.

Because there have been only limited studies specifically related to the effects of religious television, in order to answer the question thoroughly the researcher in religious television is forced to extrapolate from empirical studies in related mass-communication areas. The problem with this, however, is that the study of mass communication has passed through several stages and allows for several very different approaches. Initial approaches to the study of mass communication effect, for example, attributed strong powers to the mass media to bring about change in viewers' attitudes and behavior. Referred to as the "hypodermic" approach, it suggested that broadcasters were able to inject their messages unhindered into the minds of the listeners, achieving whatever effect they desired. The social psychologist Dorwin Cartwright in 1949 expressed this attitude in his comment: "It is conceivable that one persuasive person could, through the use of mass media bend the world's population to his will."[1] We have noted also that some religious broadcasters still reflect this understanding, thinking that once they are able to attract an audience to their program changing that audience to their point of view is simply a matter of technique.

In the 1940s and 1950s, however, several studies began to demonstrate a more complex picture of the flow and effect of mass communication. From this matrix, subsequent research slowly began to identify a range of different variables that intervened between the message communicated and the effect produced on the person receiving the message.

The situation today is a complex one. Several major research directions have emerged involving not only personal but also social and cultural dimensions in the mass-media process, so that it is difficult to integrate these into a single theory of mass-media effect which has not only explanatory but also predictive ability. In order to cope with this diversity in the evaluation of religious television, it is necessary to break down the subject into several specific issues (covered in this chapter and the following two chapters). In this chapter, the major focus will be personal effects of religious television, understood primarily in terms of change in personal attitudes and behavior. Subsequent chapters will focus on two other major areas of religious television effect: the effects of religious television in relation to the local church and in relation to the broader cultural environment.

One of the most useful models for evaluating the personal effects of religious television programs is found in *Television and Human Behavior* by George Comstock and his associates. The authors looked at more than 2,500 books, articles, reports, and other documents in an attempt to derive an empirically based and comprehensive statement of the effects of television on human behavior. Included in this broad analysis is a psychological model for understanding the effects which television may have on individual attitudes and behavior. It is the opinion of this author that this model is of significant value for the religious communicator because of its empirical basis, its comprehensiveness, its clarity, and its applicability in understanding the religious television situation.

The authors of *Television and Human Behavior* recognize that such a model must be seen as a hypothetical postulation of the actual process of television effect. Nevertheless, it has the value of providing a sound structure by which present research may be integratively understood and future research stimulated and organized. With the advantage of this overarching theoretical framework, otherwise insignificant pieces of research on aspects of religious television may be of great value in illuminating aspects of the model as it applies to religious television. It is intended in this chapter to examine relevant aspects of the model, and how research in the area of religious television relates to it.

A Psychological Model of Television Effect

The central thesis of the model is described by the authors in the following way:

The likelihood of a given person's behaving in conformance with a given "act" is a function of three factors: "salience," the degree to which the particular behavior exists psychologically for the person; "repertoire," the summed salience of all possible acts for the person in his present situation (any single act is a fraction of repertoire); "arousal," which is the extent to which the person is activated to perform *any* act in his present situation.[2]

The authors present this thesis as a mathematical equation in the following form:

$$act = \frac{salience}{repertoire} \cdot arousal$$

The implications of expressing the thesis as such an equation are (1) if the viewed action is not at all salient for the person (i.e., = 0) the action will not affect the viewer's behavior ("act"); (2) the chance that a particular viewed action will affect a person's behavior will decrease to the extent that they have other alternatives in their "repertoire"; and (3) if the individual is not aroused to act he will not exhibit the viewed behavior, no matter how salient it is. If it is the only act in the person's repertoire then it is maximally likely to be exhibited, limited only by the degree of arousal. Television is able to affect an individual's behavior by effecting change in each of these three factors.

1. Changes in Salience of an Act

Television is able to affect the salience of an act by: (1) demonstrating the act to be performed and (2) attaching negative or positive values to the act through perceived consequences and perceived reality of the act. The salience of a particular viewed action is also postulated as an equation:

salience = past consequences + (perceived consequences × perceived reality)

The implications of this equation are (1) if the degree of perceived reality is zero, the increment in salience of a viewed action will also be zero; (2) if no evaluative consequences are associated with the viewed action, salience will not result regardless of the extent to which the portrayal is seen as realistic.

The salience of a particular viewed action for the viewer is dependent to a large extent on the perceived consequences of performing the act. These consequences are seen as a function of several factors.

(1) *Anticipated reward and punishment.*   A viewed behavior will be encouraged to the extent that a reward is attached to it, and disinhibited to the extent that punishment is attached to it. The research suggests that reinforcement factors are applicable to a wide range of behaviors, though reinforcement appears to apply specifically to the performance of a behavior and not to its cognitive acquisition.

(2) *Justification.*   Justification appears to operate primarily as a disinhibiting factor, countervailing against negative perceived consequences more than providing a positive stimulus. The research indicates that justification interacts with the motive state of the individual viewer. The more closely the rationale for justifying the model's otherwise negative behavior coincides with the immediate arousal of the viewer, the stronger is the disinhibiting effect.

The salience of viewed behaviors for the viewer is dependent also on the perceived reality of the behaviors. The reality of a perceived act on television derives mainly from the viewer's perspective, with a good deal of variation in the degree to which different viewers perceive a portrayal as realistic. To a large extent, the cue properties of a situation within which the viewer finds himself or herself after observing a television portrayal govern the influence of that portrayal. The salience of a particular perceived behavior for a viewer is also dependent on the patterns of reinforcement that the viewer has experienced for similar behaviors in the past.

2. Changes in the Viewer's Repertoire

Television portrayals are able to affect a person's repertoire of available appropriate behaviors in two basic ways: (1) by changing the salience of particular acts within the repertoire, and (2) by the addition of new, salient alternatives.

The probability of a person's performing a viewed action is decreased to the extent that he or she has other possible acts in his or her repertoire. A television portrayal, however, may change the salience of a particular action by demonstrating its effectiveness or ineffectiveness in a specific situation.

The extent to which television is able to add new, salient alternatives to the person's repertoire is dependent on gaining the person's attention, achieving retention of the behavior, and the person's ability and motivation to perform the act. When a behavior that has been observed fails to be imitated immediately, however, it cannot be necessarily inferred that it was not learned in the limited sense represented by the observed behavior. If incentives and opportunity later occur, the behavior may be displayed.

3. Changes in the Arousal Level of the Viewer

Arousal is proposed as a necessary condition for the expression of overt behavior. If a viewer is not at all aroused to act, that viewer will not exhibit the viewed behavior, no matter how salient it may be. Arousal is highly situational, with the level fluctuating markedly. It is intuitively obvious that a person can be aroused by many situational factors in daily life, and there is evidence to suggest that both the content and form of televised portrayals can be arousing.

Arousal by television itself is not necessary for television to have an influence on behavior. When arousal is sufficiently heightened by sources other than television to activate the factors encompassed by the proposed model, the television-related influences can play an important role.

A further significant element within the model is that of opportunity. Social learning will be most likely when television portrays acts which the person has many opportunities to perform. But opportunity is not just a situational contingency pertinent to only one act. Rather, behaviors for which there is more frequent opportunity will be displayed more often and this will in turn reinforce these acts at the expense of others. Some increase in salience is added each time a behavior is displayed; therefore, television and environmental events tend to be mutually reinforcing. One should not expect mass-media portrayals to stimulate or disinhibit behaviors for which opportunity is rare and not contiguous to the viewing situation.

Therefore, if the value of "act" is greater than zero as a consequence of the equation,

$$\frac{\text{salience}}{\text{repertoire}} \times \text{arousal}$$

we could expect the viewed behavior to occur if "opportunity" is present. If not, we could expect the person to seek "alternatives" to the extent that he or she remains aroused. If such behavior is exhibited it may be reinforced depending on the real consequences, thus increasing the salience of that behavior. Such behavior also reduces arousal, bringing the person back to the starting point of the model.

When applied to religious television, we might predict that religious television programs will have their greatest effect on a viewer when the viewer is aroused because of a particular need; when the recommended action on the religious program becomes salient to the person because of a lack of other options within their repertoire; when the action is perceived as being a realistic and rewarding solution to the need; when the viewer has experienced favorable consequences as a result of the action in the past; and when the program presents options for action that the viewer has opportunity to perform.

These optimal conditions for effect are not always present, of course. The research suggests in fact that they are rarely present. Most effects of religious television programs are strongly modified by variations in most elements of the model, making it extremely difficult to predict with any certainty what the particular effect of any program will be. There are, however, several studies which illuminate aspects of the model as it applies to religious television programs.

Several studies indicate that religious television programs can be effective in stimulating people to consider religion as a subject and to modify their attitude toward it. The Mennonite Church in 1970 produced and aired nationally a series of television spots oriented toward the family. A subsequent national survey indicated that 4 percent of the people who recalled having seen the spots said they had been stimulated to talk with someone else about the subject.[3] Donigan, in a study of broadcasting by the Mormon Church, found that the broadcast programs were effective in creating favorable impressions of the church among nonmembers and the broadcasts were one of the factors influential in the respondents' desire to know more about the Mormon Church.[4] The Gallup Poll in the "Unchurched American" found that religious programs may also be effective in stimulating thought among viewers who do not have an active connection with a church. The poll found that 14 percent of those unchurched who had listened to or watched a religious radio or television program in the past 30 days had considered becoming active in a church again as a result of it. Of itself, of course, this finding says little: it gives no indication of the extent to which these people were actually aroused to this course of action. On the other hand, it ties in with another finding of the same study: that 52 percent of the unchurched could see a situation where they could become a fairly active member of a church and would be open to an invitation from a church community.[5]

Two experimental studies conducted on religious television programs support the thesis that viewing these programs can change attitudes toward religion. Rockenstein in 1966 and Klos in 1978 studied the effects of selected Christian children's programs on informational and attitudinal tests administered to selected groups of children in controlled laboratory situations before and after viewing. They found that the religious programs were effective in teaching the children facts and attitudes about the subject matter of the programs.[6]

The general body of research indicates, therefore, that religious television programs do have the potential to change people's attitudes toward religious faith in general and toward specific aspects of religious faith and practice in particular. To the extent that religious television programs are able to do this, religious television could play a valuable complementary role to the functioning of the local church by laying a groundwork in the cultivating of favorable attitudes toward religious faith. This function is frequently described as a "preevangelistic" function.

The model presented by Comstock and his associates highlights the multitude of variables that tend to qualify this effectiveness: salience of the acts presented, the viewer's repertoire, the viewer's state of arousal at the time, the past and perceived future consequences of the behavior, the perceived reality of the behavior, and the opportunities present for its performance. It is obvious that more extensive research is needed to clarify the nature and conditions necessary for such effectiveness to take place.

Other research directions illuminate further characteristics in the understanding of religious television effect. The nature of the effect gained will vary according to the centrality and function of the attitude within the human psyche. Katz has identified four major functions served by attitudes within the human personality: (1) the utilitarian function, by which certain attitudes enable maximization of rewards and avoidance of pain in adjusting to one's environment; (2) the ego-defensive function, by which specific attitudes protect the ego; (3) the value-expressive function, by which particular attitudes provide satisfaction from personal values and self-concept; and (4) the knowledge function, by which certain attitudes satisfy the need to structure and understand one's universe. Attitudes that exist on the periphery of one's psyche, such as those related to the knowledge or utilitarian functions will be more susceptible to modification than will those that are central to identity formation and continuity.[7]

Mechanisms of defense, such as selectivity of exposure, distortion of perception, and group pressure act continually, and frequently subconsciously, to protect the individual against messages that challenge fixed and functional ideas, attitudes, and behaviors. These mechanisms tend to direct people not only to seek and choose communications that are favorable to their own predispositions, but also to misperceive and misinterpret other persuasive communications in accordance with those established predispositions.[8]

These mechanisms are especially pertinent to religious broadcasting, which is concerned not only with adjustments in people's knowledge and operation of life situations, but also in change within central life commitments and values. The operation of these defense mechanisms is seen in the structure of the religious television audience: most viewers of religious programs on television are those who are already in strong agreement with message of the program. The more specified the message, the more specified also becomes the audience for that program.

The effect of these mechanisms was also apparent in the laboratory studies of Rockenstein and Klos. Rockenstein found that there were significant differences in information acquisition and attitude change between churched children and nonchurched children: churched children gained more of the information and accepted more of the attitudes communicated by the televised programs than did the nonchurched children. Similarly, he found that Protestant Ecumenical children—those whose religious tradition was similar to that of the program—gained more information and accepted more of the attitudes communicated by the program than did Catholic children and Protestant Evangelical children.

Though the preevangelistic opportunities offered by television may be a valid justification for the religious use of television, the qualifications on the effectiveness of this use should be noted: religious television programs will be most effective in those situations where no strong attitudes or behavior patterns exist on the point in question, where the change is an extension or redirection of an old strong attitude, or if the attitude being proposed is perceived by the receiver as being salient to a specific unsatisfied need-state existing at the time.

However, even where genuine attitude change or behavior change may take place under the impact of a televised religious message, the longitudinal durability of such changes are uncertain. Research indicates that when opinions, attitudes, or behavior do shift under the impact of communications, they tend to regress to the preexisting position unless they are reinforced by events, other communications, or group pressures. Hence Comstock et al. suggest that those attitudes and behaviors for which there is more frequent opportunity for expression within the immediate environment will tend to be displayed more often and in turn reinforced at the expense of others. Mass media, therefore, should not be expected to stimulate or disinhibit attitudes or behaviors for which opportunity is rare.[9]

For these reasons, as Schramm notes, in major decisions which involve significant and central attitude change, the channels of interpersonal communication and influence are far more effective than mass media because of the opportunities they present for reinforcement of response and ongoing group support. However, failure to reinforce an acquired attitude may give it an unfavorable reinforcement record and result in its being rejected on future occasions as a viable response alternative.[10]

The necessity of proximate opportunity for behavior expression will be seen to be a major issue in considering the contribution religious television programs are able to make to the growth of the membership of local churches. Viewers are more likely to express influences of religious programs in actions which are proximate to the television screen, such as contacting or subscribing to a religious broadcast organization rather than through the more distant option of initiating a relationship with a neighborhood church. Realization of the importance of reinforcing appropriate supportive behavior by viewers has also led the broadcasters to encourage formation of an interactive relationship between viewers and themselves rather than attempting to direct them to a local church.

In summary, therefore, the research indicates that religious television programs could be effective in influencing viewers' attitudes and opinions on certain subjects and in producing certain types of behavioral response. Because of the strong dynamic of defense mechanisms, the major effect of religious television programs will be one of reinforcement of existing attitudes that most viewers would hold in harmony with the broadcaster.

The persuasiveness of religious programs toward change appear to be greatest when they are viewed by a person who is in a state of attitude imbalance or transition and seeking new forms of gratification for his or her needs; when they are viewed by a person for whom religious faith has always been a viable, if not vital, option; when the options being presented are seen as realistic and leading to a desirable end; when opportunity for demonstration exists in proximate distance to the viewing situation; and when the attitude or behavior is not central to the individual's self-concept and ego-functioning.

The presence of religious programs on television does serve the function of maintaining religious faith as an option to be considered in the search for salient sources of need-gratification. The religious perspective presented on television may also serve to create an imbalance in an otherwise balanced need-state in the direction of development of religious faith. However, for significant and permanent changes in attitudes and behavior toward religious faith, religious programs need to be complemented by interpersonal contact and continuing group support. It will be noted later in this chapter that the failure of broadcasters in this regard may have significantly reduced the effectiveness of their contribution to the mission of the church.

Can Religious Programs on Television Convert People to Religious Faith?

We noted initially, in looking at the empirical evidence for this question, that the theological concept of conversion as held by Protestants is different from what is usually meant by the term in empirical analysis. In theological terms conversion is used to describe the moment when a person for the first time comes to a personal realization of the grace and forgiveness of God and accepts that theological reality as relevant for his or her life. Within Protestant theology it is this moment when one is acknowledged as becoming a Christian. Acceptance of this reality may or may not result in any immediately observable change in overt behavior, though over a period of time it is expected that the person would demonstrate increased qualities of love and acceptance to others, patience, and self-control. As with many theological affirmations, there is no empirical way of testing the existence or reality of such conversion. Compare this concept to the more general use of the term conversion, which is applied to a situation where a person demonstrates marked change in behavior, often resulting in a stance which is diametrically opposed to a previous stance.

While it is not possible empirically to verify the validity of a theological reality, it is possible empirically to clarify several things related to religious television's claim of success in converting people. One is the assessment of their claims made of situations of radical change in behavior i.e., where the theological reality is accompanied by significant change in attitude and behavior. Another is an evaluation of the extent to which the broadcasters' claims of influence on people's lives are supported by people's own perception.

While the dominant function of television has been noted as the reinforcement of existing attitudes, there is some evidence to suggest that radical change in attitudes and values may occur in response to a mass-communicated message. Though defense mechanisms act to protect functional attitudes against threat and change, these defense mechanisms are not absolute. Berelson and Steiner note that "even in extreme cases, there is usually a sizable minority of people who read or listen to material against or indifferent to their prior position—out of curiosity, accident (i.e., no foreknowledge of what the content will be), lack of predispositional strength or, importantly, simple accessibility of materials."[11] Accidental exposure is especially effective in bypassing defense mechanisms because the mechanisms have not had the chance to be aroused. This could be particularly pertinent to American television where a large amount of viewing is nonpurposive. It could also be relevant to the use of religious spots, which are often interspersed within general programming and are free of the trappings and identification that accompany longer religious programs.

Radical change of attitude may also take place when existing attitudes are no longer adequate to satisfy the related need-state of the viewer. As needs change because of changes in sociophysical or biophysical conditions, former patterns of attitudes or behaviors may no longer be perceived as satisfying. This condition prompts an active or passive search to match newly salient needs with available sources of gratification.[12] In this situation, a mass communication might engender redefinition of attitudes or personal images in several possible ways: through addition, clarification, or even radical reorganization.[13] Such redefinition can also occur at many different levels of personality structure or attitude centrality. Religion on television may be particularly effective in stimulating attitude change because of the "personal" attributes of much of religious programming and also the immediacy of religious television's presence in the home, a place where defense mechanisms are usually less active.

There is research which questions the number of "conversions" claimed by the paid-time religious broadcasters. James Engel of Wheaton Graduate School of Communication surveyed a sample of viewers of the religious station WCFC-Channel 38 in Chicago who had called the station in response to the invitation given on the station to "accept Christ," a term used in evangelical circles as equivalent to religious conversion. Though the survey sampled only those who had called the station within the past two and a half years to accept Christ, 29.92 percent of the respondents said that they had been Christians for longer than three years. Further, he found that only 19.69 percent of the respondents associated their decision to accept Christ with either watching television or praying with a television counselor. The remaining 60.65 percent who said they had had a religious conversion experience identified this experience with a church, a friend, or other situation. The call to the station appears to have been an expression of this earlier decision or a confirmation of it. While such a study does not attempt to evaluate the significance of the experience on the persons involved, it does call into question the accuracy of the broadcasters' claims of effectiveness in evangelism. In terms of observable behavior, the study reveals that for most of those involved the call to the station was not a radical change in behavior, but rather an extension of already well-established behavior patterns. More than half the respondents indicated that they attended church at least once a week (almost half that number attended twice a week) before the call and another 13.39 percent said they attended monthly or several times a year. A large majority of the callers—63.78 percent—had called the station before.[14]

While it is possible for television to trigger a radical change in behavior in certain persons under certain conditions, most paid-time broadcasters present this dramatic effect as the norm for their programs. The research indicates, however, that the figures given particularly by the paid-time religious broadcasters in support of this claim are sweeping overstatements: they do not attempt accurately to assess the situation of the person involved in the decision making before claiming them as a conversion statistic, nor do they take into account the durability of the change which, it is claimed, is produced. Under certain conditions a dramatic change may occur within a person's attitudes and behavior; however, research on persuasion and attitude change indicates that these changes will not endure unless they are reinforced by rewarding experiences, other communications, or group pressure.[15] Within Protestant thought one of the extablished criteria for genuine conversion is subsequent moral behavioral change and continued Christian group involvement. As will be noted in the following chapter, the record of religious television in this regard is quite dismal. There are very few people who may experience some form of religious conversion by television alone who continue in that change through extended involvement within an interactive Christian group.

Notes

1. Dorwin Cartwright, "Some Principles of Mass Persuasion: Selected Findings of Research on the Sale of U.S. War Bonds," *Human Relations* 2, July 1949, pp. 253–67.
2. The model is presented in Comstock, *Television and Human Behavior*, chapter 8.
3. Mennonite Advertising Agency, "Report of Family Life Television Spots—Series II, 1970," Harrisonburg, 1970.
4. Robert W. Sonigan, "A Descriptive Analysis of the Effectiveness of Broadcasting by the Church of Jesus Christ of Latter Day Saints in the Northern States Mission Area," M. A. thesis, Brigham Young University, 1964.

5. Gallup, "Unchurched American," pp. 57–58. This 14 percent represents 3.93 percent of the total unchurched population.
6. W. H. Rockenstein, "Children and Religious Television: An Experimental Study of the Reactions of Children in the Fifth, Sixth, Seventh, and Eighth Grades in Monogalia County, West Virginia to Children's Religious Television Programming," Ph.D. dissertation, Northwestern University, 1966, pp. 161–75; Frank Klos, "A Study of the Origin, Utilization, and Impact of the 'Davey and Goliath' Series 1959–77 and Its Present Effectiveness in Teaching Religious Values to Children," Ed.D. dissertation, Temple University, 1979, pp. 177–82.
7. Daniel Katz, "The Functional Approach to the Study of Attitudes," *Public Opinion Quarterly*, 24, 1960, pp. 163–204.
8. Bernard Berelson and Gary A. Steiner, *Human Behavior: An Inventory of Scientific Findings*, New York: Harcourt, Brace and World, 1964, pp. 529–30, 536.
9. Comstock, *Television and Human Behavior*, pp. 447–48.
10. Wilbur Schramm, *Mass Media and National Development*, Stanford: Stanford University Press, 1964, pp. 132–39.
11. Berelson, *Human Behavior*, p. 531.
12. John W. Dimmick et al., "Media Use and the Life Span," *American Behavioral Scientist*, September/October 1979, p. 10.
13. Wilbur Schramm and Donald F. Roberts, eds., *The Process and Effects of Mass Communication*, revised edition, Urbana: University of Illinois Press, 1971, p. 364.
14. Engel, "Pilot Research Study," pp. 26–32.
15. Berelson, *Human Behavior*, p. 543.

11
Religious Television and the Local Church

One of the major areas of conflict that has occurred as a result of the rapid growth of paid-time religious broadcasting has been the threat it has posed to the established church, particularly in relation to its traditional local organizations. The development and nature of this conflict has been analyzed in detail in chapter 5. It was noted there that so far there has been little empirical evidence to clarify the validity both of the criticisms and defense of the paid-time broadcasters.

In this chapter, we intend to clarify this question by examining what the research available on the subject says about it. As in the other chapters in which empirical evidence is considered, relevant findings from general communication research will be considered along with research focused specifically on aspects of religious television.

The question of the effect of religious television programs on the local church has both short-term and long-term dimensions. Because of the complex interaction of religious broadcasting with other social characteristics such as broader religious and cultural movements, changing social uses of mass media, and changing historical circumstances, it is unlikely that a simple cause–effect relationship between the viewing of religious programs on television and individual faith and church interaction could ever be isolated. However, it is possible, on the basis of consistent findings drawn from a wide range of studies over a reasonable period of time to indicate areas of significant possibility and concern. While a definitive answer to the question of whether present religious television programs are having a beneficial or detrimental effect on local churches will not be found, areas of reasonable probability will be identified.

In this chapter, the principal area of focus will be the relationship between religious television and the local church. The broader and more indirect effects, such as the contribution of religious broadcasting to broader cultural changes that might affect the church along with other cultural institutions will be examined further in the following chapter. The major questions to be examined in this chapter are: What responses can religious programs elicit from viewers? Are religious television programs increasing the membership of local churches? Are religious television programs encouraging the transfer of loyalty away from local churches? Have religious programs reduced people's giving to their local church?

What Responses Do Religious Programs Elicit From Viewers?

There are a variety of opportunities made available to viewers of religious programs to establish contact with the broadcaster, ranging from a one-time contact to an ongoing relationship of support and interaction. The research indicates that religious broadcasters receive a significantly large response from viewers, depending on the situation and the broadcast organization.

The largest response is evoked when something free is offered to viewers by a program. Broadcasters frequently use this device both to supplement their televised message with printed and taped materials and to procure names for their mailing lists. From Spring 1963 to Spring 1966 the mainline-network program "Frontiers of Faith" ran 85 weeks of Bible Tele-courses— lectures with visual aids—on biblical and ethical subjects. Giveaways such as free study guides, lesson summaries, and bibliographies were offered on the programs. In that period 31,017 requests for the materials were received from viewers—an average of 365 a week.[1] In the year 1978–79 the Southern Baptist Convention's Radio and Television Commission received 8,223 requests for material offered on its four television programs "Human Dimension," "JOT," "Listen," and "The Athletes."[2] Even the unusual national advertising campaign by the Passionist Fathers seeking recruits for the priesthood, featuring seven different spots that were broadcast hundreds of times on 74 television stations and more than 200 radio stations, resulted in 1,800 letters over three years being sent to the Order seeking more information about the priesthood.[3]

These figures pale into insignificance, however, when compared to the response gained by major religious broadcasters. The present paid-time religious broadcasters offer items such as religious badges, pins, record albums, pendants, and jewelry to any person who calls or writes. Though no specific figures are available on the response to offers of this kind, the "Old Time Gospel Hour" in 1979 purchased two million "Jesus First" pins as giveaways to viewers.[4]

The personal nature of the evangelical programs, with their emphasis on offering help to viewers, appears to be especially effective in attracting this personal response from viewers. After a five-day nationally broadcast crusade from Philadelphia in 1960, the Billy Graham association received over 600,000 letters in a five-day period. In 1978 it received more than one million letters from its radio and television audience.[5] The "Old Time Gospel Hour" in 1978 received an average of 10,000 letters each working day and the Oral Roberts' organization receives such a volume of mail that it has established a mail room with a handling capacity of 20,000 letters a day.[6]

More direct and immediate personal contact is possible where the program provides opportunities for telephone contact, and many of the paid-time religious broadcasters now have this facility. The PTL Network and CBN both staff telephone banks with volunteer counselors who are frequently shown on the air seated behind the host and his guests. Viewers are often invited during the program to call these counselors with their concerns, problems, or prayer requests. As was noted earlier, the PTL Network claims that in 1979, more than 478,000 calls were received on these "prayer lines."[7]

The CBN organization has decentralized these counseling facilities, having established regional counseling centers in different parts of the country. These serve as call-in centers as the program is being broadcast. WXNE-Channel 25 in Boston, for example, was built as a network station by CBN and since October 1977 has served as the regional counseling center for the network in New England. Reference has been made previously to some characteristics of the calls received at this center. Table 11.1 provides full details of the calls received at this center during the period 1977–79. Each call is categorized by the telephone counselor as it is received and recorded for subsequent computerization at the central office in Virginia. Explanation of the categories was given by Jack Kincaid, Spiritual Life Director for CBN Boston at the time. No attempt is made by this author to justify the validity of the categories nor the accuracy of the categorization of the counselors. The figures give only a guide to the nature of calls received by this paid-time religious organization.

What stands out in a consideration of the figures in Table 11.1 is the large number of calls directed to the simple sharing of a concern with another and the seeking of support through a "prayer request." This tendency provides an insight into the function which religious programs fulfill in the lives of many people.

The research indicates that those who use such facilities have strong common characteristics. Bailey in 1972 found that those who responded to the program "Herald of Truth" were largely married housewives on a low income, who attended church services regularly, and who were loyal "Herald of Truth" viewers or listeners.[8] In 1978 the Christian Broadcasting Network studied characteristics of the partners who used their telephone counseling services. They also found that there were shared characteristics

TABLE 11.1   Counseling Calls Received at CBN Boston, 1977–79

	1977–78	1978–79
Total Number of Calls	15,253	20,972
Salvations	1,246	1,478
(i.e., Number of people who call in response to an appeal on the program or who are saved by the telephone counselor after conversation)		
Prayer Requests	14,569	21,928
(Number of people for whom a prayer request is made. One call could include several such prayer requests.)		
Holy Spirit Baptisms	150	296
(Number of people who call to enquire about or to report a "baptism in the spirit.")		
Answers to Prayer	773	758
Referrals and Clergy Contact	601	517
(Number of people referred to or requesting referral to a clergyman or church)		
Family Problems	1,338	2,317
Drug Problems	125	195
Emotional Problems	939	1,134
Alcohol Problems	289	484
Sexual Deviance	62	102
Suicide	55	89

SOURCE: CBN, Boston, "Monthly Statistical and Activity Report."

in the type of people who used these counseling facilities. Females call more frequently than males: 64 percent compared to 48 percent. Those of lower education and lower income call more than those of higher education and higher income: 63 percent compared to 48 percent. Members of the "700 Club" call more than nonmembers, and long-term members call more often than recent members. Those with a church affiliation use these counseling facilities more often than those without a church affiliation: 61 percent of those with a church affiliation compared to 50 percent of those without.

When adjusted for different proportions of persons in each of these categories, the following profile of the CBN partners who have called a CBN counseling center emerges: 80 per cent are women; 91 percent are "700 Club" members; 94 percent have been a "700 Club" member for one year or more; 70 percent are over the age of 35; 84 percent have no college education; and 90 per cent are affiliated with a church.[9] These figures suggest that, far from being a complementary activity to the church in reaching and providing care for those outside the church, the counseling activities of CBN and perhaps for all the major paid-time religious broadcasters, appear more as a service supported by older, female church members without a college education, primarily for their own support and companionship.

The implications of this alternative counseling service provided for church members must be considered in evaluating the effect of paid-time religious programs on the life of the local church: is it a complementary service or a substitutionary one?

Are Religious Television Programs Increasing the Membership of Local Churches?

There are several ways in which religious programs on television may be effective in building the membership of local churches: One is by the addition of new members, the other is by the reactivation of old ones. The available research indicates that religious television programs demonstrate little ability to stimulate formation of a relationship between viewers and a church where a previous relationship did not exist. There is little evidence to support the contention that religious programs on television are increasing the overall membership of the church.

When attempting to understand the reasons for the failure of religious programs to increase local church membership, several possible explanations emerge. First, one needs to look at the dominant characteristics of the religious television audience: most viewers are people who are already active church members. The more a particular program emphasizes strong religious attributes conducive to church attendance, the more selective the audience becomes and the fewer nonchurch members are in the audience. Second, one needs to recognize the substantial difference that exists between a response to a specific proposition gained by a broadcaster from viewers in front of a television set and the transference of that response to other situations of new behavior. We have noted already the research insight that the mass media cannot be expected to stimulate or disinhibit behaviors which are not contiguous to the viewing situation. It cannot be assumed, therefore, that because individuals have a change in attitude toward religious faith while watching religious television they will be motivated to adopt behavior perceived by the broadcaster to be related but which is not related within the environment of the viewers. That this failure to link attitude change to church attendance occurs appears to be supported by research. When persons watching television are motivated to change their attitude toward religious faith, even to make a religious commitment of some sort, most frequently they integrate that decision within their existing environment rather than changing their environment. Their newly acquired religious faith, where it persists, more frequently than not is oriented around the television set and the television preacher than around an external local church that has not been associated with the experience.

This behavior is reinforced by the broadcasters' general lack of emphasis on the centrality of the local church to Christian faith and their apparent unwillingness to channel persons who contact them toward involvement in a local church or to encourage local church members to establish contact with the respondent.

A unique opportunity to study the effectiveness of television in contributing to the growth of a church was provided in Tallahassee, Florida, in 1974, where the Christian and Missionary Alliance denomination strategically planned for the establishment of two new congregations. In establishing the congregations, the Alliance employed a variety of forms of mass and personal communication. The mass communication employed was:

Radio—a five-minute daily program on one of the local radio stations, along with occasional spots.
Newspaper—weekly ads in the church page and ads on special occasions
Television—fifteen 30-second ads in September 1973 inviting people to attend the churches
Highway signs
Direct mail—to those people who moved into or within the city.

In addition to these forms of mass communication designed to reach those who did not attend church regularly, the churches conducted door-to-door visitation within the area of the churches.

In order to measure the comparative effectiveness of these various means of communication, George Thompson drew a random sample of those who had attended the church and filled out visitor cards (N=192) and a random sample of the general population from telephone books (N=251). He found that at the end of the 18-month project period, 40 percent of the general population and 82 percent of those who had attended one of the churches had heard of the sponsoring denomination, the Christian and Missionary Alliance. The main source of acquaintance for both the church sample and the general population sample was direct mail, which was named in 72 percent of the cases. Friends were the second major source, named in 25 percent of the cases. The television ads were named by only 5 percent of the respondents.

When those who had attended the church were asked what the reason was for their attendance, 86 percent of respondents said they had attended because of a personal invitation. The second most important reason—the newspaper ads—was named by only 8 percent of the respondents. None of those who attended said they were motivated to attend because of the television ads.

While there was no effort made in the study to control the particular input of each information variable, it is interesting to note the significant difference between the contribution of the mass media to the information function compared to the attendance function. Thompson concluded from

his research that while mass communication is able to fulfill some information function when used widely and to advantage, actual behavior change
or response such as attendance at a church, requires personal contact.[10]

This inability of mass communication to stimulate formation of *novel*
relationships with the church has been demonstrated in several other studies
of mass campaigns, even when the campaigning organization works closely
with the local churches. *Church Growth: America* magazine undertook
research of the Billy Graham crusade in Greater Seattle in 1976. One year
later they sampled the 18,136 people who came forward or stood in their
place in response to the call to accept Christ. Of that number, 30.6 percent
were found to be for "conversion" reasons, but 53.6 percent of these were
found to have been already attending a church. Of those who made a
"decision" at the crusade, however, only 11.2 percent started participation
in a subsequent Crusade-sponsored nurture group and only 8 percent
finished the group program.[11]

The magazine also studied a "Here's Life, America" campaign in
Indianapolis and Fresno, a multi-media evangelistic campaign based in local
churches and drawing heavily on personal contact by telephone. The study
found that of the 1,665 people who "made a decision to accept Christ,"
only 242, or 14.5 percent, began to participate in subsequent organized
Bible studies and only 101, or 6 percent of respondents completed them.[12]

These results suggest that mass-communicated messages alone are
limited in their ability to introduce new members to the church. This is not
an isolated finding, but is also supported by the weight of other communication research. An individual stands within a strong system that reinforces certain life-styles, attitudes, and behaviors. While particular acknowl-
edgements may be made in response to a mass-communicated message, the
extension of this acknowledgement into sustained change in behavior requires strong personal support, encouragement, and demonstrated viable
alternatives. To this extent, it is significant that personal contact has frequently been identified as one of the major contributive factors in the establishment of novel church attendance. In the *Church Growth: America* study
of the Billy Graham Seattle Crusade, it was found that of the 7 percent of
conversions from the Crusade who were involved in a church a year later,
82.8 percent of them had a friend and/or relative in that particular congregation. The magazine in other research asked over 4,000 people in 35 states and
three countries why they had become part of a local church. Between 75
percent and 90 percent responded that friends or relatives had been the
"door of the church" for them.[13] Bibby and Brinkerhoff in their study of
membership additions to conservative churches found that of the 9 percent
of the new members who had become members through a novel proselyte-
type conversion, 32 percent were either married or engaged to a member of
the church at the time of their conversion.[14] This personal influence has been
noted in other research on behavior change as well.[15]

In spite of these findings, most religious broadcasters make little effort to establish personal contact between respondents to their programs and a local church, though they frequently claim to be supportive of the idea. It has been noted that between 1977 and 1979 CBN Boston received 36,225 phone calls at its counseling center. Of the 2,724 of these calls that were identified as being for "salvation," only 1,118 referrals were made to local clergymen or churches, and many of these were for other counseling reasons. (See Table 11.1.) A study of the direct-mail follow up procedures used by the paid-time broadcasters in 1981 for persons who seek information on religious conversion indicates that church attendance is rarely mentioned or encouraged. Following an enquiry about conversion by the author to five paid-time religious broadcasters, a total of 54 mailings were received in the following nine-month period. Only six of the mailings were directed to answering the original enquiry; the remainder were directed primarily to fund solicitation by the broadcaster. Suggestions of the enquirer's becoming involved in the life of a local church were minimal and none of the broadcasters referred the enquirer's name to a local church for subsequent follow-up.

It is more likely that any effect that religious programs may have on church attendance and membership lies in their possible reactivation of inactive members or the channelling of members from one church to another. Engel's survey of respondents to Channel 38 in Chicago revealed that 33.86 percent of the respondents said that their church attendance had increased since their phone calls to accept Christ were made to the station. While there is no breakdown of these figures into differences between those who had not previously been attending a church compared to those who had, the figures indicate that in many cases this attendance was an increase from occasional attendance to regular attendance.[16]

In a survey of its partners, CBN found that 36 percent of its partners with a church affiliation reported increased involvement with their local church because of their viewing of CBN programs. This figure was substantially lower (19 percent) for those who had no current church affiliation. Those who were not affiliated with a church also reported a greater tendency to become less involved than those with a church affiliation.

It is possible that religious television programs for church members fill a complementary role, maintaining and increasing their enthusiasm by providing alternative ideas for local church development, maintaining their level of personal inspiration, or by supplying things which are not otherwise available at their local church.

A major effect of the religious programs on church membership may be the channelling of church members from one church to another. This channelling effect has been one of the major results associated with religious television's functioning. Through the vitality perceived within evangelical programs, a viewer who is dissatisfied with the functioning of his present church may come to associate vitality with evangelical churches as a whole. This behavior ties in with research on need gratification in a situation of imbalance, and with the tendency to seek gratification of existing needs within areas perceived to be similar to previous behavior patterns rather than in areas perceived to be radically different. If the viewer has formed an attraction to a particular program or its host, the movement to a church more closely identified with the preferred program may cement the loyalty perceived in the relationship. Movement to a church of similar content and association as the television program may also remove discordance felt by the viewer between the message received through television and the message received through his or her church. The dominance of paid-time religious programs on television at present is possibly creating a substantial status-conferral effect. Viewers are more likely to associate the Christian viewpoint with the paid-time religious stance seen on television, especially in situations where the viewer lacks other points of reference.

Are Religious Television Programs Detrimental to the Local Church?

There are several research findings suggesting that religious television programs may be detrimental to the local church. A religious program on television may be effective in awakening within viewers dissatisfaction with their present situation, prompting them to begin a search for a satisfying answer to newly aroused religious questions and needs. However, research on television and human behavior indicates that a particular answer to this search will probably not be chosen if there are easier, cheaper, or otherwise more desirable actions apparently leading to the same goal. This process has been described as "satisficing" behavior i.e., where choices of behavior to meet felt needs proceed by the seeking and choosing of alternatives that are easy and satisfactory rather than optimal. The person will tend to stop seeking once a *desirable rather than optimal* level of gratification is achieved in order to preserve time and energy. There is a tendency then for individuals consciously or subconsciously to reduce their expectations of satisfaction in order to match and live with the levels of actual achievement.[17]

This evidence, which appears in general communication research, suggests that while religious programs on television may be effective in motivating a person to consider religious questions and needs, they may also project themselves as being the satisfactory answer to those needs. As we have seen, there are strong economic pressures on the paid-time religious broadcasters to project such an image in order to maintain the loyalty and contributions of their audiences. Perhaps in recognition of the realities of psychological reinforcement, broadcasters have developed services for their viewers which previously were considered appropriate only to a local church. Far from being a complementary service to the local church, therefore, religious broadcasters appear to be providing an overlapping service, one traditionally provided by the local church. Counseling materials sent to enquirers about religious faith place little or no stress on the need to become involved in a local church and few referrals of enquirers are made. A content study of 15 paid-time religious programs by Hilton in 1980 found that in none of them was the local church ever mentioned. This was true even for Robert Schuller, even though it is claimed of Schuller that he frequently encourages his television audience to attend a local church.[18]

There is a small detrimental effect present and this is shown to be greater among those who have no established church affiliation or who are dissatisfied with their current church affiliation. Hilton in his study of the use of television worship services by the members of the Irvington Presbyterian Church found that 9 percent of the members of that church have stayed home on occasion to watch television worship services rather than gone to the local church to worship, and 3 percent of the members said the television worship services had caused them to be less involved in their local church.[19]

The CBN study of its partners found that only 2 percent of its partners reported becoming less involved in their local church because of their viewing of CBN programs. When broken down into categories of members, the number increased to 9 percent of those without a current church affiliation compared to 2 percent for those with a church affiliation.[20]

It is unlikely that paid-time television programs alone will sway individuals who are deeply rooted in their local church and finding satisfaction within that church. As noted, the majority of the audience of religious television programs are people who are already actively involved in a local church and there is therefore little empirical evidence to support the contention that religious programs on television are "draining people out of the local churches." However, for people who are dissatisfied with their local church, who have little established connection with a local church, or whose religious consciousness may be awakened by a viewed religious program, the research indicates that paid-time religious programs, by presenting themselves as competent alternatives to the local church, offering a range of services similar to the local church, and not referring respondents or enquirers to a local church, may be acting as a barrier to people's developing their faith most fully within this interpersonal context.

Have Paid-Time Religious Programs Reduced People's Giving to their Local Church?

A contentious issue, particularly between the mainline churches, the income of which in the 1960s and 1970s has been decreasing, and the religious

TABLE 11.2   Incomes of Major Paid-Time Religious Broadcasters, 1979

	Audience Contributions	Other Income	Total Income
	($ millions)		
Old Time Gospel Hour	38.4	7.9	46.3
Hour of Power	16.8	-	16.8
PTL Club	51.8	.8	52.6
Rex Humbard			30.0*
Billy Graham (1978)	32.0	8.0	40.0

SOURCES: Thomas Road Baptist Church and Related Ministries, "Consolidated Statement for the Year Ended June 30, 1979"; "Financial Report: Hour of Power Television, 10th Anniversary Year, 1970–80"; "Summary of Financial Information, Fiscal Year Ended May 31, 1979," Action, March 1980; Billy Graham Evangelistic Association and Related Ministries, Annual Report, 1978.
* 1980 budget estimate given by Rex Humbard Ministry in personal correspondence, July 9, 1980.

broadcasters whose income in the same period has been steadily increasing, has been whether local church contributions have been reduced because of contributions to television religious programs. What does the research say?

The paid-time religious broadcsters have certainly been effective in their money-raising ability. Table 11.2 lists the incomes of several of the major paid-time religious broadcasters for 1979, as drawn from their organization's public financial statements.

Though public statements are not available for other broadcasters, the more reliable estimates are: Oral Roberts, $60 million (1978); Christian Broadcasting Network, $46 million (1979); Jimmy Swaggart, $20 million (1979). Several broadcasters and newspapers suggest that the total contributions for these broadcasters and the numerous other smaller radio and television ministries exceed one billion dollars each year.[21] Is it possible that such a large amount of money could be given above and beyond what is otherwise given to a local church?

Evangelicals in general, who comprise the majority of the audience of the paid-time religious programs, are more generous givers to religious organizations than other church members.[22] Christian television-program viewers in particular have also been found to be more generous givers to a church or other religious organizations than nonviewers. The following table from a Gallup poll presents responses to the question: What percentage of your income do you contribute to your church or other religious organization? The study does not differentiate between contributions given to a church and contributions given to a religious broadcast organization. It does reveal that religious television viewers are more generous contributors than nonviewers.[23]

	10% or more	5% – 9%	Less than 5%	None	Don't know
General Public	16%	13%	33%	26%	12%
Watches Religious TV	26%	12%	32%	19%	11%
Does Not Watch	11%	13%	34%	30%	12%

Not all viewers of programs are supporters. Ben Armstrong quotes a 1978 NRB study which indicated that only between five and 10 percent of viewers contributed financially during the course of a year and of those less than 25 percent sent gifts regularly.[24] The size of the audiences over the course of a year and the generosity of those who do contribute appear to compensate for such a low percentage. It was noted, for example, that the average contribution to the "Old Time Gospel Hour" in 1976–77 was $23.[25]

A study of former partners of CBN found that 42 percent of those interviewed said that the greatest amount of their financial support went to their local church: only 11 percent said that CBN receives the greatest share of their giving. Former partners are those who had been regular contributors to CBN but who had discontinued regular support during the most recent 12-month period. The average annual contribution to CBN by these discontinued partners during the twelve-month period was $107, which represented only 19.4 percent of their total giving to religious organizations.[26]

A panel study of 18 CBN partners and eight prospective partners revealed that very few of the panelists supported CBN exclusively, even though many were regular monthly supporters. Nearly all of the panelists professed to be involved in a local church of one denomination or another and admitted that they gave first to their local church and then to CBN and others. The majority of the panelists said they tithed and gave the majority of this to their church first. The single most important reason given by the panelists for supporting CBN was "to get the Gospel out." In this regard CBN was seen as complementing the work of their local church, not replacing it. For this reason they felt justified in supporting both.[27]

These studies suggest that contributions given to paid-time religious broadcasters by evangelicals are not replacing giving to their local church, but are in addition to it. There is only limited research to indicate the position of contributors from the mainline denominations. In his study of Irvington Presbyterian Church, Hilton found that 15 percent of his sample of members had given money to television worship services. Twenty-five percent of inactive members were among these contributors. Of this 15 percent, 87 percent said it was money that would not have otherwise gone to the local church; 13 percent said it was. Hilton concluded his research by stating that his research had found little to substantiate the fear that the electric church was draining money away from the local churches, though he also found little support for the broadcasters' contention that the broadcasters were generating money for the local church by building up the commitment of believers.[28]

The research implies that for those who are actively involved in a local church and therefore (one might assume) among its chief supporters, the church remains central to their understanding of the Christian mission and as a result the object of their major support. It is unlikely that paid-time religious organizations will change that focus of commitment as long as the church remains satisfying to its active members' needs. Should the broadcast organization come to be the primary source of gratification for the needs of its audience, or to be seen as a functional substitute for the local church, the direction of an individual's financial support could change, though such a change does not appear to be occurring to a great extent at present.

Of concern to all churches, however, should be the approach the broadcasters take in attempting to raise money from their viewers. Little emphasis is placed on responsible stewardship of finances and possessions. The major methods used to elicit support are threat (removal of the program from the viewer's area), pathos (appeal on the basis of the broadcaster's being personally damaged by a financial shortfall), enticement (receiving a desired object that is otherwise unavailable), fear (protection against a common enemy), superstition (gaining something from God for a gift given), and selfishness (receiving more from God than the value of the gift given). The habituating effect of these constant appeals is now being reflected in the increasingly bizarre methods adopted in fund raising.

A survey of the research allays some fears of a dramatic undermining or replacement of the local church by paid-time religious programs. Where an effect may be taking place, it is more likely to be in the nature of channelling members of churches away from those churches that are not represented on television toward those that are. The research gives little support to the contention that the religious broadcasters as yet are draining money from the local churches into their own organizations. Unsupported also, though, is the claim made by religious broadcasters that they are helping build local churches through the introduction of new members. The research indicates that few new members are brought into the church by religious programs on television, and that increases in membership in particular churches are due primarily either to movement from other churches or to the establishment of personal contact by another member of that congregation.

Further research is needed to clarify the contributory part religious programs may have played in that process and also the long-term effects of many religious programs' avoidance of reference to the local church and their development of services in competition with the local churches.

Notes

1. Broadcast and Film Commission, "Frontiers of Faith," p. 3.
2. Radio and Television Commission of the Southern Baptist Convention, "Program Response Report," October 1978 to September 1979.
3. Terry Ann Knopf, "Advertising for Priests," *Boston Globe*, March 24, 1980, pp. 21–22.
4. Montgomery, "Electric Church," p. 29.
5. Robinson, "Study of the Audience," p. 119; Armstrong, *Electric Church*, p. 97.
6. Montgomery, "Electric Church;" Sholes, *Prime-Time Religion*, p. 1.
7. "PTL Counseling."
8. Edward J. Bailey, "An Analysis of Respondents to 'Hearald of Truth' Radio and TV Programs," M.S. thesis, Iowa State University, 1972.
9. Market Research Group, "National CBN Partner," Table 90.
10. George S. Thompson, "The Effect of the Use of Mass Media to Establish a Local Church: A Study of the Pilot Church Project of the Christian and Missionary Alliance in Tallahassee, Florida" Ph.D. dissertation, Florida State University, 1975, pp. 141–44.
11. Win Arn, "Mass Evangelism—The Bottom Line," *Church Growth: America*, January/February, 1978, pp. 4ff.
12. Win Arn, "A Church Growth Look at 'Here's Life, America,'" *Church Growth: America*, January/February, 1977, p. 4.
13. Arn, "Mass Evangelism," p. 6.
14. Reginald W. Bibby and Merlin B. Brinkerhoff, "The Circulation of the Saints: A Study of People who Join Conservative Churches," *Journal for the Scientific Study of Religion* 12, September 1973, pp. 277–80.
15. Schramm, *Mass Media and National Development*, pp. 132–39.
16. Engel, "Pilot Research Study," pp. 26–32.
17. J. W. Johnstone, "Social Integration and Mass Media Use among Adolescents," in Blumler and Katz, *Uses of Mass Communication*, pp. 35–47.
18. Armstrong, *Electric Church*, p. 10.
19. Hilton, "Influence of Television," p. 56.
20. Market Research Group, "National CBN Partner," Table 183.
21. See Bisset, "Religious Broadcasting," p. 29.
22. Stark and Glock, *American Piety*, pp. 81–107.
23. Gallup, "Evangelical Christianity."
24. Armstrong, *Electric Church*, p. 151.
25. Montgomery, "Electric Church."
26. Market Research Group, "National Former Partner," p. 2.
27. Market Research Group, "Report on Finances," pp. 5–9.
28. Hilton, "Influence of Television," p. 95.

12

Religious Television and American Culture

A major public concern has been that the paid-time religious broadcasters, through their media activities, exercised a disproportionate power over the American electorate. Though only a few of the broadcasters were politically involved, their wide constituency which was made possible by the mass media and the passionate loyalty which they appeared to engender from this constituency made them a minority group whose power exceeded their number. Particular focus of this concern centered on the fundamentalist preacher and churchman, Jerry Falwell and his related organizations, Moral Majority and the Religious Roundtable. These preachers, representing traditions that had previously played little active part in national elections, entered the political arena not just with a general message for Christians to be politically involved but with a specific agenda of policies and preferences and formed political alliances to further the cause of these preferences.

Social commentary on the broadcasters at the time of the elections reached close to a fever pitch, with fears being expressed that the broadcasters held such power as to hold the key to the election outcome. The election of Ronald Reagan as president, the paid-time broadcasters' chosen candidate, provided for many evidence to justify their fears. Now that much of the preelection tension and anxiety has abated, however, a more calculated analysis of the broadcasters' actual and future potential influence in the political sphere can be made.

Subsequent research on the political influence of the religious broadcasters indicates that they were not a major influence in the actual election outcome. There are several pieces of evidence for this conclusion. First, many of the fears expressed developed around the belief that the broadcasters were drawing comparatively large audiences containing a broad representation of the American population. As has been noted in chapters 8 and 9, audience research indicates that the broadcasters consistently were watched by a significantly smaller audience than was generally believed; and that this smaller audience was not universally representative of the American population but was a highly segmented one in terms of demographic characteristics.

Subsequent research also indicates that the potential influence claimed by the broadcasters in relation to their actual supporters was exaggerated. Hadden and Swann note, for example, that during the 1980 campaign Jerry Falwell claimed that Moral Majority had from two to three million members, which included 72,000 pastors. However, the circulation of their newsletter, *The Moral Majority Report*, at election time was only 482,000. It is unlikely that such a vital communication as the regular newsletter would be sent to only 16–24 percent of the supposed membership: the more likely assumption is that the total membership of Moral Majority was in fact substantially lower than what Falwell claimed. The figure of 482,000 also parallels more closely the projected national membership total based on state membership figures.[1]

The case studies presented by Moral Majority of candidates who were unexpectedly defeated in Senate and Congressional elections because of Moral Majority opposition—Senators Birch Bayh and George McGovern and Representative John Brademas, for example—are neutralized by other case studies of politicians who had been targeted for defeat by the New Right coalition but who retained their seats. Jewish representative Barney Frank, for example, in Massachusetts retained his seat in a heavily Roman Catholic area despite late, strongly directed attacks by the conservatives and the Roman Catholic Archbishop in the area over the issue of abortion.

Further research verifies that evangelicals and fundamentalists as groups are not as politically homogenous as the broadcasters had hoped. Polls conducted throughout the campaign indicated that political preferences among "born-again" voters showed a consistent split between Reagan and Carter. A voter-exit poll conducted by *The New York Times* and CBS showed that white "born-again" Protestants voted 61 percent for Reagan and 34 percent for Carter, a split which closely parallels that of other sectors of society.[2]

Subsequent research has sought to identify the influence of religious broadcasters and the Christian right on voters' choices. Johnson and Tamney studied 262 voters from "Middletown," a population representative of the voting patterns of the whole country. In their study of the factors influential in the choice of a particular candidate, they measured such variables as party preference, perception of political ideology, and religious attitudes on various issues. Their findings indicated that in terms of a general index devised to measure identification with the Christian Right, there was no difference in the percentage who chose Reagan compared to the general population. The authors found that the major independent variable that identified preference for Reagan was perceived political ideology, (i.e., those with a conservative political ideology voted for Reagan more than did the moderates). However, the conservative–moderate political ideology was found to be unrelated to religious preference. The most significant variable found in determining Reagan's election, according to this study, was the issue of inflation. *Finally, people made their presidential decision on the basis of who they perceived would best solve the problem of inflation.* The authors concluded from their research that: "In the 1980 Presidential election, the Christian Right had virtually no influence at all . . . the most important issue was inflation and those who picked it voted for Reagan 2 to 1."[3]

Because of the large number of variables that intervene between the message of a television personality and final political choices, it is unlikely that the contributory effect of a single factor could ever be isolated definitively. The weight of research into political decision making and the influence of mass media in this decision making suggests that most voters have established patterns of political choices. Television's main effect is in crystalizing or reinforcing these predispositions rather than in changing them. At the same time, the research indicates that television can have a significant effect on those who are politically undecided by helping them define issues and identify personalities. Given the small margins which typify many elections, this small influence could have a major social impact.[4]

The research mentioned above, however, suggests that in the 1980 election the political activities of the religious broadcasters were not a significant factor in the election outcome. There is no reason to assume, however, that the broadcasters could not be a significant influence in the future, given a situation where the issues on which they choose to focus attention become critical issues in the eyes of the electorate, and where a marginal influence may play a major part in determining the outcome. If American leaders and the American population learn from their historical experiences, however, it may be more difficult in the future for religious leaders to exert their influence primarily by bluff and threat: their future claims may be received more critically following the experience of exaggeration in 1980.

The more significant effect of recent trends in religious broadcasting may not be the immediate actual influence or lack of influence which religious broadcasters had on the outcome of the 1980 national elections, but the contributory effects which current religious television has on conservative trends in America and other Western countries. More significant also may be the particular effect the broadcasters have had on the development of American religious culture.

Stewart Hoover has noted that the greater influence of television lies not in its ability to brainwash or radically change people's minds on particular issues but in its ability to coalesce an audience around a particular issue.[5] Jerry Falwell's major success in 1980 may have lain not in achieving the dramatic effects of which he boasted but in demonstrating for religious and social leaders the potential of television and its associated media to bring together elements of society that had previously been scattered. There has always been a significant fundamentalist movement in American society: Falwell did not create it. However, fundamentalism in American society has typically consisted of unrelated, often antisocial small pockets of society. Falwell was able to put together a religious and social media package which brought together a diversity of people in a potentially dramatic way. It is quite likely that many of these were people who did not agree with all of Falwell's package, nor even with his central Fundamentalist theology, but who felt otherwise disenfranchised over a particular issue of concern to them, whether it be deterioration of the family, the spread of pornography, abortion, prayer in the school, or the restoration of traditional American life. In the absence of any possible alternative action, many may have moved behind Falwell on the basis of agreement with only one of his issues.

That this group was not radically influential in the 1980 election has already been suggested by the research: the dominant concerns were not those represented by Falwell, but rather the single issue of inflation. However, the potential for future influence among these people remains strong. As we noted earlier, attitude change by the media is most effective where the new attitudes being promoted are seen as being extensions of old, existing attitudes. Where there is an identification with a personality such as Falwell on one issue of concern, the possibility is greater for the extension of his attitudes to other areas of the viewers' thought and behavior. The influence that religious broadcasters may have is more significant, therefore, when they are viewed within the broader context as indicators of a general cultural trend among groups of disenfranchised citizens.

The influence of paid-time religious television also takes on a wider significance when considered within the broader context of the structures of the mass media in their political and economic dimensions. It is wrong simply to view the owners of mass media as the sole determinants in the shaping of media organizations and messages. They stand within a larger historical context and are themselves played upon by historical events and the circumstances these events thrust upon them. Horace Newcomb has noted that the ideas and symbols in American television have not been created there but frequently have a history in American culture.[6] Television is rarely an innovator of social forms or ideas but is more commonly a purveyor and reflector of those forms. Should the television programmers move too far away from what is publicly perceived as historically and socially appropriate, they would soon lose the attention of their audiences.

Similarly, as stated previously, the current evangelical–fundamentalist phenomenon on television is not a new one in American life. The major aspects of its message and its media style can be seen in earlier fundamentalist movements, particularly in the distinctive style of revivalist tent meetings, emotional expressions, dramatic incidents, and vitriolic challenge. Never before, though, has this minority movement been able to dominate a medium to the virtual exclusion of other religious expressions as it has on television in recent years.

The significance of this domination for religious culture lies not in its individual characteristics, but in its relationship with the media themselves. For while the media, and particularly television, serve mainly as mediators of the culture, the political and economic interests of the media controllers pass the culture through discreet but generally well-defined filters which are effective in serving their own purposes, namely reinforcing the economic status quo and suppressing challenge in the form of specific critique or overall diversity. Michael Real has noted in his recent work *Mass-Mediated Culture* that:

Mass-mediated culture primarily serves the interests of the relatively small political–economic power elite that sits atop the social pyramid. It does so by programming mass consciousness through an infrastructural authoritarianism that belies its apparent superstructural egalitarianism.[7]

This dynamic was identified more than 35 years ago by the media researchers Lazarsfeld and Merton and presented in their seminal article "Mass Communication, Popular Taste and Organized Social Action:"

The social effects of the mass media will vary as the system of ownership and control varies. . . . Since the mass media (in America) are supported by great business concerns geared into the current social and economic system, the media contribute to the maintenance of that system . . . not only from what is said, but more significantly from what is not said.[8]

In the early years of television, this establishment of authoritarian interest was occasionally apparent in overt conflicts between management, producers, and advertisers. Descriptions of these conflicts are provided by such practitioners as Eric Barnouw (*Tube of Plenty*) and Fred Friendly (*Due to Circumstances Beyond Our Control*). Given the primarily economic motive of the American broadcasting industry, it was finally the advertisers in their relation to the media management who gained the upper hand. Having won this battle for power over the forces of innovation and independent creativity, these established political and economic interests have become institutionalized within the industry. Challenges today in the name of diversity, realism, and innovation are discreet and usually ineffectual, strongly contained within the general parameters which have been set by the media controllers. One may note, for example, the description of the television creative process given by a leading Hollywood television writer:

You have an idea and you make an appointment (with a network executive). It's usually easy to get in the door. Your first meeting is with a Vice President in charge of programming—a tasteless thug who was once a network salesman. With him are four flunkies. All of them have titles—Assistants in Program Development. All of them put in their "two cents worth." . . . Then you go through the usual steps—more meetings, more suggestions from the flunkies. After a while you begin not to care about your original idea—you just hang on to see if you come out the other end.[9]

•One of the important issues arising out of recent trends in religious television lies in the symbolic and actual implications of religion's acquiescence to this process and the subjugation of religion on television to this normalizing process. The Christian church had been one of the few remaining alternative ideologies to remain in creative interaction with the television industry. In its local organization, the church remained a culture counter to the highly centralized, individualized, and depersonalized culture represented by general television programming. Though many compromises had been made to accommodate the distinctive features of the television medium and management, sustaining-time religious producers retained their ties to the local church and retained significant control and input into program content from their perspectives. Because sustaining-time programs were not placed under the same demands to maintain or increase ratings as were other television programs, sustaining-time programs were able to maintain a greater community representativeness and integrity of content. This perspective is reflected in the freedom apparent in the comments by CBS religious programs producer, Pam Ilott in 1970:

When asked about the low ratings her programs had, she replied that if she were only after ratings, she could add pop groups or produce something like Bishop Sheen. She is content, she said, with the million or million-and-a-half viewers she now has who "get something out of the programs and take it a step beyond—discussing it with their friends or taking action." . . . This is more valuable, she said, than a mass audience.[10]

The paid-time religious producers sacrificed that freedom of programming when they made themselves dependent on their popularity with their television audience.•This placed them in a situation where they were forced to blend into the television culture in order to appeal to those for whom this culture was realistic. The preceding comments by Pam Ilott can be compared with the philosophy reflected by the paid-time religious broadcasters:

•One of the unwritten laws of mass communication is that the more people you reach the further your dollar goes but the more it costs overall. Another unwritten law is that you can get your share of the audience only by offering people something they want. There's an additional law in religious broadcasting—the larger the audience, the greater the response in terms of lives changed.[11]

The author of the statement, Ben Armstrong, does not appear to recognize the innate contradiction in his statement: the essential distinction between giving people something they want and something that will change them.

The key in the difference between the two broadcasting approaches lies in the economic basis and this, it has been noted, was the issue over which programming issues were first raised in the early years of television in the 1950s. The growth of paid-time religious programming and its adaptation to and endorsement of the economic competitive basis of American broadcasting represents in many ways the final takeover by television of the last of its programming to be independent of its economic intentions. This is another of the significant issues in the recent growth of paid-time religious programming: by displacing all other types of religious programming, the paid-time religious broadcasters have virtually eliminated the community-responsibility orientation of media functioning in America which had been represented by public-service programming, much of which was religious in orientation. The paid-time religious broadcasters have reinforced the economic competitiveness of the television industry as the adequate basis for the maintenance and development of social thought; they have challenged the practice of religious diversity by the presentation of only one strand of American religious culture; they have endorsed the normalizing of religious thought to that which corresponds to existing mass-media mythology and intent.

The effects of this endorsement of the normalization of religious thought by the paid-time religious broadcasters may be twofold. First, it has reinforced the power of television, with its limited views, to act as an adequate determinant of the presentation of religious cultural thought. The fundamentalist view has come to be preferred because of the economic advantage it offers to the television industry and because elements within this thought are in harmony with television's goals of reinforcing the social status quo with the economic basis of American broadcasting, and with the promotion of a consumer orientation toward social issues and human relationships. There is no reason to believe that such a preferential relationship between broadcasting and paid-time religion will continue, however. It is likely that only as long as paid-time religion serves the interests of the broadcast industry will it remain in the preferred situation which it now enjoys.

The second effect to be considered is that on American religious culture as a whole. While television is not the only source of American culture and thought, it has a significant effect in the conferral of status on particular movements and issues, and in the setting of personal and social agendas. While there remains a significant diversity in American religious culture, of which fundamentalism and evangelicalism are still only minority views, the presence of these two traditions on television is reinforcing the perception that they are in fact the dominant expressions of Christianity in American society.

The further danger is that while mass-mediated religions can effectively transmit certain aspects of religious faith and practice, they tend to vitiate other aspects. Religion on television, for example, cannot fully convey the participatory elements of religious faith and practice, the emotive impact of silence in worship, or the indispensable theological aspects of awe and mystery. Yet by excluding these elements the mass media effectively rob religious faith of its essence and mutate it into being primarily information about religious occurrences or observed spectacles. No longer is the viewed presentation distinctively Christian, nor for that matter essentially religious. It has sold its rich birthright of meaning, fellowship, and joy for a potage of public exposure, and has become indistinguishable from other elements of television entertainment, simply another part of the total mass media environment to which modern people have become enslaved.

It is difficult to measure specific effects of paid-time religious television on American religious faith and practice. However, several research perspectives suggest possibilities. The cultural indicators research program has demonstrated that the major effect of television lies not in its stimulation of direct imitation, but in its steady cultivation within viewers of assumptions and perceptions about the nature of life and the world. By measuring the patterns of reality presented on television, it is possible to predict the influence they will have on those who are heavy consumers of these patterns. If it is the recurring patterns as presented on the major social forms of communication which are effective in the molding of culture, greater attention needs to be given to the study of the dominant patterns and images shown on religious television programs and how these relate to other and traditional expressions of religious faith. To what extent are paid-time religious programs consistent with traditional Christian thought, and to what extent are they shaped by the environment in which they have been cast? Of interest also is the phenomenon already noted: the extent to which paid-time religious programs on television are bypassing reference to the group expressions and aspects of religious faith in favor of an individualized and privatized faith.

The paid-time religious broadcasters have not created this trend. Other studies indicate that there are strong individualistic conceptions of religious faith in America. A Gallup Poll in 1978 revealed that 80 percent of Americans believe that "an individual should arrive at his or her own religious beliefs independent of any churches or synagogues," and 76 percent believe that a person can be a good Christian or Jew even if he or she doesn't attend church or synagogue.[12] In their lack of reference to church involvement, the religious broadcasters possibly recognize this social reality. By acquiescing to it and avoiding reference to the necessity of corporate dimensions of religious faith, however, the broadcasters simply reinforce the individualized social conception and extend its application.

Virginia Stem Owens in her book *The Total Image* notes how the mass-cultural acquiescence seen in the paid-time religious broadcasters is part of a broader infatuation by evangelical and fundamentalist Christianity with mass commercial and advertising culture. Lying at the base of it is the adoption of "image advertising" in the promotion of religious faith, the technique by which one paints for the customer "a total picture of the kind of person he would like to be and then makes him believe your product is a necessary part of that picture." The problem, according to Owens, is that the elements of the image created by these religious communicators in their presentation of the Christian faith are less determined by the original Gospel message and more by the expectations created by the commercial world. The goal, or at least the effect, of such image adaptations of the Christian faith to the culture is to erase the distinctions between the Christian message and the cultural environment. Influenced again by the dominant functioning of the mass media, the method employed in mass religious communication lies in demonstrating that acceptance of the religious message involves not a radical change (repentance and conversion) but simply a modification of outlook—a slight cultural readaptation. In this form of religious communication, therefore, similarities between the message and one's existing lifestyle are stressed and affirmed, while dissimilarities are deemphasised. Central to the process appears to be the marketing of prepackaged Christian lifestyles:

To an outsider it must often seem that what commercial Christianity is promoting is a certain certified life-style. . . . The life-style shopper "buys into" the chosen fashion in much the same way and for the same reason that he opts for polyester double-knit or prewashed denim. And the lines of demarcation between the styles, even though both consider themselves Christian, are not friendly frontiers. A certified feminist in her peasant blouse and jeans does not fit among the Total Woman in pegnoirs. An OK guy cannot function as a Bill Gothard father. However all of these can blend inconspicuously into the surroundings of their secular counterparts.[13]

Religious faith cannot be culturally ascetic, but what is absent in these expressions of Christianity is the culturally critical dimension which, in its original expressions elevated not the culturally acceptable but the socially outcast and despised as the paradigms of divine favor and blessedness.[14] This message of elevation of the socially despised is, of course, antithetical to current commercial advertising and the consumer society, though it is likely that should such genuine Christianity become a powerful expression again the industry would mold it into a new image as it did with the counterculture movement in the 1960s.

In his cultural study of Billy Graham, Michael Real provides a case study of the shaping effect the mass media have on those who progress to become its celebrities. Real suggests that while Graham is not solely a media creation, he has succeeded in the media because of basic similarities between his message and the goals of mass-mediated culture. In the process, however, Graham has served to extend the goals of these media and in some way to provide a religious imprimatur for some of its un-Christian cultural aberrations. Real notes in particular Graham's unique identity as the god-father of American nationalism.

The variety of religion that Graham represents is a blend of Reformation Protestantism and economic capitalism. Graham's evangelism fits the dominant political economy in the United States and its allies, providing a combination of individual righteousness and social authoritarianism. One ethical result is that strange Watergate morality of private machiavellianism overlaid with public puritanism.[15]

There have always been different positions held within Christian thought concerning the relationship of the church and the Christian message to the culture within which they find themselves.[16] These different positions have generally acted in correction of the biases present within the other Christian positions. The present paid-time religious broadcasters have lacked any depth of social critique and as such have found themselves in a position of having been used by the more powerful interests of commercial television. It remains to be seen whether other expressions of Christianity will be able to correct some of the imbalance shown by these broadcasters, or whether the power of mass-mediated culture may also successfully neutralize such a challenge to its functioning either by displacement or subsumption.

The power to correct the situation may lie finally in the hands of the local church: those face-to-face, interactive groups in which the essence of Christianity as a genuinely social yet personal religious movement is maintained. The strongest ally of the Christian faith in resisting the shaping effect of mass culture may lie not in a charismatic leader who satisfies the image functions of mass media, but in strong and virile groups of interactive, compassionate, and sensible Christians who genuinely care for each other, who are active in reaching out to need within their environments, and who creatively relate the historic dimensions of their faith to their present experience. These nontechnological, decentralized expressions of Christian community may well be the best defense against the manipulative, homogenizing drive of commercial mass culture.

Notes

1. Noted in Hadden and Swann, *Prime-Time Preachers*, p. 164.
2. Ibid., p. 163.
3. Stephen D. Johnson and Joseph B. Tamney, "The Christian Right and the 1980 Presidential Election," *Journal for the Scientific Study of Religion* 21, 2, pp. 123–131.
4. Comstock, *Television and Human Behavior*, p. 362.

5. Stewart M. Hoover, *The Electronic Giant*, Elgin: The Brethren Press, 1982 p. 125.
6. Horace Newcomb, "Assessing the Violence Profile Studies of Gerbner and Gross: A Humanistic Critique and Suggestion," *Communication Research*, Vol 5, No 3, July 1978, pp. 264–81.
7. Michael R. Real, *Mass-Mediated Culture*, Englewood Cliffs: Prentice-Hall, 1977, p. xi.
8. Lazarsfeld and Merton, "Mass Communication." p. 567.
9. Quoted in Tracy Westen, "Barriers to Creativity," *Journal of Communication*, Spring 1978, pp. 36–42.
10. Kahle, "Religion and Network Programming," p. I.6.
11. Armstrong, *Electric Church*, p. 137.
12. Gallup, "Unchurched American," p. 9.
13. Owens, *Total Image*, pp. 36–37.
14. See particularly the beatitudes, Matthew 5:3–12.
15. Real, *Mass-Mediated Culture*, p. 201.
16. For a useful discussion of these, see H. Richard Niebuhr, *Christ and Culture*, New York: Harper and Row, 1951.

PART III

The Future of
Religious Television

13

The Future of
Current Trends

Central to an understanding of what will be the future of religious television in America is the fact noted in the research on audience sizes: that the audiences for paid-time religious programs as a whole reached a plateau around the year 1977. This fact has important implications for religious television.

First, this fact served to demystify evangelical and fundamentalist television programming. Prior to this, paid-time religious programming had been growing without interruption not only from the early 1970s but also from the beginning of television itself. The fears that emerged during the 1980 national elections were understandable: Was paid-time religious programming the correct model for electronic communication, destined to become the new form of Christianity in the modern age? And was paid-time religious programming on the way to becoming a major force in American society, to the point of replacing established institutions and transforming the nature of religious belief from its traditional diverse personal and corporate, mystical and conceptual, practical and inward expressions to an almost totally individualized, consumer commodity?

The plateau reached in 1977 and the demographic characteristics of the audience attained at this point provide a different picture and a different perspective: that *paid-time religious programming on television is not a universal model of religious faith for the future but is primarily a specialized programming service for a specialized audience.* In 1977, it appears that that segment of the total television audience to a large extent was at saturation point. In that year, the broadcasters had largely reached the type of audience they were going to reach with their current contents and formats. The very specific nature of their content had for the most part excluded other viewing

165

groups. While one may reasonably expect some movement within the total picture it is unlikely that the overall size and characteristics of the paid-time religious program audience will vary significantly. Recent increases in the level of audience sizes of 1977 may be considered variations rather than significant increases.

To understand fully the implications of the characteristic audience of paid-time religious programs, one must consider the historical context of the changes that have taken place in religious broadcasting over the past 15 years. Paid-time religious programming has justified its dominance of the religious television field in recent years by suggesting that with its independent financial resources gained through audience cultivation and support it has been able to overcome the limitations experienced by mainline broadcasters as they worked with the local stations and networks on a public service basis. By strong audience cultivation and solicitation, paid-time religious broadcasters claimed that they have been able to buy their way out of the religious ghetto and exert an influence never before possible in televised religion.

Recent trends in the syndication and audience demographics of paid-time programming suggest that the evangelical and fundamentalist strategy in relation to television has also failed. While the evangelical and fundamentalist broadcasters have been successful in raising money, in building large organizations and support services, in utilizing new technologies, and in providing sophisticated religious programming for evangelical viewers, they have not demonstrated any greater capacity or ability to get their message across to the larger television population.

In the process they may have done considerable damage to the wider movement of religious broadcasting. They have created a situation of injustice in the representation of religious faith on the media of social communication through endorsing lack of representation of the range of religious faith. Their willingness to pay for air-time in competition with religious groups has set a precedent for the television industry and has given the television industry the means for exploitation of differences between religious groups for the industry's own economic advantage. They have reinforced and contributed substantially to the commercialization and consumerization of religious faith.

Some paid-time religious broadcasters now recognize these limitations and see the overcoming of them as the challenge of this new decade for evangelicals. Tom Bisset, an evangelical broadcaster, suggested in an article recently that the challenge of the future for evangelical broadcasting included reaching a greater number of nonevangelicals, speaking prophetically to current social issues, and upgrading program content.[1] Ironically, evangelical broadcasters in the 1950s criticized mainline religious broadcasting for its attempts to do these things and presented themselves and their approach as the answer. What is not readily admitted by evangelicals is that if these qualities were not present in evangelical broadcasting in its zenith, it is unlikely that they will be developed in its wane. What is also not realistically acknowledged is that the current paid-time religious broadcasters have acquired their current audiences by doing as Ben Armstrong has intimated, namely, giving people what they want. It is unlikely that, in the face of declining audiences and increased pressure from an increasing number of other paid-time religious broadcasters seeking the same audience, that broadcasters will begin to change to a less popular form of programming.

Part of the persistent problem has been the paid-time religious broadcasters' unwillingness to take seriously the limitations of television as a means of religious communication. This naive delusion is continued in the renewed expectations being thrust upon cable television as the new mission field, without recognizing also that the same limitations apply. The paid-time religious broadcasters have been so enamored of television's potential that, like lovesick adolescents, they have been blind to its faults. This blindness again reflects the particular emphases of their theological and ethical outlook.

In the light of these limitations, it is interesting to note the recent movements of some of the mainline churches. The United Methodist Church has been attempting for several years to raise funds to finance extensive television programming aimed at its own specific audiences. The Southern Baptist Convention has announced also its intention to purchase its own network of television stations to attempt to recapture some of its own constituents' loyalty. The Roman Catholic Church has begun its own programming network as well.

These efforts appear designed to break into the monopoly held by the independent evangelical organizations, and hold possibilities for restoring some representativeness to religious programming on television. None of the activities, though, has indicated anything of a new strategy to deal with the implications of television programming in general or to counter the demonstrated limitations of religious television communication. They have fallen well into television's mold by acquiescing to television's moral bases: air-time will be given or sold to those who succeed most in meeting television's criteria for attractiveness, competitiveness, and economic ability. The distinctive challenge religious faith could have made to television's functioning within American society—the challenge for commercial television to give representation to socially powerless groups as well as the powerful, and to decentralize television's decision-making processes—has been laid aside by churches in their clamor to protect their own interests and to survive by television's unquestioned rules of economic competitiveness.

The saturation characteristic of paid-time broadcasting of religion has had a second major implication for religious television as a whole. The paid-time broadcasters will now be faced with the need to meet ever-increasing costs and heavy financial commitments with a declining—or at best level—base of financial support. This pressure is greatest for those who are solely dependent on audience support for their existence. With the added pressure on major religious broadcasters now being brought by saturation characteristics and a constant flow of new charismatic figures, there is pressure to find a new thrust. Whether this is possible depends on several unpredictable circumstances.

Much of the growth of evangelical programs in the past was due to the coincidence of its strongly authoritative and traditional message and the confusion felt by many in the wake of the social turmoil of the 1960s. It remains to be seen whether these broadcasters' message will be perceived by many as an adequate answer to some of the problems facing American society as it nears the end of a century: the persistent problems of economics, inflation and unemployment; the growing shortages of energy, water, and space; the changing identity of America in international relations; and the rising threat of nuclear holocaust. In the absence of adequate political answers, or if the religious broadcasters can again affiliate themselves with a vital political movement, they may regain some of the influence that appears to have been lost in the wake of the 1980 elections.

Much of the influence in those elections, however, was derived from the momentum which the broadcasters projected: evangelicalism was seen as a movement that had experienced no setbacks, which was continually expanding in outreach and influence, and which projected an image of continuing in this way until its goals had been achieved. It was this image that aroused emotions, reaction, and to a large extent support. Much of that momentum, though, has now been lost. It is possible that a new momentum may be found through the conception of a new type of broadcasting which captures the public imagination as Oral Roberts did in 1970, or through the emergence of new personalities. In this regard it is interesting to note that many of the original major broadcasters are getting on in years: Oral Roberts, Rex Humbard, Robert Schuller, and Billy Graham will soon have to pass on to others the enterprises which have been built largely on their own personal charisma. Very rarely does a second generation of a charismatic movement retain the vitality of the first. Though each of these major broadcasters appears to have been cultivating one of his male offspring for this purpose, it remains to be seen whether these men can adequately fill their fathers' shoes or even give a new impetus to their fathers' respective foundations.

Much of the influence which the paid-time broadcasters wielded in the past was also due to the novelty of their enterprises and the mystique surrounding their rapid rise. As this novelty wears off, and as the mystique is demystified by social analysis and research, this influence may be further diminished.

Much of the future influence of the paid-time religious broadcasters may also be modified by the opportunities which they are given to exert it. The hold mainline broadcasters had on religious programming in the 1950s and early 1960s was taken out of their hands through the growing commercialization of religious air-time. While the current paid-time religious broadcasters retain the means to continue to purchase air-time, the television industry will determine whether the same amount of air-time will remain available. With the rapid changes taking place in electronic technology and the increasing deregulation of the broadcasting industry, it is difficult to predict how the future of broadcast television will develop.

At this crossroads in their development, the paid-time religious broadcasters appear to be faced with several possible options. One is to maintain the present level of religious content in their programs and to tolerate the inevitable drop in audience and development because of the increasing fragmentation of the religious market. This option appears to be consistent with the evangelical concern for lack of compromise in content—"Woe is me if I preach not the gospel!"

The further segmentation of the market appears to be an increasing possibility. With the mainline bodies beginning to develop their own programming in an attempt to regain the financial support of their own constituents, and the rapidly increasing number of smaller paid-time religious broadcasters making their inroads through the cheaper medium of cable, the already highly segmented audience for religious television is likely to become even more segmented and the battle for the loyalty of supportive viewers even more frantic.

The effects of this decrease in audience for some of the broadcasters could be made more significant because of their theological positions. Because audience loyalty to these programs has been built so much on images of growth and success as indicators of God's direct blessing, cutbacks could have theological as well as psychological effects, producing a further loss of support from loyal viewers. Few people want to back a losing horse, psychologically or theologically. Oral Robert's recent vision of a 900-foot Jesus standing beside his beleagured City of Faith complex could be evidence of the tremendous pressure on broadcasters to maintain an image of divine approval in the presence of considerable and apparent setbacks. This need for evidence of theological approval may result in a constant change of scene within religious broadcasting. Like fashion trends, religious broadcasting may demonstrate the characteristics of continual movements of passing the mantle from the old to ever emerging new charismatic figures.

It is possible, therefore, that some of the paid-time religious broadcasters may show signs of becoming more "established," consolidating basic identities and service functions in order to maintain their audiences similar to an extended congregation, withdrawing their programs from areas that are no longer profitable, and developing as extended independent church organizations in line with their particular theological emphases.

Another option is for audience-supported broadcasters to try to develop alternate bases of revenue in an effort to stabilize their vacillating financial base. Those broadcasters who have previously invested excess income in revenue-producing activities such as their own stations or other industries appear to be in a healthier position than others who have invested in liabilities such as buildings or dependent schools. Unless the broadcaster has already substantially developed such activities, however, it may be too late to consider them an option because of already decreasing reserves and income.

A third option the current paid-time religious broadcasters may choose is to attempt to expand their audience base and thus broaden their range of supporters. One way of doing this is to expand international activities, and there are indications that some broadcasters are pursuing this avenue more aggressively. It is unlikely, though, that the overseas market will be as lucrative or supportive as the American market has been.

Another way to expand one's audience base is to offer a less specific religious content that would appeal to a broader group of Christians or even non-Christians and to promote the cause in less specifically religious terms in order to attract more general financial support. There are some indications that some of the paid-time religious broadcasters are beginning to do this. The Christian Broadcasting Network, for example, has recently expanded the format of the "700 Club" to include among other features a regular segment on home decorating and the decor of luxury hotels and vacation spots. One could observe on occasion the interesting phenomenon of the "700 Club" host carefully restraining an overzealous religious guest in order to maintain the new, less religious format. CBN has also been decreasing the amount of religious programming on its Boston station, even on Sundays, in order to build a larger general audience and thus increase advertising revenue. This is apparently a network-wide strategy to develop an alternate source of income to support the basic religious programming of the network.

While the managerial dynamics behind these changes can be appreciated, the implications for religious programming are profound. One of the persistent criticisms of mainline religious programs made in the past by the evangelicals was that the mainline programs had compromised the gospel message and lacked distinctive Christian content. One of the basic tenets in the formation of National Religious Broadcasters was to protect the right of evangelical broadcasters to preach doctrinal sermons on the air. The evangelicals now appear to have been forced into the same compromise as they perceived the mainline broadcasters had done many years before. However, whereas for the mainline broadcasters their content was a result of theological intent in line with their perception of the appropriate use of television, the evangelicals have been forced into a similar situation almost solely for economic reasons, a factor illustrating again the awesome levelling and censoring power of the commercial television industry.

This problem illuminates again the particular deficiency of the evangelical strategy toward mass communication. While their strength has been in their enthusiasm for preaching and in their technological enterprise, they have been deficient in sound theological reflection on the nature of technology. Any deficiencies or limitations, they consider, are to be overcome by a more appropriate or extended application of further technology: a stance identified by Frederick Ferre as "technolatry," the belief that "every apparent evil brought on by technique is to be countered by yet greater faith in technique."[2] The inherent limitations now being experienced, however, indicate that the upsurge in evangelical broadcasting in the 1970s has not resolved but simply postponed the inevitable confrontation between traditional Christian faith and the technologies of communication.

Notes

1. Tom Bisset, "Religious Broadcasting Comes of Age," *Christianity Today*, September 4, 1981, pp. 33–35.
2. Frederick Ferre, *Shaping the Future*, New York: Harper and Row, 1976, p. 43.

14

A Strategy for the Religious Use of Television

Television must be recognized as a significant form of social communication within American society and one that exerts a major influence on the lives of individuals and groups. As Comstock and his associates note: "Television has introduced a fifth and artificial season to the four natural ones around which people have always organized their lives. . . . It differs from the natural seasons by remaining with us in some guise throughout the year."[1] Television has been documented as having influenced the way in which people perceive social groups and trends, the nature of life and reality, and the way in which people organize and live their lives. If the church is meant to be concerned about what things influence poeple's thought and behavior, it must be actively concerned with television.

A review of the history of religious uses of television suggests that religious television at present is at a crossroads in its development. The evangelical and fundamentalist strategy of building programming on direct audience support and purchasing air-time for religious programming for the purpose of evangelism has been shown to have not succeeded. The paid-time religious programs' audience sizes have levelled off with only a small minority of Americans viewing; their syndication patterns and audience characteristics indicate that they have not been effective in reaching to a great extent outsiders to the Christian faith nor in achieving their theological objectives; and they face mounting financial pressures with a possible decreasing base of support. The actions of some mainline groups in beginning development of their own television ministries pose an added competitive element.

172

Changes within the television industry also suggest a crossroads point for religious television. The deregulation of the television industry carries implications which could affect religious television. The rapidly changing medium of cable television is creating new opportunities and dangers and posing a challenge to the established understanding of broadcast television.

These changes suggest that the present time might be an appropriate one for the churches to develop an approach to communication by television which is both realistic and effective, one which takes seriously both theological intentions of such communication and empirical insights. If there is to be any learning from the past experiences of religious broadcasters, however, future actions must be directed by a well-thought-out strategy rather than mere opportunism or impulse. The religious broadcaster must not only have a clear idea of what he wants to achieve but also have a clear idea of what is achievable through this particular medium. Future planning for religious uses of television should take seriously those insights provided by empirical research both into general television use and effects and into specifically religious television use and effect.

A proposal for elements of such a strategy is presented below. The details within these elements will no doubt be elaborated according to the particular theological and practical emphases of each denomination or tradition, though firm consideration of each element is considered necessary if religious television is to take seriously the realities of television communication and the lessons of the past.

1. The religious broadcaster must articulate the goals of any mass-communication effort, articulating also how the demands of the medium are to be incorporated and how the limitations of the medium are to be compensated.

Much of the problem posed by paid-time religious broadcasters has been due to their reticence to recognize that television is limited in its capacities to communicate the full depth of the Christian message and that television imposes demands on any message communicated by it, demands which shape that message. Future uses of television must be closely controlled and specified so that those demands and limitations do not detract from the integrity of the Christian faith.

The objectives of the religious television program need to be spelled out first in terms of what audience it hopes to target. Research indicates that at present, with only a few exceptions, such definition does not take place in program development. Is a program being aimed at the unchurched, the fringe-churched, or the well-churched? Is a program aimed at children, youth, young families, middle-aged persons, or older persons? Is a program designed for those of lower education or higher education, specific employment status or the unemployed?

There is a need to be realistic in this area. The research indicates that the dominant audience of religious programs on American television is people who are already religiously interested and church attenders. •The more specific the religious content of a program, the more specific this characteristic of the audience becomes. The tenacity of this characteristic has strong roots in the selective nature of American television viewing and the dominant functions that television fulfills in American society. The research indicates that even within this general variable of religious interest, further discrimination is possible: not all religiously interested people are viewers of religious television programs. Religious programs on American television have traditionally been viewed by older rather than younger people; females rather than males; and the less-educated rather than the more-educated. These particular characteristics also have deep roots in the traditional uses made of television by the American population.

•While it is possible to reach a greater unchurched audience by modifying the religious content of programs, the objectives of such programming must be suitably modified also.

Once the audience of a program is defined, the objectives of the program in relation to that audience need to be specified. Are the purposes of the program simply to affirm the status of that person or group in their present situation or to extend them toward a desired status? Is the purpose to present a particular denominational image? Is it to advertise a certain local church? Is it to stimulate counseling follow-up opportunities? Is it simply to maintain a presence for the denomination on television? Is it to raise questions designed to stimulate thought on specific religious issues? Is it to raise money for a particular or general purpose?

Not only does the definition of the specific objectives of a program provide clarification of the best means by which to achieve the objectives, but it provides an externalization of the demands which the television process will impose on that particular communication. This definition opens the possibility for the religious communicator to control the communication rather than letting the television industry do so. It is an indictment on the paid-time religious broadcasters, for example, that while they maintain their stated aims of evangelism and raise substantial amounts of money from viewers for that purpose, the content, syndication, and audiences of their programs are contrary to a genuine evangelical situation.

•The research indicates that the major effect of religious television on audience attitudes toward religion is likely to be one of reinforcement of existing attitudes or the channelling of existing attitudes into closely related areas. Some attitude change is possible and likely through the viewing of religious programs on television. However, the extent of this change is significantly modified by a wide range of social and personal variables such as the functions that are being served for the individual by the attitudes in question; the satisfaction the individual derives from existing attitudes; the strength of existing defense mechanisms and group pressures surrounding those attitudes; patterns of reinforcement for similar attitudes in the past; other alternatives available to the viewer; and the current psychological state of the viewer. These variables act to protect the viewer from demanding changes in attitude and behavior.

It is perhaps not surprising to find that the dominant functions served by current religious programs for the majority of their audiences appear to be personal inspiration, companionship, support, and reinforcement of evangelical beliefs and aspirations. Given the specific characteristics of current paid-time religious programs, determined to a large extent by their need to elicit financial support from viewers, they attract people who are already familiar with and in agreement with the theological and organizational goals of the program.

•The research casts doubt on the validity of the goal of evangelism in the use of television. Evangelism in this regard is defined as establishing contact with those outside the Christian faith, bringing them to a realization of the relevance of the Christian faith for their lives, and establishing them in a process of continuing growth in faith and service within a Christian community. Though television does provide some contact with those who are otherwise religiously uninterested or uncommitted, because of the randomness of television viewing in general or the use of religious television to satisfy other than religious needs, research indicates that religious programs consistently reach only a small and segmented portion of this population. There are also strong pressures on the religious programmer which shape program syndication and content in ways that mitigate against genuine efforts to establish contact with and address relevantly the situation of the religiously unconvinced.

Further, while television in some situations may stimulate an immediate radical change in attitude, emotions, or behavior, alone•it lacks most of the capacities required to maintain the durability of that change or to extend it into other areas of a viewer's behavior. The evidence indicates that even where an unchurched person may have a significant experience of religious faith while viewing television, rarely is that experience extended into an ongoing relationship with a supportive and stimulating Christian interactive community within which other dimensions of the faith experience may be explored and appropriated.

A review of the research suggests that the most effective uses of television in relation to those outside the normal reach of the Christian faith lie within the areas of imparting information about religious issues or organizations, the suggestion of religious questions for consideration by the viewer as applicable to his or her life, and the maintenance of a positive image in relation to general or specific religious issues or organizations. Each of these reflects a *preparatory* rather than a *consummatory* role in relation to the mass communication of religious faith. The Christian faith remains an essentially social or interpersonal as well as an individual experience. As television distances people from each other and tends toward the privatization of experience, its most appropriate uses in religious communication should be in preparing the way for this subsequent interpersonal interaction.

When the preparatory emphasis in religious mass communication is retained, there is also a greater chance of remaining open-ended and thus controlling the dictatorship of the medium. When a consummatory role is sought from religious television, such as in seeking a faith commitment from viewers, the medium exerts strong pressures on how the matter is to be "closed," and essential elements of the Christian faith which cannot be communicated en masse by television are necessarily excluded. The Christian faith loses its sovereignty and is forced into a position of subservience to the limitations of the mass-communication process and structures.

Once the target audience and objectives have been defined, the method by which the two are to be connected must also be defined. What type of program format is desired and what are the implications for that format? Is air-time suitable for the purpose of reaching the target audience available? What are the advantages and limitations of the specific method chosen to achieve the goals? Does the method meet the requirements of theological integrity, empirical validity, and technical competence?

When this process has been worked through, it may be determined that television communication is not adequate to the objectives being sought or the particular population group being targeted, and an alternative communication strategy may be adopted. Such freedom is more possible where the television communication is only one option or aspect of a wider communication strategy. This raises the issue covered by the following strategic element, that of seeing the television ministry within the total context of the wider church.

2. The religious use of television must restore emphasis on its role as a service function to the church, with an articulated strategy indicating how its various activities and objectives are related to the general functions of the church.

This element within an overall strategy has both empirical, theological, and practical foundations.

• Empirically it has been demonstrated that changes in deeply entrenched attitudes and behavior, as are implied in religious conversion and growth, need the cathexis of the personal presence of one who is significant to the person concerned. While lightly held attitudes may be molded by the information and attitudes presented on religious television, significant changes for an individual are generally dependent on the stimulus and reinforcement of another significant individual. Research on religious television and other mass communication of religious faith reinforces this finding. The link between a faith experience gained in front of a television set and subsequent involvement within a local church or Christian group is usually provided by the bridge of personal relationship. Initial changes in attitudes and behavior will tend to regress to the preexisting position unless they are reinforced in this way by rewarding events or group pressures. These findings suggest that if the purpose of religious programs on television is to produce change in the direction of acceptance of the Christian faith, religious broadcasters should take every opportunity possible to relate viewers, and particularly respondents to programs, to interpersonal and interactive Christian groups. The failure of most current broadcasters to do this has tended to minimize the lasting effect they have on the furtherance of the mission of the church.

•Theologically, the message and activities of religious broadcasting are seen as inadequate and incomplete expressions of the Christian message. They lack essential qualities recognized in theological definitions of the church and hence are more properly understood as agencies of the church fulfilling specialist functions. The programs should be in constant liaison with parent churches and under the discipline of these churches. The temptation of religious television programs and organizations is to act and promote themselves as self-sufficient religious entities. This is frequently the case where a broadcast organization has no other constituency except for the viewing audience, or where the viewing audience is the major constituent group. It becomes a major temptation also where the broadcaster is dependent on this constituency of the audience for financial support. The local church has remained the model for the embodiment of the message of the Christian faith since its inception. The lack of liaison between religious broadcasters and local churches both through program content and counseling referral suggests a loss of the service identity and relationship by most current religious broadcasters.

Practically, the resources of the local churches offer valuable support and service opportunities that cannot be provided by the religious broadcasters in their highly centralized and generally impersonal structures. Local churches offer continuity of relationship and support for viewers in need; personal compassion; individualized teaching and stimulation; corporate worship opportunities; and personal discipline and challenge within a supportive group. In the light of this great potential for extension of initial contacts made by broadcasters, it is damaging to the mission of the church that current broadcasters have made so little effort to develop this potential.

3. The church needs to establish a watchdog agency which would conduct continuous research and debate to ensure that the message and practice of religious programs remains congruous with established Christian thought.

Television is not simply a neutral tool of technology available for use by anybody in the way they choose. There are strong pressures within the medium which shape any message communicated by it. These pressures are a combination of several things: the nature of the television technology; the social and economic organization of the television industry; and the dominant social uses made of the medium by individuals and social groups. The combination of these factors has resulted in the historical development of strong common elements in most general television programming.

An analysis of current religious programming on American television reveals the influence of this shaping effect on religious programming also: particular religious traditions are presented to the exclusion of others; there are apparent similarities between the content of many religious programs and general television programming; and there are similarities in religious program formats and content even in programs from a range of different theological traditions and experience.

Television is not a unique situation. Each cultural context in which the Christian faith is expressed plays some part in determining the nature of the expression. Yet any new expression of the gospel must be continually evaluated to determine the extent to which it remains congruous with the gospel's essential message. This process of apologetic and dogmatic has formed the dynamic of the history of Christian thought. The adaptation of the gospel to television is no different: there needs to be a clear and impartial analysis of the message and practices of those programs and organizations that call themselves Christian in order to determine how they stand in relation to the historic tenets of the Christian faith. Where persistent aberrations do occur, they need to be confronted clearly.

Such challenges to religious programs would be most effective if they came either from churches within the same traditions as the broadcaster or from the viewer's own denomination. Where significant challenge comes from those who stand within the same traditions as the broadcaster, the likelihood of theological prejudice is minimized and the broadcaster is more likely to be confronted with the appropriateness of the challenge. Where criticism comes from the viewer's own denomination, the basis of common concern is maximized and the viewer is encouraged to view religious programs critically in order to discern that which is dissonant with other aspects of their faith.

Included in this strategic element is the need for ongoing research on the extent to which goals established for religious uses of television are being achieved. In the past, the tendency has been to undertake little evaluation of the effectiveness of religious broadcasting. If broadcasters are genuinely concerned with achieving certain goals, a continual process of evaluation and redirection will be necessary.

Some areas of immediate research interest should be: To what extent does the content of Christian programs reflect the shaping influence of the television medium? What is the spectrum of effects for Christian television programs and what are the relative frequencies of occurrence of each effect?

What functions do Christian television programs serve for the different segments of their audiences and in what way do these programs fulfill these functions in comparison with the local church? What are the characteristic patterns of Christian television organizations' counseling activities, and how do these relate to other counseling opportunities available to viewers? What may be the long-term effects of current Christian television programs?

4. Religious television programmers need to resolve the issue of program financing.

It has been noted that the major discriminating variable for identifying different types of religious programs is the manner in which they are funded. Because television is a capital-intensive industry, the matter of where the money is to come from is one of central importance, for it has been demonstrated that the source of the finances for religious programming plays a major part in shaping the nature of the program.

The most desirable situation is one in which neither the television station nor the network nor the audience is the primary source of funding. Freedom from dependence on each of these removes a significant pressure in the determination of the nature of programming. Such a situation, though, may be too idealistic for application. In whatever financial situation, however, it is essential that the programmer identify and articulate the demands which are made on the programmer by the source of finance and decide whether these demands are consistent with the theological goals. Failure to do so usually results in indiscriminate asquiescence to prevailing forces, with a consequent modification of one's message.

5. Religious programming on television should exist as only a part of a recognized broader ministry within the television field.

It is possible for a religious group to become too enamored of television programming because of its visibility and ignore other equally important areas of the religious response to television.

The church must concern itself with media education. Christ's concern for individuals enslaved by the products of their sinful condition should be motivation enough for Christians to concern themselves with people today who are increasingly demonstrating the signs of electronic narcosis, with consequent effects of isolation, alienation, fear, abnegation of responsibility, and loss of joy. The answer does not lie in transferring their narcosis from nonreligious to religious programs; it lies in liberation from dependence on mediated experience and escapist material. As one of the few remaining personal interactive communities within society, the church has a responsibility and unique opportunity to embody the redemptive love of Christ.

In line with this, ♦Christians should develop a strong critique of television content in general in order to counter the dehumanizing and humanly destructive aspects of television programming. While some attention has been drawn in recent years to the Christian critique of sex and violence in television programming, the critique must also include other dehumanizing aspects such as consumerism, limited access for such groups as minorities and older people, and the continuing commercial exploitation of children and youth. The effectiveness of this critique is substantially weakened when Christian programs, in their effort to be seen as relevant and sophisticated, adopt the same images of glamour and success.

A critique should also focus on the relative absence of sensible and informed religious faith from general programming. Although slightly less than half of the American population are church attenders, rarely in general television programming is church attendance portrayed as a desirable attribute; rarely are religious people or representatives presented in other than negatively stereotyped portrayals; and rarely is the religious perspective presented favorably. Much more effective than all the religious programs presented in "ghetto hours" may be the frequent portrayal of an attractive, sensible, and compassionate religious person in general television drama. Religious programmers should also seek other opportunities to increase the presence of religious persons on television programming, such as on news programs and talk shows. Given the dominant functions of television in status conferral and image creation, religious uses of television may more effectively be achieved through secular programming than through religious programming.

Religious broadcasters should also be aware of the importance of working in television as advocates for those who are otherwise powerless. The Christian approach to television will be deficient if all that is attempted and achieved is the furtherance of its own particular interests. If Christian programming is to bear the mark of integrity it must be supported also by an active program of action for equity and justice on behalf of those who lack the social and economic power to act on their own behalf.

This study has suggested that the Christian use of television needs to be significantly demythologized in relation to its ability to contribute to the ongoing mission of the church, and restored to a more realistic appreciation of what may be achieved through programming. In 1979 television researcher George Comstock, in assessing the impact and achievements of the educational television series "Sesame Street" observed that, "We simply do not know what we thought we did, but the lesson appears to be that too much can be expected from a mass medium even when, by its own terms, it is performing superbly."[2] Religious media practitioners have frequently been hypnotized by the potential of television and lost sight of the particular part which it may play within the total mission and communication activity of the church. It is hoped that through this study a more realistic understanding of the part to be played by television communication within the total life of the church may have been attained.

It has been indicated that there is also the need for significant changes within the present structure of religious television, both in terms of integrity of message and practice, in representativeness of a diversity of religious traditions and viewpoints, and in the relation of communication efforts to the wider work of the church. Realistically, it must be noted that there are powerful and vested interests which militate against such changes. Within a broader perspective, George Comstock has noted the pressures which resist change even when that change is perceived by many to be necessary. His comments are apt also for religious television.

The system is likely to continue much as it is for reasons of sociology and politics. A society does not dismantle its major institutions in the absence of public displeasure and usually that displeasure must reach the level of fury for such transformations to occur. . . . Furthermore, the present system has created in the broadcasters which benefit from it a very powerful set of vested interests opposed to change.[3]

We have seen, however, that internal and external changes may have placed religious broadcasting at a crossroads at which constructive change may be timely. It is the opinion of this writer that reasonable and constructive change is more likely to occur, and to be more effective in its occurrence, if analysis, debate, and action are based not merely on opinion and speculation but on researched and informed insight. It is hoped that through this work a basis may be laid for a more accurate understanding of the effects and effectiveness of the religious use of television and a more informed consideration of its future directions. The sustaining theological motive for this effort is reflected by H. Richard Niebuhr in his discussion of the historic debate on the relationship of faith and culture:

It is helpful to recall that the repeated struggles of Christians with this problem have yielded no single Christian answer, but only a series of typical answers which together, for faith, represent phases of the strategy of the militant church in the world. . . . The belief which lies back of this effort, however, is the conviction that Christ as living Lord is answering the question in the totality of history and life in a fashion which transcends the wisdom of all his interpreters yet employs their partial insights and their necessary conflicts.[4]

Notes

1. Comstock et al., *Television and Human Behavior*, p. 1.
2. George Comstock, "A Critical Look at Television and Learning: A Review of *Sesame Street Revisited*," *NCCT Forum*, Fall 1979, pp. 37–38.
3. George Comstock, "The Role of Social and Behavioral Science in Policy-making for Television," *Journal of Social Issues* 32, 4, 1976, pp. 174–75.
4. H. Richard Niebuhr, *Christ and Culture*, New York: Harper & Row, 1951, p. 2.

Bibliography

Allen, Robert J. "Catholic Social Doctrine in National Network Catholic Television Programs in the U.S., 1951–68." Ph.D. dissertation, New York University, 1972.

Armstrong, Ben, ed. *Annual Directory of Religious Broadcasting, 1979*. Morristown, N.J.: National Religious Broadcasters, 1979.

———. *The Electric Church*. Nashville: Thomas Nelson, 1979.

Arn, Win. "A Church Growth Look at 'Here's Life, America.'" *Church Growth: America* (January/February 1977): 4–30.

———. "Mass Evangelism—The Bottom Line." *Church Growth: America* (January/February 1978): 4–16.

Avery, Robert K. "Adolescents' Use of Mass Media." *American Behavioral Scientist* 23 (September/October 1979): 53–70.

Bachman, John W. *The Church in the World of Radio-Television*. New York: Association Press, 1960.

Bailey, Edward J. "An Analysis of Respondents to 'Herald of Truth' Radio and Television Programs." M.S. thesis, Iowa State University, 1972.

Ball, Samuel. "Methodological Problems in Assessing the Impact of Television Programs" *Journal of Social Issues* 32 (1976): 8–17.

Bamberger, Stefan. "Reflections on the Ecclesiological Aspect of Group Media." In *Multimedia International Yearbook, 1978*, pp. 5–18. Rome: Multimedia International, 1978.

Barnouw, Eric. *Tube of Plenty: The Evolution of American Television*. New York: Oxford University Press, 1975.

Baum, Gregory, and Greeley, Andrew, eds. *Communication in the Church* (Concilium Series: Religion in the Seventies), A Crossroad Book. New York: The Seabury Press, 1978.

Benson, Dennis. *Electric Evangelism*. Nashville: Abingdon, 1973.

Berckman, Edward M. "The 'Old Time Gospel Hour' and Fundamentalist Paradox." *Christian Century* 95 (March 29, 1978): 333–37.

Bethell, Tom. "The Common Man and the Electric Church." *Harpers* (April 1978): 86–90.

Berelson, Bernard, and Steiner, Gary A. *Human Behavior: An Inventory of Scientific Findings.* New York: Harcourt, Brace and World, 1964.

Bettinghaus, Erwin P. *Persuasive Communication.* New York: Holt Rinehart and Winston, 1968.

Bibby, Reginald W., and Brinkerhoff, Merlin B. "The Circulation of the Saints: A Study of People Who Join Conservative Churches." *Journal for the Scientific Study of Religion* 12 (September 1973): 273–83.

Biernatzki, W. E. *Catholic Communication Research: Topics and a Rationale.* London: Research Facilitator Unit for Social Communication, 1978.

Billy Graham Evangelistic Association and Related Ministries. *Annual Report, 1978.* Minneapolis: Billy Graham Evangelistic Association, 1978.

Bisset, J. Thomas. "Religious Broadcasting: Assessing the State of the Art." *Christianity Today* 24 (December 12, 1980): 28–31.

———. "Religious Broadcasting Comes of Age." *Christianity Today* 25 (September 4, 1981): 33–35.

Bloesch, Donald. *Essentials of Evangelical Theology.* Vol. 1, *God, Authority and Salvation.* San Francisco: Harper and Row, 1978.

Bluck, John. *Beyond Neutrality, A Christian Critique of the Media.* Risk Books Series, No. 3. Geneva: World Council of Churches, 1978.

Bluem, A. William. *Religious Television Programs: A Study of Relevance.* New York: Hastings House, 1969.

Broadcast and Film Commission, National Council of the Churches of Christ. "Frontiers of Faith—Report of Research." New York, 1966. (Mimeographed)

———. "The Message and the Media: Co-operation in Mass Communication." New York, n.d. (Mimeographed)

Broadcast Institute of North America. *Religious Programming on Television: An Analysis of a Sample Week.* New York: Broadcast Institute of North America, 1973.

Brown, James A. "A History of Roman Catholic Church Policies Regarding Commercial Radio and Television Broadcasting in the U.S., 1920 through 1961." Ph.D. dissertation, University of Southern California, 1970.

Brown, Robert McAfee. *Frontiers for the Church Today.* New York: Oxford University Press, 1973.

Brunner, Emil. *The Divine Imperative.* Philadelphia: Westminster Press, 1947.

Buddenbaum, Judith M. "The Audience for Religious Television Programs." M.A. thesis, Indiana University, 1979.

Butler, Phill. "The Christian Use of Radio and Television." *Interlit* (December 1977): 2–15.

Buursma, Bruce. "Retiring Communicator Targets Television Evangelists." *National Catholic Reporter* (April 6, 1979): 4.

Carter, Betsy. "The Lord's Network." *Newsweek* (March 20, 1978): 80–81.

Cartwright, Dorwin. "Some Principles of Mass Persuasion: Selected Findings of Research on the Sale of U. S. War Bonds." *Human Relations* 2 (July 1949): 253–67.

Casmir, Fred L. "A Telephone Survey of Religious Program Preferences among Listeners and Viewers in Los Angeles." *Central States Speech Journal* 10 (Spring 1959): 31–38.

Chaffee, Steven M. "Television and Adolescent Aggressiveness (Overview)." In

Television and Social Behavior. Vol. 3, *Television and Adolescent Aggressiveness*, pp. 1–34, edited by G. A. Comstock and E. A. Rubenstein. Washington: Government Printing Office, 1972.

Chambers, Curtis A. "An Informal Review of Certain Contemporary Religious Uses of Television: A Report on a Sabbatical Study Project." October 29, 1979. (Mimeographed)

Children and Television: Senate Standing Committee on Education and Arts Inquiry into the Impact of Television on the Development and Learning Behaviour of Children. Canberra: Australian Government Publishing Service, 1978.

Christian Broadcasting Network. "Monthly Statistical and Activity Reports, October 1977 to September 1979." Boston. (Mimeographed)

Chu, Godwin C., and Schramm, Wilbur. *Learning from Television: What the Research Says.* Washington: National Association of Educational Broadcasters, 1968.

Communications Research, Corporation for Public Broadcasting. *The Effect of Television on People's Lives: A Qualitative Study.* Washington: Corporation for Public Broadcasting, 1978.

Comstock, George A. "A Critical Look at Television and Learning: A Review of *Sesame Street Revisited.*" NCCT Forum 2 (Fall 1979): 37–38.

———. *The Evidence on Television Violence.* Santa Monica: The Rand Corporation, 1976.

———. "The Impact of Television on American Institutions." *Journal of Communication* 28 (Spring 1978): 12–28.

———. "The Role of Social and Behavioral Science in Policymaking for Television." *Journal of Social Issues* 32 (4, 1976): 157–76.

Comstock, George, Chaffee, Steven, Katzman, Nathan, McCombs, Maxwell, and Roberts, Donald. *Television and Human Behavior.* New York: Columbia University Press, 1978.

Comstock, George, with the assistance of F. G. Christen, M. L. Fisher, R. C. Quarles, and W. D. Richards. *Television and Human Behavior: The Key Studies.* Santa Monica: The Rand Corporation, 1975.

Coon, Roger W. "The Public Speaking of Dr. William A. Fagal of 'Faith for Today:' America's First National Television Pastor." 2 vols. Ph.D. dissertation, Michigan State University, 1969.

Cox, Harvey. "Bad News for the Good News." *The American Baptist* (January 1979): 2–3.

———. *The Seduction of the Spirit: The Use and Misuse of People's Religion.* New York: Simon and Schuster, 1973.

Dabney, Dick. "God's Own Network." *Harpers* (August 1980): 33–52.

Davis, R. "Television and the Older Adult." *Journal of Broadcasting* 15 (1971): 153–59.

Davis, R., Edwards, A., Bartel, D. J., and Martin, D. "Assessing Television Viewing Behavior of Older Adults." *Journal of Broadcasting* 20 (1976): 69–76.

De Fleur, Melvin, and Ball-Rokeach, Sandra. *Theories of Mass Communication*, 4th ed. New York: Longman, 1982.

Dennis, J. L. "An Analysis of the Audience of Religious Radio and Television Programs in the Detroit Metropolitan Area." Ph.D. dissertation, University of Michigan, 1962.

Dick, Donald. "Religious Broadcasting 1920–65; A Bibliography." *Journal of Broadcasting*, 9 (1965), pp. 249–79, 10 (1976), pp. 163–80, 257–76.

Dimmick, John W., McGain, Thomas A., and Bolton, W. Theodore. "Media Use and the Life Span: Notes on Theory and Method." *American Behavioral Scientist* 23 (September/October 1979): 7–31.

"Displaying Crystal." *Eternity* (March 1980): 14.

Donigan, Robert W. "A Descriptive Analysis of the Effectiveness of Broadcasting by the Church of Jesus Christ of Latter Day Saints in the Northern States Mission Area." M.A. thesis, Brigham Young University, 1964.

Dudley, Carl S. *Where Have all our People Gone? New Choices for Old Churches.* New York: Pilgrim Press, 1979.

Dulles, Avery, *The Church Is Communications.* Rome: Multimedia International, 1971.

Ellens, J. Harold. *Models of Religious Broadcasting.* Grand Rapids: W. B. Eerdmans, 1974.

————. "Program Format in Religious Television: A History and Analysis of Program Format in Nationally Distributed Denominational Religious Television Broadcasting in the United States of America, 1950–70." Ph.D. dissertation, Wayne State University, 1970.

Emery, Fred and Emery, Merrelyn. *A Choice of Futures: To Enlighten or Inform.* Canberra: Center for Continuing Education, Australian National University, 1975.

Engel, James F. *Contemporary Christian Communications.* Nashville: Thomas Nelson, 1979.

————. "A Pilot Research Study of Channel 38, WCFC, Chicago." Wheaton: Wheaton College Graduate School, 1979. (Mimeographed)

Epstein, Edward J. *News from Nowhere: Television and the News.* New York: Random House, 1973.

Fant, Charles. "Televising Presidential Conventions, 1952–80." *Journal of Communication.* 3 (Autumn 1980): 130–39.

Federal Communication Commission. "Submission by the Communications Committee of the United States Catholic Conference and Others in the Matter of Amendment of the Commission's Rules Concerning Program Definition for Commercial Broadcast Stations by Adding a New Program Type Community Service and Expanding the Public Affairs Program Category and Other Related Matters." BC Docket No. 78–335, RM-2709, 1979.

Ferre, Frederick. *Shaping the Future.* New York: Harper and Row, 1976.

"Financial Report, 'Hour of Power' Television, 10th Anniversary Year, 1970–80." (Brochure)

Fore, William. *Image and Impact: How Man Comes Through in the Mass Media.* New York: Friendship Press, 1970.

————. "Mass Media's Mythic World: At Odds with Christian Values." *Christian Century* 94 (January 19, 1977): 32–38.

————. "A Short History of Religious Broadcasting." In *Religious Television Programs: A Study of Relevance*, pp. 203–211, edited by A. William Bluem. New York: Hastings House, 1969.

————. "There is No Such Thing as a TV Pastor." *TV Guide* (July 19, 1980): 15–17.

Frady, Marshall. *Billy Graham: A Parable of American Righteousness.* Boston: Little, Brown, 1979.

Frank, Ronald E., and Greenberg, Marshall G. *The Public's Use of Television: Who Watches and Why.* Beverly Hills: Sage Publications, 1980.

Friendly, Fred W. *Due to Circumstances Beyond Our Control.* New York: Vintage Books, 1968.

Gerbner, George, with Kathleen Connoly. "Television as New Religion." *New Catholic World* (May/April 1978): 52–56.

Gerbner, George and Gross, Larry. "Living with Television: The Violence Profile." *Journal of Communication* 26 (Spring 1976): 173–99.

Gerbner, George, Gross, Larry, Jackson-Beeck, Marilyn, Jeffries-Fox, Suzanne, and Signorielli, Nancy. "Cultural Indicators: Violence Profile No. 9." *Journal of Communication* 28 (Summer 1978): 176–207.

Gerbner, George, Gross, Larry, and Melody, William, eds. *Communications Technology and Social Policy: Understanding the New "Cultural Revolution."* New York: John Wiley and Sons, 1973.

Gerbner, George, Gross, Larry, Morgan, Michael, and Signorielli, Nancy. *Violence Profile No. 11: Trends in Network Television Drama and Viewer Conceptions of Reality, 1967–79.* Philadelphia: Annenberg School of Communications, University of Pennsylvania, 1980.

Gerbner, George, Gross, Larry, Signirielli, Nancy, Morgan, Michael, and Jackson-Beeck, Marilyn. "The Demonstration of Power: Violence Profile No. 10." *Journal of Communication* 29 (Summer 1979): 177–96.

Goethals, Gregor T. *The TV Ritual: Worship at the Video Altar.* Boston: Beacon Press, 1981.

Gorfain, Louis. "Pray TV." *New York* (October 6, 1980): 47–57.

Graham, Billy. *World Aflame.* Garden City: Doubleday, 1965.

Graney, Marshall, and Graney, Edith. "Communications Activity Substitutions in Aging." *Journal of Communication* 24 (Autumn 1974): 88–89.

Graves, S. B. "Television's Impact on the Cognitive and Affective Development of Minority Children." Paper presented at University of California, Los Angeles, 1978.

Griffin, Emory A. *The Mind Changers: The Art of Christian Persuasion.* Wheaton: Tyndale House Publishers, 1976.

Griswold, C. T., and Schmitz, C. H.. *How You Can Broadcast Religion.* New York: National Council of Churches of Christ in the U.S.A., 1957.

Grounds, Vernon. *Revolution and the Christian Faith.* Philadelphia: Lippincott, 1971.

Hadden, Jeffrey. "Some Sociological Reflections on the Electronic Church." Paper presented at the Electronic Church Consultation, New York University, February 6–7, 1980.

Hadden, Jeffrey, and Swann, Charles. *Primetime Preachers: The Rising Power of Televangelism.* Reading, Mass: Addison-Wesley, 1981.

Halloran, James D. "Communication and Change." *WACC Journal* 21 no. 4 (1974): 34–41.

Hanford, William J. "A Rhetorical Study of the Radio and Television Speaking of Bishop Fulton J. Sheen." Ph.D. dissertation, Wayne State University, 1965.

Hart, Nelson. "Bishop Sheen's Television Techniques." *Today's Speech* (September 1962): 18–21.

Hegstad, Roland. "Washington for Jesus—Really?" *Liberty* (September/October 1980): 3–27.

Hemphill, Paul. "Praise the Lord—and Cue the Cameraman." *TV Guide* (August 12, 1978): 4–9.

Henry, Carl F. H. "Evangelicals: Out of the Closet but Going Nowhere?" *Christianity Today* 24 (January 1980): 16–22.

Hilton, Clifford T. "The Influence of Television Worship Services on the Irvington Presbyterian Church, Indianapolis, Indiana." D.Min. thesis, Drew University, 1980.

Hoge, Dean, and Roozen, David. *Understanding Church Growth and Decline, 1950–78.* New York: Pilgrim Press, 1979.

Holt, B. Russell. "Superbowl Christianity." *Ministry* (May 1980): 19.

Hoover, Stewart M. *The Electronic Giant: A Critique of the Telecommunications Revolution from a Christian Perspective.* Elgin: The Brethren Press, 1982.

Independent Broadcasting Authority. *Lonely People and the Media.* London: Independent Broadcasting Authority, 1978.

Jackson, B. J., ed. *Communication for Churchmen.* Nashville: Abingdon.
  Vol 1: *Communication Learning for Churchmen*, 1968.
  Vol 2: *Television-Radio/Film for Churchmen*, 1969.
  Vol 3: *Audiovisual Facilities and Equipment for Churchmen*, 1970.

Jacquet, Constant H., Jr., ed. *Yearbook of American and Canadian Churches, 1980.* Nashville: Abingdon, 1980.

Jennings, Ralph M. "Policies and Practices of Selected National Religious Bodies as Related to Broadcasting in the Public Interest." Ph.D. dissertation, New York University, 1968.

Johnson, Daniel L. "Electronic Fundamentalism: Supply and Demand." *Christian Century* 99 (May 28, 1980): 606–7.

Johnson, Nicholas. "The Careening of America." *The Humanist* (July/August, 1972).

———. *How to Talk Back to Your Television Set.* Boston: Little, Brown, 1967.

Johnson, Stephen D. and Tamney, Joseph B. "The Christian Right and the 1980 Presidential Election." *Journal for the Scientific Study of Religion,* 21 (2, 1982): 123–31.

Johnson, Stuart. "Contemporary Communications Theory and the Distribution Patterns of Evangelical Radio Programs." Ph.D. dissertation, North-western University, 1978.

Johnstone, Ronald L. "Who Listens to Religious Radio Broadcasts Anymore?" *Journal of Broadcasting* 16 (Winter 1971–72): 91–102.

Kahle, Roger. "Religion and Network Television." M.S. thesis, Columbia University, 1970.

Katz, Elihu. "The Two-Step Flow of Communication: An Up-to-Date Report on an Hypothesis." *Public Opinion Quarterly* 21 (Spring 1957): 61–78.

———, Blumler, Jay G., and Gurevitch, Michael. "Uses of Mass Communication by the Individual." In *Mass Communication Research: Major Issues and Future Directions,* edited by W. P. Davidson and F. T. C. Yu. New York: Praeger, 1974.

————, Gurevitch, Michael, and Haas, Hadassah. "On the Use of Mass Media for Important Things," *American Sociological Review* 38 (April 1973): 164–81.

————, and Lazarsfeld, Paul F. *Personal Influence: The Part Played by People in the Flow of Mass Communication.* Glencoe: The Free Press, 1955.

Keckley, Paul H., Jr. "A Qualitative Analytic Study of the Image of Organized Religion in Prime Time Television Drama." Ph.D. dissertation, Ohio State University, 1974.

Kehl, D. D. "Peddling the Power and the Promises." *Christianity Today* 24 (March 1980): 16–19.

Kelman, Herbert C. "Processes of Opinion Change." *Public Opinion Quarterly* 25 (Spring 1961): 57–78.

Klos, Frank. "A Study of the Origin, Utilization, and Impact of the 'Davey and Goliath' Series 1959–77, and Its Present Effectiveness in Teaching Religious Values to Children." Ed.D. dissertation, Temple University, 1979.

Knopf, Terry Ann. "Advertising for Priests." *Boston Globe* (March 24, 1980): 21–22.

Kuhns, William. *The Electronic Gospel.* New York: Herder and Herder, 1969.

Lacey, Linda-Jo. "The Electric Church: An FCC 'Established Institution?'" *Federal Communications Law Journal* 31 (No. 2, Spring 1979): 235–75.

Lasswell, Harold D. "The Structure and Function of Communication in Society." In *The Communication of Ideas*, pp. 37–52, edited by Lyman Bryson. New York: Institute of Religious and Social Studies, 1948.

Lazarsfeld, Paul F., and Merton, Robert K. "Mass Communication, Popular Taste and Organized Social Action." In *The Communication of Ideas*, pp. 95–118, edited by Lyman Bryson. New York: Institute for Religious and Social Studies, 1948.

Limburg, Val E. "An Analysis of Relationships between Religious Broadcasting Programming Objectives and Methods of Presentation Used by Selected Major Religious Program Producers, as Compared with the Church of Jesus Christ of Latter Day Saints." M.A. thesis, Brigham Young University, 1964.

Macquarrie, John. *Principles of Christian Theology.* London: SCM, 1966.

Mander, Jerry. "Four Arguments for the Elimination of Television." *Co-Evolution Quarterly* (Winter 1977–78): 39–52.

Mann, James, with Sarah Peterson. "Preachers in Politics: Decisive Force in '80?" *U.S. News and World Report* (September 15, 1980): 24–26.

Market Research Group. *National CBN Partner Survey.* Southfield, Mich.: Market Research Group, 1978.

————. *National Former '700 Club' Partner Survey.* Southfield: Market Research Group, 1978.

————. *Report on '700 Club' Finances and Direct Mail Focus Group Panel Discussions, Detroit, Michigan.* Southfield: Market Research Group: 1978.

Marsh, Spencer. *God, Man, and Archie Bunker.* New York: Harper and Row, 1975.

Martin, William. "The Birth of a Media Myth." *The Atlantic* (June 1981): 9–16.

Marty, Martin. "The Electronic Church." *Missouri in Perspective* (March 27, 1978): 5.

————. *The Improper Opinion: Mass Media and the Christian Faith.* Philadelphia: Westminster Press, 1961.

————. "The Invisible Religion." *Presbyterian Survey* (May 1979): 13.

————. "Needed: A Christian Interpretation of the Media World." *Lutheran World* 19 (No.2, 1972): 105–14.

Matthews, Donald C. "Commercial Religion and the Public Interest." Paper presented at the Electronic Church Consultation, New York University, February 6–7, 1980.

Mayer, Allan J. "A Tide of Born-Again Politics." *Newsweek* (September 15, 1980): 28–36.

McAnany, Emile G. "Television: Mass Communication and Elite Controls." *Society* (September/October 1975): 41–46.

McBrien, Richard P. "The Electronic Church: A Catholic Theologian's Perspective." Paper presented at the Electronic Church Consultation, New York University, February 6–7, 1980.

McCombs, M. E., and Shaw, D. L. "The Agenda-Setting Function of the Mass Media."*Public Opinion Quarterly* 36 (1972): 176–87.

McLoughlin, William G. *Revivals, Awakenings, and Reform*. Chicago: University of Chicago Press, 1978.

McLuhan, Marshall. *Understanding Media*. New York: Signet Books, 1964.

Megill, Virgil. "An Analysis of Religious Programming on Television." In *Religious Broadcasting Sourcebook*, rev. ed., pp. D-17-18, edited by Ben Armstrong. Morristown: National Religious Broadcasters, 1978.

————. "The Origins of National Religious Broadcasters." In *Religious Broadcasting Sourcebook*, rev. ed., pp. N-1-2, edited by Ben Armstrong. Morristown: National Religious Broadcasters, 1978.

Menendez, Albert J. "Who Are the Evangelicals?" *Christianity Today* 22 (January 1978): 42.

Mennonite Advertising Agency. "Report of Family Life Television Spots—Series II, 1970." Harrisonburg, Va.: Mennonite Advertising Agency, 1970.

Mielke, Sharon. "Press Told to Aid Powerless." *United Methodist Reporter* (May 23, 1980): 3.

Moberg, David O. "Fundamentalists and Evangelicals in Society." In *The Evangelicals*, edited by David Wells and John Woodbridge. Grand Rapids: Baker Book House, 1977.

Montgomery, Jim. "The Electric Church." *The Wall Street Journal* (May 19, 1978): 1,29.

Moyer, Ivan. "A Study of Audience Reactions to Religious Television Programs on Basis of Viewer's Socio-Economic Status." M.A. thesis, Pennsylvania State University, 1966.

Muggeridge, Malcolm. *Christ and the Media*. Grand Rapids: W. B. Eerdmans, 1977.

Nelson, J. Robert. *Criterion for the Church*. London: Epworth Press, 1963.

Newbigin, Lesslie. *The Household of God: Lectures on the Nature of the Church*. London: SCM Press, 1953.

Newcomb, Horace. "Assessing the Violence Profile Studies of Gerbner and Gross: A Humanistic Critique and Suggestion." *Communication Research* 5 (July 1978): 264–81.

————. "Toward a Television Aesthetic." In *Television: The Critical View*, pp. 273–89. New York: Oxford University Press, 1976.

Nichols, Joseph B. "Religious and Iconic Implications of Televised Corporate Oil

Advertising, 1969–74." M.A. thesis, Annenberg School of Communication, University of Pennsylvania, 1977.

Niebuhr, H. Richard. *Christ and Culture*. New York: Harper and Row, 1951.

Ong, Walter. "Communication Media and the State of Theology." *Cross Currents* 19 (Fall 1969): 462–80.

Owens, Virginia Stem. *The Total Image or Selling Jesus in the Modern Age*. Grand Rapids: W. B. Eerdmans, 1980.

Park, Jeff. "PTL Encounters the FCC: Truthful Probe or Witch Hunt?" *Action* (March 1980): 10–14.

Parker, Everett C. "Christian Communication and Secular Man." New York: 1966. (Mimeographed)

———. *Religious Television: What to Do and How*. New York: Harper and Bros., 1961.

Parker, Everett C., Barry, David W., and Smythe, Dallas W. *The Television-Radio Audience and Religion*. New York: Harper and Row, 1955.

Pierard, Richard V. *The Unequal Yoke: Evangelical Christianity and Political Conservatism*. Philadelphia: J. B. Lippincott Co., 1970.

Plowman, Edward E. "Carter's Presence Confirms Clout of Evangelical Broadcasters." *Christianity Today* 24 (February 1980): 268–69.

Pool, Ithiel de Sola. "Direct-Broadcast Satellite and Cultural Integrity." *Society* (September/October 1975): 47–56.

———. "The Mass Media and Politics in the Modernization Process." In *Communication and Political Development*, pp. 234–53, edited by Lucien W. Pye. Princeton: Princeton University Press, 1963.

Princeton Religion Research Center and the Gallup Organization, Inc. "Evangelical Christianity in the United States: National Parallel Surveys of General Public and Clergy." Study conducted for *Christianity Today*. Princeton: Princeton Religion Research Center, 1978.

———. "The Unchurched American." Study conducted for the Religious Coalition to Study Backgrounds, Values and Interests of Unchurched Americans. Princeton: Princeton Religion Research Center, 1978.

"PTL Counseling." Leaflet published by the PTL Network, Charlotte, N.C. n.d.

Quebedeaux, Richard. *The Worldly Evangelicals*. New York: Harper and Row, 1978.

———. *The Young Evangelicals*. New York: Harper and Row, 1974.

The Radio and Television Commission of the Southern Baptist Convention. "Audited Financial Statements and Other Financial Information." Fort Worth, September 30, 1979. (Mimeographed)

———. "Program Response Reports, October 1978 to September 1979." Fort Worth. (Mimeographed).

Real, Michael R. *Mass-Mediated Culture*. Englewood Cliffs, N.J.: Prentice-Hall, 1977.

"Rex Humbard Ministry Costs." Brochure of the Rex Humbard Ministry. n.d.

Rice, Berkeley. "Call-In Therapy: Reach Out and Shrink Someone." *Psychology Today* (December 1981): 88.

Rice, Phyllis Mather. "Interview with Martin Marty." *Your Church* (November/December 1979): 5–6, 48–49.

———. "Interview with Pat Robertson." *Your Church* (May/June, 1979): 5–15.

Ringe, R. "An Analysis of Selected Personality and Behavioral Characteristics which Affect Receptivity to Religious Broadcasting." Ph.D. dissertation, Ohio State University, 1969.

Robinson, Haddon W. "A Study of the Audience for Religious Radio and Television Broadcasts in Seven Cities throughout the U.S." Ph.D. dissertation, University of Illinois, 1964.

Robinson, J. P. "Television's Impact on Everyday Life: Some Cross-National Evidence." In *Television and Social Behavior.* Vol 4, *Television in Day-to-Day Life: Patterns of Use,* pp. 410–31, edited by E. A. Rubenstein, G. A. Comstock, and J. P. Murray. Washington: Government Printing Office, 1972.

———. "Toward Defining the Functions of Television." In *Television and Social Behavior.* Vol. 4, *Television in Day-to-Day Life: Patterns of Use,* pp. 568–603, edited by E. A. Rubenstein, G. A. Comstock, and J. P. Murray. Washington: Government Printing Office, 1972.

Rockenstein, W. H. "Children and Television: An Experimental Study of the Reactions of Children in the Fifth, Sixth, Seventh, and Eighth Grades in Monongalia County, West Virginia, to Children's Television Programming." Ph.D. dissertation, Northwestern University, 1966.

Romero, Charles I. "An Analysis of Organization in Selected Television Addresses of Bishop Fulton Sheen." M.A. thesis, University of Arizona, 1962.

Sanders, Frederick B. "A History of the Lutheran Television Production 'This Is the Life' from 1952 to 1958." Ph.D. dissertation, University of Michigan, 1961.

Saunders, Lowell S. "The National Religious Broadcasters and the Availability of Commercial Radio Time." Ph.D. dissertation, University of Illinois, 1968.

Schramm, Wilbur. "Aging and Mass Communication." In *Aging and Society.* Vol. 2, *Aging and the Professions,* pp. 352–75, edited by Matilda White Riley, John W. Riley, Jr., and Marilyn E. Johnson. New York: Russell Sage Foundation, 1969.

———. *Mass Media and National Development.* Stanford: Stanford University Press, 1964.

Schramm, Wilbur, and Roberts, Donald F. *The Process and Effects of Mass Communication,* rev. ed. Urbana: University of Illinois Press, 1971.

Schreiber, Elliot S., and Boyd, Douglas A. "How the Elderly Perceive Television Commercials." *Journal of Communication* 30 (Winter 1980): 62–70.

Sheen, Fulton J. *Treasure in Clay: The Autogiography of Fulton J. Sheen.* Garden City: Doubleday, 1980.

Sholes, Jerry. *Give Me That Prime-Time Religion.* New York: Hawthorn Books, 1979.

Shriver, Donald. "The Temptation of Self-Righteousness." *Christian Century* (October 22, 1980): 1002.

"Signs of Trouble in Southern Baptist Convention." *Context* (February 1, 1978): 1.

Singer, J. L., and Singer, D. C. "Can Television Stimulate Imaginative Play?" *Journal of Communication* 26 (Autumn 1976): 74–80.

Solt, David C. "A Study of the Audience Profile for Religious Broadcasts in Onondaga County." Ph.D. dissertation, Syracuse University, 1971.

"Some True Beliefs about Religious Programming." *P. D. Cue* (April 1977): 8–14.

Spargur, Ronn. "Can Churches Break the Prime-Time Barrier?" *Christianity Today* 14 (January 16, 1970): 3–4.

Stager, Robert C. "A Critical Analysis of Bishop Fulton J. Sheen's Use of Invention in Selected Radio and Television Talks Regarding Communism from 1936 to 1953." M.A. thesis, Bowling Green University, 1955.

Stark, Rodney and Glock, Charles Y. *American Piety: The Nature of Religious Commitment.* Berkeley: University of California Press, 1968.

"Stars of the Cathode Church: Television-Radio Preaching: A Controversial Billion Dollar Industry." *Time* (February 4, 1980): 64–65.

Stauffer, David D. "Description and Analysis of the Historical Development and Management Practices of the Independent Christian Church Religious Television Program Syndicators." Ph.D. dissertation, Ohio University, 1972.

Steel, William E. "A Survey of Religious Television Broadcasting in the Los Angeles Metropolitan Area and Proposals for Change: New Strategies for Mainline Churches." D.Min. thesis, School of Theology at Claremont, 1979.

Strober, Gerald, and Tomczak, Ruth. *Jerry Falwell: Aflame for God.* Nashville: Thomas Nelson, 1979.

"Summary of Financial Information, Fiscal Year Ended May 31, 1979, The Heritage Village Church and Missionary Fellowship, Inc., and Related Corporations." *Action* (March 1980): 15.

Swann, Charles E. "The Electric Church." *Presbyterian Survey* (May 1979): 9–16.

Szalai, A., ed. *The Use of Time, Daily Activities of Urban and Suburban Populations in Twelve Countries.* The Hague: Mouton & Co., 1972.

Taylor, James A. "No Miracles from the Media." *Christian Century* (May 30, 1979): 613–15.

———. "Progeny of Programmers: Evangelical Religion and the Television Age." *Christian Century* (April 20, 1977): 379–82.

Thomas Road Baptist Church and Related Ministries. "Consolidated Statement for the Year Ended June 30, 1979." Lynchburg, Va. (Mimeographed)

Thompson, George S. "The Effect of the Use of Mass Media to Establish a Local Church: A Study of the Pilot Church Project of the Christian and Missionary Alliance in Tallahassee, Florida." Ph.D. dissertation, Florida State University, 1975.

Tillich, Paul. *Systematic Theology*, 3 vols. Chicago: University of Chicago Press, 1951–63.

United Methodist Communications. "What Happens to All That Money." Booklet of United Methodist Communication. n.d.

Van den Heuvel, A. "Effects and Counter-Effects of Media in Evangelization." *WACC Journal* 24 no. 4., (1977): 2–5.

Wagner, C. Peter. "Who Found It?" *Eternity* (September 1977): 13–19.

Wenner, Lawrence. "Functional Analyses of Television Viewing for Older Adults." *Journal of Broadcasting* 20 (1976): 79–88.

Westen, Tracy A. "Barriers to Creativity." *Journal of Communication* (Spring 1978): 36–42.

"What's Wrong with Born-Again Politics?" *Christian Century* 97 (October 22, 1980): 1002–4.

Williams, Russ. "Heavenly Message, Earthly Designs." *Sojourners* (September 1979): 17–20.

Woodward, Kenneth. "A One Million Dollar Habit." *Newsweek* 98 (September 15, 1980): 35.

World Council of Churches. "The Church and the Media of Mass Communication." In *The Uppsala Report, 1968*, Appendix XI. Geneva: World Council of Churches, 1968.

Yablonsky, Mary J. "A Rhetorical Analysis of Selected Television Speeches of Archbishop Fulton J. Sheen on Communism, 1952–56." Ph.D. dissertation, Ohio State University, 1974.

Yancey, Philip. "The Ironies and Impact of PTL." *Christianity Today* 23 (September 21, 1979): 28–33.

Youngblood, Gene. "The Mass Media and the Future of Desire." *The Co-Evolution Quarterly* (Winter 1977/78): 7–16.

Zweier, Robert, and Smith, Richard. "Christian Politics and the New Right." *Christian Century* 99 (October 8, 1980): 937–42.

Index